APACHEAN CULTURE HISTORY AND ETHNOLOGY

ANTHROPOLOGICAL PAPERS OF
THE UNIVERSITY OF ARIZONA
NUMBER 21

APACHEAN CULTURE HISTORY AND ETHNOLOGY

KEITH H. BASSO and MORRIS E. OPLER, *editors*

collaborating authors

William Y. Adams
Harry W. Basehart
Keith H. Basso
Michael W. Everett
P. Bion Griffin
Dolores A. Gunnerson
James H. Gunnerson

James J. Hester
Harry Hoijer
Gordon Y. Krutz
Louise Lamphere
Mark P. Leone
Morris E. Opler
Mary T. Shepardson

THE UNIVERSITY OF ARIZONA PRESS
TUCSON, ARIZONA 1971

THE UNIVERSITY OF ARIZONA PRESS

CONTENTS

MAPS AND FIGURES

TABLES

PREFACE

This volume grew out of a symposium held at the sixty-ninth Annual Meeting of the American Anthropological Association in November 1969 at New Orleans, Louisiana. The "Apachean Symposium," as it came to be called, was designed to provide an opportunity for scholars engaged in research on southern Athapaskan cultures, past and present, to report upon their findings and, wherever possible, to link them to known fact and existing theory.

No restrictions were imposed on the participants with respect to the selection of topics or type of analytic treatment nor, as sometimes happens in symposiums of this kind, were they asked to discuss their material in reference to a particular theoretical model or position. Each participant was urged to focus upon a problem he felt was important and to approach it with methods he considered applicable and illuminating. For these reasons, it is hardly surprising that the papers presented at the symposium, and those contained in this volume, deal with a variety of empirical and theoretical issues. Despite this diversity—or, more probably, because of it—the work represented here adds significantly to our knowledge of Apachean cultures. It is equally important, if not more so, that each of the contributions also pertains directly to wider spheres of anthropological concern.

In Part One, "Apachean Culture History," Harry Hoijer examines the relationship of the Apachean languages to the Athapaskan stock as a whole, a topic of certain interest to all involved with the reconstruction of North America's prehistory. The same may be said of the following article by James and Dolores Gunnerson which, though primarily aimed at the identification and location of extinct Apachean groups on the southern Plains, clarifies many other aspects of this region's archaeological past.

Morris Opler's study of Jicarilla pottery-making and use presents data which have long been unavailable but, more significantly, demonstrates how ethnographic materials can contribute to the definition and elucidation of archaeological problems. Harry Basehart then investigates the structure of Mescalero bands and leadership roles in a work which employs the results of exacting documentary scholarship to reveal important principles of social organization. Basehart's paper may be read as a study in the methodology of ethnohistory as well as a valuable contribution to Mescalero ethnography.

James Hester's paper deals with Navajo culture change. Beginning with the arrival of Athapaskan-speaking peoples in the American Southwest, Hester traces the full course of Navajo history, partitions it into periods of major change, and then isolates a set of key processes that appear to have regulated successive transformations of Navajo culture up to the present time. Hester's scope is wide indeed, and his work warrants the attention of all scholars concerned with American Indian acculturation.

The final article in Part One, largely the work of Bion Griffin and Mark Leone, evaluates a specific "materialist" hypothesis of cultural development against data drawn from Western Apache ethnohistory and the archaeological investigation of an abandoned Apache farm site. While concluding that the hypothesis is untenable, at least insofar as the Western Apache are concerned, this study nevertheless reflects the authors' opinion that, in addition to the documentation of prehistory, archaeology should address itself to the formulation of explicit principles concerning the growth of social forms.

Part Two, "Apachean Ethnography and Ethnology," begins with a study in which William Y. Adams examines the economic and ecological adjustments of a Navajo community with reference to the pervasive effects in these areas of Navajo value orientations. At a more general level, Adams' work suggests that rigidly "materialistic" explanations of cultural adaptation run the risk of oversimplification and misinterpretation by failing to acknowledge the powerful—and sometimes critical—influence of ideology.

In a study on contemporary Navajo political organization, Mary Shepardson analyzes some absorbing case materials and reaches a set of conclusions directly relevant to modern theories of factionalism and dispute. Louise Lamphere then provides a penetrating discussion of Navajo concepts of cooperation and autonomy and, on the basis of what is termed a "social network model" of Navajo social structure, offers a fresh interpretation of gossip and witchcraft accusations. Lamphere's article is followed by an historical study of Western Apache wage labor in which William Y. Adams and Gordon Krutz discuss some of the factors that have retarded economic development on the San Carlos Reservation in Arizona. This study will be of immediate interest to all anthropologists who would seek to understand the role that a capricious Anglo economy has played in shaping the conditions which prevail today on America's Indian reservations.

In a paper dealing with Western Apache medical behavior, Michael Everett makes use of decision-making theory in an attempt to construct a model that depicts the types of information White Mountain Apaches attend to when they select among alternative treatment procedures. And, finally, in a paper that combines principles from both "ethnoscience" and sociolinguistics, Keith H. Basso investigates the types of social situations in which Western Apaches regularly refrain from speech. An hypothesis is advanced to account for why the

Apache keep silent when they do, and additional data are presented which indicate that this hypothesis may have relevance to the explanation of silence behavior in other cultures.

The foregoing summary is intended to give some indication of the wide-ranging interests of anthropologists currently engaged in Apachean studies. Moreover, it serves to illustrate that the articles collected here, though firmly grounded in empirical fact, are aimed at more than the mere presentation of data. Without exception, they are also directed toward the critical reexamination of accepted concepts and assumptions and/or toward the creation and implementation of new ones. It is clear that, together with other scholars in the field of Apachean research whose work, unfortunately, is not represented here, the contributors to this volume have ably demonstrated that the study of southern Athapaskan cultures continues to be a viable and creative force in modern cultural anthropology. Moreover, these authors have clarified some of the lines along which future work is likely to proceed—a service, we hope, to which students and professionals alike will respond with enthusiasm and sustained interest.

In conclusion, we want to express our sincere thanks to those individuals whose talents and efforts were essential in bringing this project to completion. Ann Fisher, who made the local arrangements in New Orleans; all the participants, whose interest and cooperation was truly remarkable and is deeply appreciated; and Marshall Townsend and Karen Thure, of the University of Arizona Press, whose editorial skills fashioned the volume into its present form. Above all—and here we know we speak for all the contributors—we thank the Apacheans.

KEITH H. BASSO

MORRIS E. OPLER

PART ONE

Apachean Culture History

Chapter 1

THE POSITION OF THE APACHEAN LANGUAGES IN THE ATHAPASKAN STOCK

Harry Hoijer

HARRY HOIJER, professor emeritus of anthropology at the University of California, Los Angeles, conducted linguistic studies among the Apachean tribes of New Mexico and Arizona from 1930–40. He is the author (with others) of *Linguistic Structures of Native America* (Viking Fund Publications in Anthropology, volume 6, 1946) and numerous monographs and articles on the Athapaskan languages.

It has long been known that the Athapaskan languages of Alaska, the Canadian Northwest, the Pacific Coast, and the American Southwest are related, despite the considerable distances that separate those of the North from those of the Pacific Coast and the Southwest. The precise terms of this relationship, however, have only recently become known, and then only in part. Most of the comparative work so far published relates in the main to the Pacific languages (Hoijer 1960, Li 1930) and to the languages of the Apachean group (Hoijer 1938). In recent years, a considerable body of data has been gathered on the northern languages, and although much of this is still in manuscript, the picture of Athapaskan relationships has become much clearer.*

In this study it is my purpose to review these data, especially in regard to the relationship of the Apachean languages to those of the North. I shall also offer a revision of my own earlier study of the Apachean languages (Hoijer 1938).

Most of the comparative studies of the Athapaskan languages have concentrated on the initial consonants of the stem syllable, a concentration imposed upon us by the fact that, for many Athapaskan languages, we possess as our only dependable lexical data more or less complete lists of stems. Despite this handicap, it is possible to reconstruct a Proto-Athapascan (PA) consonantal system with a fair degree of accuracy. It also becomes apparent that the PA consonants reveal major differences in development mainly in respect to fifteen consonants, out of a total of forty-one. These PA consonants may be listed as follows:

1. ĝ   ḵ   ḵ̓
2. ĝʷ ḵʷ ḵ̓ʷ
3. g   k   k̓
4. dz ts t̓s
5. dž tš t̓š

This system of consonants remains intact, so far as we now know, only in Minto, Central Tanana (both in Alaska), Kutchin, and Han. In all the remaining languages of Northwest Canada, and in the languages of the Pacific Coast and the American Southwest, the consonants of line 2 (ĝʷ, ḵʷ, ḵ̓ʷ) merge with, respectively, dž, tš, and t̓š of line 5. Because of the wide distribution of this merger, we can set up a second proto-system (PCPA, i.e. Proto-Canadian-Pacific-Apachean), a system which developed in the North, at a time well before the speakers of the Pacific and Southwestern languages migrated southward. The PCPA system may be reconstructed as follows:

1. ĝ   ḵ   ḵ̓
2. g   k   k̓
3. dz ts t̓s
4. dž tš t̓š   (< lines 2 and 5 of PA)

---

*The Alaskan data have been collected by Michael Krauss, who has generously given me by correspondence his as-yet-unpublished material on the relationships of the Alaskan languages.

3

One group of Canadian languages preserves this system intact, although not in terms of the phonetics implicit in the PCPA system. Thus, in Chipewyan and Slave, we find the following system:

g	k	k̓	(< PCPA line 2)
dδ	tθ	t̓θ	(< PCPA line 3)
dz	ts	t̓s	(< PCPA line 4)
dž	tš	t̓š	(< PCPA line 1)

In Carrier the system is:

ĝ	ḳ	ḳ̓	(< PCPA line 1)
g	k	k̓	(< PCPA line 2)
dδ	tθ	t̓θ	(< PCPA line 3)
dz	ts	t̓s	(< PCPA line 4)

Dogrib reveals a somewhat greater phonetic diversity but a phonemic system identical with that of PCPA:

g	k	k̓	(< PCPA line 2)
gʷ	kʷ	k̓ʷ	(< PCPA line 3)
dz	ts	t̓s	(< PCPA line 4)
dž	tš	t̓š	(< PCPA line 1)

In Hare we find two additional mergers, but it is clear that the Hare system can easily be derived from the PCPA system:

g	k	k̓	(< PCPA line 2)
fʷ		ẇ	(< PCPA line 3, with an additional merger of PCPA dz and ts to fʷ)
dz	ts	t̓s	(< PCPA line 4)
dž	tš	t̓š	(< PCPA line 1)

Finally, we note a system in Nabesna (or Tutchone) which is like that found in Hare:

g	k	k̓	(< PCPA line 2)
θ		t̓θ	(< PCPA line 3, with, as in Hare, a merger of PCPA dz and ts to θ)
dz	ts	t̓s	(< PCPA line 4)
dž	tš		(< PCPA line 1)

A second group of Canadian languages—made up of Sarsi, Beaver, Kaska, Sekani, and probably Tahltan—is distinguished from the first group by a merger whereby the consonants in PCPA lines 3 and 4 go to dz, ts, and t̓s. The system in all five languages appears to be the same:

g	k	k̓	(< PCPA line 2)
dz	ts	t̓s	(< PCPA lines 3 and 4)
dž	tš	t̓š	(< PCPA line 1)

In my 1938 comparative study of the Apachean languages, I divided them into two groups: Western Apachean (Navajo, San Carlos, Chiricahua, Mescalero) and Eastern Apachean (Jicarilla, Lipan, Kiowa Apache). The principal criterion for this classification is the development in Apachean of PCPA *t and *k. These consonants remain in Western Apachean but merge to k in Eastern Apachean. However, it was also noted that k in Kiowa Apache appears only before a and o; before e and i, PCPA *t and *k become tš, so merging with the tš derived from PCPA *tš.

A not-yet-published lexicostatistical study of the Apachean languages reveals the percentages of shared cognates shown in Table 1.

It is obvious that this study reveals:

1. That Navajo, San Carlos, Chiricahua, Mescalero, Jicarilla, and Lipan are simply closely related dialects of a single language.

2. That Kiowa Apache is a second Apachean language equidistant from each of the six dialects.

These conclusions, it is evident, don't agree with my 1938 classification, and they have led me to reexamine the Apachean subgroup to determine, by the comparative method, if the 1938 study can be justified or if it requires considerable modification.

1. Lines 1 (ĝ, ḳ, ḳ̓) and 3 (dz, ts, t̓s) of the PCPA consonant system merge to dz, ts, t̓s in Navajo, San Carlos, Chiricahua, Mescalero, Jicarilla, and Lipan, but not in Kiowa Apache.

2. In Kiowa Apache, lines 1 (ĝ, ḳ, ḳ̓) and 4 (dž, tš, t̓š) merge to dž, tš, t̓š.

3. As noted above, PCPA *t and *k merge to k in Jicarilla and Lipan, and to k (before a and o) and tš (before e and i) in Kiowa Apache.

TABLE 1

Shared Cognates in Apachean Languages

	S.C.	Chir.	Mesc.	Jic.	Lip.	K.A.
Nav.	94	95	95	94	92	75
S.C.	x	96	94	93	90	74
Chir.		x	97	95	93	75
Mesc.			x	96	95	74
Jic.				x	94	76
Lip.					x	75

4. PCPA *n is retained in Navajo and San Carlos, becomes ⁿd in Chiricahua, Mescalero, Jicarilla, and Lipan, and becomes d in Kiowa Apache, d representing a merger of PCPA *n and *d.

These facts suggest that the Athapaskan peoples who moved southward to the American Southwest were not uniform in language. Indeed, it is quite likely that the merger of PCPA *t and *k took place before any considerable movement southward took place, a fact which receives some confirmation from the recent discovery that the same merger is found in a Chipewyan dialect (Haas 1968). It is also likely that the migration southward, presumably along the eastern foothills of the Rockies, took place first by the groups we now know as the Navajo, San Carlos, Chiricahua, and Mescalero, followed by but still in contact with the Jicarilla and Lipan. The Kiowa Apache clearly came much later: James Mooney in Hodge's *Handbook of the American Indians North of Mexico* (1907) says that the Kiowa Apache were associated with the Kiowa from the earliest known period and that the Kiowa Apache were never linked with other Apaches but were always a Plains people. As late as 1805, "Lewis and Clark described the Kiowa Apache as living between the heads of the two forks of the Cheyenne river in the Black Hills of northeastern Wyoming" (Mooney 1907:701). It seems quite clear, then, that the relationship of Kiowa Apache to the rest of the Apachean languages is the result of their early separation, probably in the North, from the southwestern Apaches.

A final question may now be raised: to what languages or language group of the Pacific Coast or the North are the Apachean languages most closely related? It is clear, from both the comparative method and lexicostatistics, that the Pacific languages are more remote from Apachean than are the languages of Canada. The comparative evidence may be found in Hoijer 1960. Percentages of shared cognates as between Hupa, Mattole, Kato, and Galice of the Pacific Coast and Navajo are, respectively, 65, 65, 69, and 73. Kiowa Apache has 57, 60, 67, and 69 percent, respectively.

In the North, the percentages of shared cognates between Hare, Dogrib, Slave, Chipewyan, Beaver, Carrier, Sarsi, and Navajo are, respectively, 71, 68, 69, 76, 70, 73, and 68, slightly higher than the percentages for Apachean vis-à-vis the Pacific Coast.

Comparative evidence yields similarly ambiguous results. Considering alone the PCPA consonants of lines 1, 3, and 4, we note that Chipewyan has a system phonemically identical with that of PCPA:

$$\text{dž} \quad \text{tš} \quad \text{t'š} \quad (< \text{PCPA line 1})$$
$$\text{d}\delta \quad \text{t}\theta \quad \text{t'}\theta \quad (< \text{PCPA line 3})$$
$$\text{dz} \quad \text{ts} \quad \text{t's} \quad (< \text{PCPA line 4})$$

From this system, however, we can derive, with almost equal ease, the system of Sarsi, southwestern Apachean, and Kiowa Apache.

Sarsi:

dz ts t̓s   (< PCPA lines 3 and 4)

dž tš t̓š   (< PCPA line 1)

Southwestern Apachean:

dz ts t̓s   (< PCPA lines 1 and 3)

dž tš t̓š   (< PCPA line 4)

Kiowa Apache:

dz ts t̓s   (< PCPA line 3)

dž tš t̓š   (< PCPA lines 1 and 4)

It is clear, then, that Sarsi, southwestern Apache, and Kiowa Apache each diverge from PCPA by a distinctive merger: PCPA lines 3 and 4 in Sarsi, PCPA lines 1 and 3 in southwestern Apachean, and PCPA lines 1 and 4 in Kiowa Apache. We can only conclude that southwestern Apachean and Kiowa Apache broke off from PCPA at about the same time; or, in other words, that neither Chipewyan nor Sarsi can be said to be closest to the languages of the Southwest.

REFERENCES

HAAS, MARY R.

1968   Notes on a Chipewyan Dialect. International Journal of American Linguistics 34:165–75.

HOIJER, HARRY

1938   The Southern Athapaskan Languages. American Anthropologist 40:75–87.

1960   Athapaskan Languages of the Pacific Coast. *In* Culture in History: Essays in Honor of Paul Radin, Stanley Diamond, editor. Published for Brandeis University by Columbia University Press, New York.

LI, FANG-KUEI

1930   Mattole, an Athabascan Language. University of Chicago Press, Chicago.

MOONEY, JAMES

1907   Kiowa Apaches. *In* Handbook of the American Indians North of Mexico, Frederick W. Hodge, editor. Bulletin of the Bureau of American Ethnology 30. Smithsonian Institution, Washington, D.C. Part 1, pp. 701–2.

Chapter 2

APACHEAN CULTURE:
A STUDY IN UNITY AND DIVERSITY

James H. Gunnerson and Dolores A. Gunnerson

JAMES H. GUNNERSON, professor of anthropology and director of the Anthropology Laboratories at Northern Illinois University, previously authored *Introduction to Plains Apache Archeology—The Dismal River Aspect* (Bureau of American Ethnology Bulletin 173:131–260), based primarily on work in Nebraska. From 1964 on, his research has been supported by grants from the National Science Foundation and has centered in Kansas and New Mexico. Dr. Gunnerson has published several articles on Apachean archaeology in *American Antiquity*, the *Plains Anthropologist*, and *El Palacio*.

DOLORES A. GUNNERSON, assistant professor of anthropology at Northern Illinois University, has done extensive archival research on Apachean culture history with special emphasis on the Jicarilla. Mrs. Gunnerson has also collaborated in Apachean archaeological research, primarily in Nebraska, Kansas, and New Mexico. Her article "The Southern Athabascans: Their Arrival in the Southwest" (*El Palacio* 63, nos. 11–12: 346–65) has provided a point of departure for much of her subsequent research.

Clark Wissler once suggested (1967:214) that the Apacheans might be remnants of a large, formerly continuous southern extension of the Na-Dene into the Plains region of what is now the United States. Certainly there is evidence to suggest that when the foremost migrating Apacheans reached the Southern Plains, apparently circa 1525 (D. Gunnerson 1956), the southward movement of this group lost momentum. Some of the Apaches who reached the Plains east of New Mexico moved westward very soon and infiltrated the Pueblo area. Those who stayed out on the Southern Plains, along with others remaining on the Plains farther north, seem to have populated, albeit sparsely, the entire Plains Corridor. Within the historic period, at the northern extremity of their range, Apacheans had occasional contacts with the Northern Athapaskan Sarsi (Mooney 1898:160). Among themselves, for some two hundred years after their vanguard reached the Southwest, the Southern Athapaskans maintained an unbroken chain of contacts that preserved similarities in language and certain other aspects of culture to which anthropologists have already called attention (e.g., Goddard 1911:7–8; Opler 1936a:202, 1936b; Hoijer 1938; Brant 1949, 1953; Sjoberg 1953).

With regard to material culture, however, work in the 1960s on Southern Athapaskan archaeology has revealed areal differences, especially in ceramics, and these differences, in turn, are compatible with historical evidence concerning the location of particular Apachean groups and their relations with neighboring non-Apachean tribes.

Various lines of evidence suggest that all the Apacheans were primarily buffalo hunters in the early 1500s and that all then possessed a homogeneous, Plains-oriented material culture that lacked pottery (D. Gunnerson 1956). However, by 1540 these Plains hunters already had well-established patterns of interaction with sedentary peoples on the margins of the main buffalo country that can, we believe, explain some of the ultimate diversity in Apachean material culture. One of Coronado's men described the situation concisely:

> . . . over these plains there roam natives following the cattle, hunting and dressing skins to

NOTE: This is a modified and expanded version of a paper entitled "Band Affiliation of Apache Archaeological Sites" presented at the Annual Meeting of the American Anthropological Association in 1969. Much of the research upon which this paper is based was supported by three grants (Nos. GS445, GS877, and GS1245) from the National Science Foundation. This support is gratefully acknowledged.

Location of Selected Indian Groups Circa 1700

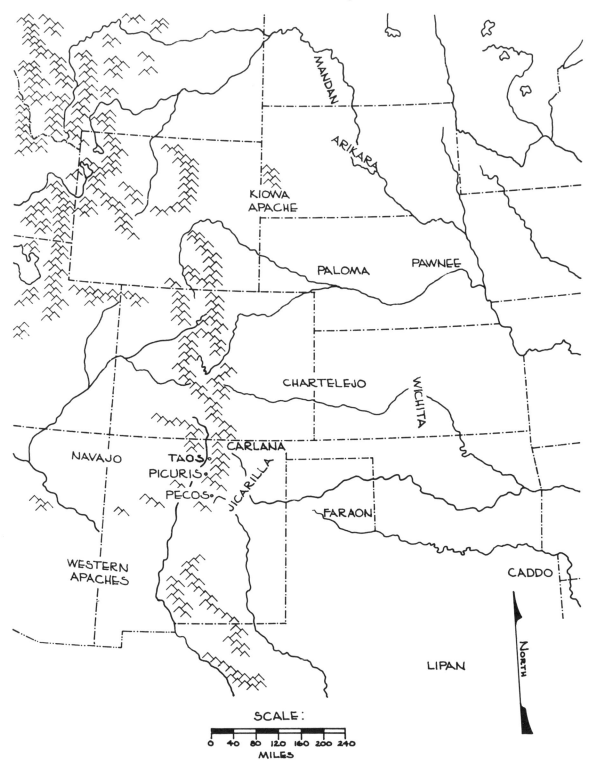

NOTE: Information for all groups is from circa 1700 excepting the Lipan, which is from 1732. Modern names, rather than those current at the time, have been used in some instances.

take to the pueblos to sell in winter, since they go to spend the winter there, each group to the nearest place. Some go to the pueblos of Cicuye [Pecos, and perhaps pueblos in the Galisteo Basin], others to Quivira [Wichita villages in central Kansas], and others toward Florida to the settlements located in the direction of that region and port [Caddo(?) villages to the east and southeast]. These peoples . . . gave reports of large settlements. (Castañeda *in* Hammond and Rey 1940:261)

This and other historical accounts, considered along with the archaeological evidence, have led us to conclude that different segments of the eastern Apacheans became semisedentary horticulturalists and pottery-makers as a result of repeated close contacts with different sedentary tribes, and that ceramic comparisons can be used to identify these Apache groups in terms of the cultural donors.

In the Central Plains, where Apachean archaeological remains are called the Dismal River aspect (e.g., J. Gunnerson 1960, 1968; Wedel 1959), Dismal River pottery literally bears the stamp, the simple stamp, of large-village-tribe pottery. The Mandan, Arikara, Pawnee, and part of the Wichita all malleated their pottery so as to produce on the surface sharply defined "lands and grooves," and so did their Apache neighbors. This "simple stamping," which was apparently usually produced with a carved bone or wooden paddle, seems to have been done earliest in the north and to have spread down the Missouri River (Lehmer 1954: 142–43, 137). Although we do not yet know much about the archaeology of the Apaches who lived nearest the Mandan and Arikara, it is at the northernmost excavated Dismal River sites that sherds with identifiable paddle-marks are most numerous. The protohistoric Pawnees (Lower Loup focus) usually smoothed the ridges created by paddling to a certain extent (e.g., Dunlevy 1936:173–74, 188), but not so completely as some of the protohistoric Wichita (Great Bend aspect, Little River focus), who usually almost obliterated the paddle-marks (Wedel 1959:237).

The importance of sheer proximity may well be indicated in the fact that the Dismal River Apaches living near the Wichita smoothed their pottery more than did those living near the Pawnee (J.

Gunnerson 1968:175–76, 180). The fact that those Plains Apaches whose hunting grounds were closest to Quivira in the 1500s customarily wintered with the Wichita could explain the later influence of Wichita pottery on Dismal River Apache ware in that area. Unfortunately, Spanish knowledge of the Central Plains did not extend much beyond Quivira in the 1500s, but it seems reasonable to assume that Apaches living close to the Pawnee at one time enjoyed good relations with those Caddoan-speakers also.

South of Dismal River territory, on the east side of the Sangre de Cristo Mountains, over the crest from Taos and Picuris pueblos, are early and late sites (circa 1550?–circa 1887) of "foothills" Apaches who made pottery from a clay that contained a large amount of mica in flake form and therefore did not require the addition of tempering material. This Apache pottery closely resembles historic Taos utility ware, called Taos Micaceous, and some of the pottery made at Picuris. Of special interest is the fact that all three of these wares show on the surface the marks of corncobs that were used to scrape or smooth the pots, whereas this surface treatment is not obvious on pottery made at other pueblos. Historical evidence makes it possible to attribute the sites in the Sangre de Cristos to Jicarilla Apaches and other closely related horticultural Apache bands whom the Spaniards were lumping with the Jicarillas by 1719. Moreover, there is an abundance of documentary evidence testifying to friendly interaction between the Jicarillas and the Taos and Picuris Indians that can explain the similarity of their pottery (Thomas 1935; J. Gunnerson 1969).

It has been suggested that historic Taos Micaceous developed between 1550 and 1600 out of an earlier Pueblo micaceous ware called smeared indented, which differed from it in paste and surface treatment (Ellis and Brody 1964:316, 318, 325). Jicarilla pottery was undoubtedly inspired by one or the other of these wares, but at the moment it is not clear to us whether the earliest form of Jicarilla pottery, called Ocate Micaceous, is derived directly from Taos Micaceous, or whether the differences that distinguish both Taos and Ocate Micaceous from smeared indented ware are innovations introduced by the foothills Apaches (see J. Gunnerson 1959, 1969).

Still another vista in Apachean archaeology has opened recently with the discovery, at various sites on the Southern Plains, of a thin, gray, non-Pueblo utility ware that we have tentatively assigned to the Faraon Apaches. Although this group has not been firmly identified with a modern Apache tribe, the Faraon Apaches, who were semisedentary horticulturalists, figured prominently in New Mexico history from 1675, the year in which they seem to be first mentioned (Forbes 1960:171), until the early 1800s (e.g., Twitchell 1914, II:405, 420, 550). The Faraons are almost always mentioned as aggressors, even against their congeners the Jicarillas (Thomas 1935:80, 159). However, they traded at times at Picuris (Espinosa 1942:227, 229; Hodge 1929; Thomas 1935:80–81), and their friendship with the Pecos Indians seems to have been one of the most intimate recorded between an Apache group and a Pueblo.

We first recovered what we now surmise to be Faraon pottery at a large "tipi ring" site on open plains east of Las Vegas, New Mexico, that may have been a way station for Faraons traveling to and from the Pueblos. The site has been named "Ojo Perdido" from a now-disused spring that was undoubtedly the reason for locating the tipi rings there. The gray utility ware from the site differs from both Dismal River Apache pottery of the central Plains, which is nonmicaceous, and from the "spangled"-appearing Jicarilla wares, which contain mica in relatively large flakes. Rather, the majority of culinary ware from Ojo Perdido, which we have called "Perdido Plain," contains very finely divided mica and crushed rock. The Ojo Perdido site also yielded painted Pueblo sherds, some from Picuris, but most from Pecos, that date from the 1600s, probably before 1680 (Helene Warren, letter, Sept. 12, 1968).

Plains Apaches ranged widely according to the season on hunting, gathering, raiding, and trading expeditions, so that the total area exploited by the Faraons far exceeded that in which they had their farming villages. It is also possible that parts of more than one modern Apache group may have formerly been included under the name. However,

in the late 1600s and early 1700s at least, particular Faraon friends of the Pecos Indians had farming villages on the Canadian River that were said to be some ten (Thomas 1935:82) to fourteen (Forbes 1960:225) days' journey east of the Pueblos. The nearest of these villages was said to be made up of thirty houses of wood entirely smeared with clay outside, and there the Faraons had underground cache pits for storing the corn that they raised (Thomas 1935:82). Thus the possibility that Perdido Plain is Faraon pottery has been strengthened by its presence in collections made by Keith Glasscock at sites nearly due east of Pecos near the Canadian River in the Texas Panhandle, and by its presence in University of Oklahoma collections from sites in western Oklahoma.

Even more significant is the 1970 discovery of Perdido Plain sherds around Pecos Pueblo itself (Gunnerson and Gunnerson 1970), where the presence of Faraon pottery would be consistent with the historical record. As early as 1641 the Pecos Indians were said to be "living" with some Plains Apaches (Forbes 1960:132). The Faraons specifically were said to have been living with the Pecos when De Vargas reconquered New Mexico, at which time the Faraons withdrew to the Plains (Thomas 1935:81). The records of the reconquest (e.g., Forbes 1960) contain frequent references to the Pecos-Faraon friendship. In 1696, for example, the priest stationed at Pecos reported that one group of Faraons was living in the pueblo, while another was camped nearby on the Pecos River (Forbes 1960:265). In 1715, the Pecos Indians and the Faraons were said to be "almost the same" (Thomas 1935:81).

Preliminary observations suggest, moreover, that Perdido Plain may be related to Pecos wares of the historic period. If, after further research, Perdido Plain can indeed be assigned to the Faraons, and if it does prove to be related to Pecos pottery, we will have a third instance of close connections between the pottery of an Apachean group and that of a non-Apachean tribe.

In terms of historic Apachean groups there is no doubt that the Dismal River aspect represents at least the two Central Plains tribes known to the Spaniards in New Mexico as the Cuartelejo and

Paloma Apaches (Champe 1949; J. Gunnerson 1960). Although no efforts at dating Dismal River sites have yet succeeded in pushing the aspect back in time to before circa 1675, and that date is only an estimated one (Champe 1946:25–27), it is probable that the Plains Apaches who were in the habit of wintering at the Wichita villages of Quivira by 1540 were already semisedentary by circa 1640. There were Apache "people of El Cuartelejo, on the frontier of La Quivira" at about that date (Hackett 1937:263–64; Forbes 1960:268), and since the term *cuartelejo* was used in the 1600s to refer to an area containing semisedentary, hut-dwelling western Apacheans (Tyler and Taylor 1958:306), it may have had the same significance when applied to the Apache country bordering the Wichita villages in central Kansas.

Sometime in the 1600s, apparently between the departure of Father Benavides in 1629 (Hodge, Hammond, and Rey 1945:4) and the arrival of Father Posada in 1650, Plains Apache-Caddoan relations changed for the worse, since Apaches began selling slaves in New Mexico on a significant scale. Posada, a resident of New Mexico between 1650 and 1665, wrote of the Plains Apaches in 1686:

> This nation is confined on the east by the Quiviras with whom they are now and have been continually at war. In the same region [the Apacha nation] also borders on the Texas nation, with whom they have always had war. Although the Quivira and Texas nations are wide and have many people, the Apacha nation in the interior bordering these nations along two hundred leagues as mentioned, has not only kept its boundaries, but has invaded those of the two other nations.

And he goes on to tell how, when he was resident priest at Pecos Pueblo, some Apaches had brought in captive Indian children from Quivira to trade for horses (Tyler and Taylor 1958:300–301).

Posada's account also reveals that the Spaniards still did not know the Pawnee country by 1680, but it seems safe to assume that the Central Plains Apaches were already enemies of the Pawnees by the time of which Posada writes: that is, by the mid-1600s. The earliest known references

to Pawnee captives in Spanish documents date from after the Pueblo Rebellion of 1680, from the period when the New Mexico settlers were living at El Paso (Bandelier 1890:185–86), but this may simply reflect the destruction of earlier New Mexico archives during the rebellion.

Members of Ulibarri's expedition of 1706 (Thomas 1935:59–80 and entire book, passim) provided the first direct historical evidence that the Cuartelejo Apaches were semisedentary people who lived in "huts or little houses" and raised crops, abandoning their several villages in winter because of lack of fuel. These Spaniards also brought back details of the warfare that the Cuartelejos were carrying on against the Pawnees and also against some "Jumanos," the geographical context suggesting that the latter name was being applied in this instance to the Wichitas. By chance, Ulibarri's journey coincided with the first recorded attack by the Comanches, who, during his absence, joined the Utes in destroying a village of the Carlana Apaches, also known as Sierra Blancas, who lived in the Raton Mesa area of southeastern Colorado.

Although the Cuartelejos continued to trade in New Mexico in the years that followed Ulibarri's visit to their territory in 1706, the next record that sheds any light on their condition is the diary of Valverde, who in 1719 went into southeastern Colorado to chastise Utes and Comanches for raids on settlements in New Mexico. On his way he found part of the Sierra Blanca Apaches under Chief Carlana living with the Jicarillas (Thomas 1935:114–16). The Utes and Comanches had chased them out of their own country, perhaps permanently, and they seem to have lived among the Jicarillas for the next several years.

Valverde did not penetrate far into Cuartelejo territory, if at all, and did not visit any of the Cuartelejo villages. However, the Cuartelejos, having heard of his expedition, came by the hundreds to visit him at a place where he encamped to wait for them on the Arkansas River. From them he learned that their settlements (in western Kansas) were now being attacked from two directions. The Pawnees and Jumanos (Wichitas?) aided by Frenchmen were striking from the east, and the

Utes (probably allied with Comanches) from the west. The Cuartelejos themselves had not yet abandoned their lands, but they had with them part of another Apache group, who were already refugees. These were variously called Calchufines (Thomas 1935:130), Escalchufines (Thomas 1935: 257) and (mainly) Palomas (Thomas 1935:132, 142, 229, 257).

The name Paloma, which generally means "dove" in Castilian Spanish but may have had a different meaning in New Mexico, was the one that survived longest. It is possible that no Spaniard had ever reached the territory of the Paloma Apaches (Thomas 1935:143). By their own account, their original lands had been "farther in from El Cuartelejo, on the most remote borderlands of the Apaches" (Thomas 1935:132). They had been driven out of their territory, where they raised corn, by Pawnees who had French allies (Thomas 1935:132, 144, 229, 232). In 1719, the refugee Palomas were in the process of settling in El Cuartelejo, but some had already left that area and dispersed themselves among other, unidentified, Apache rancherías because of the attacks being made by the Utes (Thomas 1935:144).

The account given by the Palomas, and the evidence bearing on the subsequent expedition of Pedro Villasur to reconnoiter the Frenchmen they described, strongly suggest that the Palomas originally lived west of the Pawnees and north of the Platte River. The Platte, called the Río Jesús María by the Spaniards (Thomas 1935:144, 163, 134, 229) and called the River of the "Panis" (Pawnees) by the French (e.g., Vermale's map of 1717 *in* Wheat 1957: op. 63) apparently divided the lands of the Cuartelejo Apaches from those of the Pawnees (Thomas 1935:163). This division leaves the Dismal River archaeological sites in the Nebraska Sand Hills and peripheral areas to be accounted for, and the Palomas are their most likely occupants. In the Sand Hills, certainly, they would have been vulnerable to attacks by the Pawnee.

For several years after 1719, the activities of the Paloma Apaches are obscure. El Cuartelejo was still occupied by the Cuartelejos and Palomas in 1726, and by then the Palomas themselves were coming into New Mexico to trade. By that year,

also, the Carlanas, who had earlier sought refuge in the Sangre de Cristos with the Jicarillas, had apparently decided to cast their lot instead with the Cuartelejos and Palomas. These three groups had banded together and, reinforced by some Frenchmen then living in El Cuartelejo, were making what may have been a last-ditch effort to drive out the Comanches (Thomas 1935:257). El Cuartelejo was still occupied in 1727, according to information given by an Apache from the "interior," and Jicarillas visiting in Taos led Governor Bustamante to conclude in that year that the French had won over the Plains Apaches (Thomas 1935:256, 258). These seem to be the last contemporary references to El Cuartelejo as Apache territory.

In and after 1730 there occur in the records tantalizing statements suggesting that the allied Carlanas, Cuartelejos, and Palomas began to live part of the time in the Sangre de Cristos and to develop closer ties with the Jicarillas, perhaps sometimes even being identified as Jicarillas. In 1730, for example, Bishop Crespo of Durango, after visiting New Mexico, stated that the priest at Taos could " if he is zealous, . . . make expeditions to Jicarilla and Cuartelejo, fifteen or twenty leagues away, where there are many pagan Indians who have formed settlements and sown land" (Adams 1953: 223–24). Although Crespo's information may have been garbled, it is possible that the Central Plains Apaches had by 1730 taken refuge with the Jicarillas, as the Carlanas alone had done circa 1719.

There is some further evidence to strengthen this idea. Not long after a mission was founded near Taos for the "Jicarillas" in 1733, some of the Apaches gathered there "returned to their place of origin, that was more than 100 leagues to the north" while others, those customarily allied with the Taos Indians, remained (Villaseñor 1748, II: 240). It may be that the mission had attempted to incorporate all the friendly Apaches, but that the Cuartelejos, Palomas, and Carlanas returned at least temporarily to the Central Plains, while the Jicarillas of the Sangre de Cristo Mountains remained. By 1748, with the sedentary villages of the original foothills Apache tribes abandoned under Comanche pressure, there seem to have been groups called Jicarillas living a less settled life in northeastern New Mexico, and they were differentiated according to whether their primary affiliation was with Taos or Pecos (Twitchell 1914, I: 148–50; Lummis 1898: 74–78).

In 1752 some Apaches called Jicarillas *and* Carlanas by the governor of New Mexico were on the Gallinas River fifteen leagues from Pecos (Thomas 1940: 108, 102), but these same Apaches were identified only as Carlanas by the parish priest at Pecos (Thomas 1940: 90). In 1752 and 1754 it was specifically the Carlanas, Cuartelejos, and Palomas who were living in or near Pecos Pueblo, except that in the latter year the Palomas are not mentioned at all. Also, in 1754, after referring to the Cuartelejos as a "subordinate" group of the Carlanas, Governor Cachupin goes on, in the same document, to refer to the Carlanas alone, and to emphasize the fact that they should be encouraged to maintain their independence (Thomas 1940: 124, 135–36). This they did, for various later archival materials show that the Carlanas (probably still including the Cuartelejos and Palomas) kept their identity, apparently even into the 1800s (e.g., Pino *in* Carroll and Haggard 1942: 128, 246).

The post-1730 archaeology of the Cuartelejos and Palomas, formerly Dismal River peoples of the Central Plains, is not yet known. We have not yet found Dismal River pottery in eastern New Mexico, although our surveys have been far from exhaustive. It is possible, however, that baking pits and certain stone and bone artifacts of Dismal River types found in a late historic context at Pecos (Kidder 1932, 1958: 119–20) represent some of these displaced Dismal River people (J. Gunnerson 1960: 241–44).

As for the Carlanas, or Sierra Blanca Apaches, who apparently absorbed the Cuartelejos and Palomas after all three tribes had become refugees, their archaeology is not yet defined on any time level. The "Sierra Blanca" in which they lived until circa 1719 may have included the main range of the Sangre de Cristos between Raton, New Mexico, and Trinidad, Colorado, but was at least the Raton Mesa that projects eastward from the main range along the present New Mexico-Colorado state line,

and in 1720 they were said to have their rancherías on its "shoulders which face south" (Thomas 1935: 142, 170, 171, 174). If the Carlanas, Cuartelejos, and Palomas eventually became the Plains band of the modern Jicarillas, they began at some point to make pottery like that of the original Mountain band, for both divisions apparently made the same kind of micaceous pottery in recent times (e.g., Gifford 1940: 50–51).

* * *

The preceding discussion of historic Central Plains Apaches, based primarily on Spanish sources, casts no light on the enigmatic Kiowa Apaches as such. However, if the lands of the Palomas before 1719 were on the "most remote borderlands of the Apaches," as these people told Valverde, and if the Palomas lived north of El Cuartelejo, as we have reasoned, then the Kiowa Apaches may have been the northernmost of the Palomas. Possibly they were already hostile toward their linguistic relatives to the south as a result of their continuing good relations with the Arikaras and their political alliance with the Kiowas, so that they preferred to remain in the north when the other Palomas fled. If the Kiowa Apaches were not among the Palomas before 1719, we do not know how to account for them in early Spanish nomenclature.

In fact, the Kiowa Apaches have long posed special problems for interested anthropologists because their cultural position as one of the Southern Athapaskan tribes has seemed incompatible with their historic geographical location far to the north of any other members of this linguistic division. Mooney assumed that the Kiowa Apaches were "practically a part of the Kiowa in everything except language" and consequently did not study them in detail. As a result he concluded, erroneously, that they had never been a part of the Southern Athapaskans (Mooney 1898: 246–48). Later anthropologists, after becoming increasingly aware of linguistic and cultural similarities between the Kiowa Apaches and the other Apacheans, have erred too far in the other direction in that they have tended to discount entirely Mooney's opinion that the Kiowa Apaches had always been a northern tribe.

Any study of Kiowa Apache history must consider the Kiowa, whose traditions, as opposed to their mythology, say they once lived on the head-waters of the Yellowstone and Missouri rivers, after which part of the tribe moved southeast, crossed the Yellowstone, met the Crows, with whom they made their "first" alliance, and settled east of this latter group (Mooney 1898:153, 246). Mooney (1898:247) concludes that the association of the Kiowa Apaches with the Kiowa "antedates the first removal of the latter from the mountains, as both tribes say they have no memory of a time when they were not together."

The relationship of the Kiowa language to Tanoan (Harrington 1910; Trager and Trager 1959) strongly suggests a Southwestern origin for this tribe (see Jelinek 1967), but this does not preclude their being on the northern Plains before 1700. Indeed, Kiowa traditions are corroborated in the main by those of other northern tribes such as the Crows and Northern Arapahos (Mooney 1898: 155–57). Statements from these tribes, however, do not include mention of the Kiowa Apaches, and it is probable that Mooney overestimated the length, as well as the nature of the relationship between the Kiowa and the Kiowa Apache. Some of his own evidence casts doubt on his interpretations (Mooney 1898:153, 155, 156). Besides the already-mentioned specific statement that the Kiowas' "first" alliance was with the *Crows*, he gives information from the Northern Arapahos that the Kiowas moved down from the mountains with the *Crows*, then eastward along the Yellowstone and later southeastward, parting with the Crows in the vicinity of Fort Robinson, Nebraska. Mooney's further statement that the Kiowas settled east of the Crows and took over the Black Hills brings them into the area where concrete Kiowa Apache traditions and history begin.

Keim, who collected the Kiowa migration legend in 1868, got no information on their home-land except that it was in the "far north" (Keim 1870:183). On the other hand, the Kiowa Apaches (whom he mistakenly identifies as Lipans) told him that ". . . many years ago they occupied the region known as the 'bad ground,' an exceedingly desolate and broken country between the head waters of

the Missouri and the Platte, and from here they wandered south until they reached Texas" (Keim 1870:190).

W. P. Clark, who collected information for his work on sign language in 1881, said, "Tradition locates the Kiowas near and to the southwest of the Black Hills, Dakota, and without doubt they had previously lived near the Missouri River. The Apaches with whom they are now associated were at this time with them" (Clark 1885:229).

Also, an old Kiowa Apache interviewed by Clark had been born near the Missouri River northeast of the Black Hills some seventy years earlier (Clark 1885:33).

When McAllister worked among the Kiowa Apaches in 1933–34, their "Medicine Lake" was said to be located in the Black Hills region of Dakota (McAllister 1937:162). In brief, neither the actual details of Kiowa migration legends nor statements obtained from the Kiowa Apaches themselves support Mooney's conclusion that the two tribes were together before the Kiowas left the mountains.

Sufficient evidence has already been presented by others to controvert Mooney's conclusions on the similarity of Kiowa Apache culture to that of the Kiowa, and McAllister's (1937:100–101) findings, as well as other evidence, suggest that the two tribes were not even particularly friendly. Goddard's (1911:7–8) brief but important statement on the relationships of the Southern Athapaskan dialects was followed by Hoijer's several detailed studies (e.g., 1938, 1948, 1956, 1958), and Brant (1949, 1953) has summarized ethnological evidence relating Kiowa Apache culture to that of the other Apacheans and differentiating it from that of the Kiowas. To account for the similarities between the Kiowa Apaches and cognate tribes, however, Brant reiterates one of Kroeber's (1947:79) views, i.e., that the Kiowa Apaches (like other Apacheans) had lived on the Plains border of the Southwest and had moved finally onto the Plains only after obtaining the horse. He considers, and rejects, the possibility that the Kiowa Apaches were among the Dismal River people (1953:200–202).

However, there is archaeological evidence of Dismal River Apache occupation in the area

traditionally and historically occupied by the
Kiowa Apache. Two sites yielding pottery very
similar to Dismal River ware have been found in
the extreme northwestern corner of Nebraska,
north of Fort Robinson, at the edge of, and in, the
badlands south of the Black Hills (J. Gunnerson
1960:226). Three such sites are located in southeastern Wyoming, one near the Platte River. What
is perhaps most significant, two sites yielding pottery very like Dismal River ware are located in
southwestern South Dakota in the Angostura
Reservoir area just southeast of the Black Hills
(J. Gunnerson 1960:266, 236–37, Fig. 13, 144).

Baking pits of Dismal River type, one of which
contained a human burial, have also been reported
from the Angostura Reservoir area. Because no
pottery was associated with these pits, they were
tentatively assigned to the Comanche by Hughes
(1949:275–76), but such pits are not found in the
Great Basin, and on the Plains they are still diagnostic of Dismal River Apaches. Such baking pits
also occurred near Glendo, in Platte County,
Wyoming (Hughes 1949:275–76), an area which
yielded Dismal-River-like sherds (J. Gunnerson
1960:236).

The historical evidence does not contradict
either Kiowa Apache tradition or the archaeology.
In 1681 or 1682, La Salle had with him in the
Illinois country a sixteen- or seventeen-year-old boy
of the "Pana" nation who apparently spoke, and
specifically understood, French. From him La
Salle learned that the "Pana" lived more than two
hundred leagues to the west on a branch of the
Mississippi. These "Pana" were neighbors and
allies of the Gattacka and Manrhoat, who lived
south of their villages and sold them horses, which
La Salle assumed had been stolen from the Spaniards of New Mexico (Margry 1875–86, II:201–2).

There can be no doubt that Gattacka is a
synonym for Kiowa Apache. Mooney (1898:246)
pointed out that Gattacka was the name by which
the Kiowa Apaches were known to the Pawnee.
Dr. Gene Weltfish (letter, Jan. 9, 1970) has kindly
provided the information that this name is a
Pawnee word properly represented as "tska-taka,"
meaning literally "face-white," and that it refers
only to the Kiowa Apaches. Moreover, these

Apaches are called "Kataka" in the treaty they
signed with the United States in 1837 (Mooney
1898:251). Lewis and Clark collected the name as
"Cat-ar-kah" at the Arikara villages in 1804
(Thwaites 1959, I:190). By this time the Gattacka
can be certainly identified as the Kiowa Apaches,
and they were still trading with the Arikara. Also,
the close relationship of the Arikara language to
Pawnee makes it possible that "Tska-taka" or a
variation of it was the Arikara name for the Kiowa
Apaches circa 1680. Since it may be difficult now
to rule out the possibility that the term Gattacka
was also applied by the Pawnee to the Paloma and
Cuartelejo Apaches before circa 1730, the identity
of La Salle's "Pana," too, becomes important for
the identification of the Gattacka who were living
south of them in 1681. Mooney (*in* Hodge 1907–10,
I:702) suggested that La Salle's "Pana" were the
Arikara. And in any case, the Arikara were at
least included in the term "Pana" or "Pani" in
early French usage (cf. Strong 1935:12–13). The
Arikaras appear under their own name on De
Lisle's map of 1718 (Tucker 1942. pl. XV), possibly
as a result of information obtained by Bourgmont
(Wedel 1959:28).

In 1719, the Frenchman La Harpe visited contiguous villages housing several tribes of the Wichita Confederacy (Margry 1875–86, VI:289). This
large settlement has been variously located on the
Cimarron near its junction with the Arkansas
(Mooney 1898:251) and on the Canadian (Wedel
1959:65). In questioning the chiefs of the tribes
who lived in this settlement, La Harpe learned that
they were allies of the "Arricaras," who lived in
seven villages 120 leagues distant to the north-
northwest. He added, "I believe that these Arricaras are part of the forty-five villages of Panis"
(Margry 1875–86, VI:292–93). This opinion, along
with other information reported by La Harpe, is
reflected on Beauvilliers' map of 1720 (Wheat 1957:
op. 70), where certain villages are labeled as those
of "Panis ou Ricara."

Thus, La Salle's "Panas" could have been
Arikaras, and, since they had an Apachean group
as an ally, they probably were. As pointed out
earlier, the Apaches living to the south of the
Pawnees in the late 1600s were the Cuartelejos,

who were almost certainly enemies of the Pawnees by that date, rather than allies. And, since the Kiowa, by their own account, were "always" enemies of the Pawnees (Mooney 1898:160), it is probable that the allied Kiowa Apaches shared their attitude.

It has been generally assumed that the Manrhoat, who were associated with the Gattacka circa 1680 as neighbors and allies of the "Pana," were the Kiowa. The fact that the Gattacka and Manrhoat both specialized in horse trading helps bear out this idea. Although La Salle assumed that these tribes stole their horses from the Spaniards in New Mexico, the method of procurement was probably far more complex, and may explain the fact that groups bearing names very like "Kiowa" and "Gattacka" were noted at times among Southern Caddoan tribes in the late 1600s and early 1700s.

La Salle, in the Illinois country, wanted to establish a trade in horses with the western tribes, including the "Pana," "Manrhout" (Kiowas?) and "Gataea" (Kiowa Apache) (Margry 1875–86, II: 168), but if horses owned by these tribes had been coming from New Mexico, that area probably ceased to be a source in 1680, when the Pueblo Indians drove the Spaniards south to the vicinity of El Paso. There are suggestions in French and Spanish documents after this date that the Kiowa and Kiowa Apache, as friends of the Arikara, had been able to develop a north-south supply route via the eastern Plains, trading with the Caddos for horses sold to these Indians by the Jumanos, who raided in Mexico.

Father Douay, who accompanied La Salle on an expedition to the Caddos in 1685, found among these Indians many items stolen by the Jumanos from the Spaniards in Mexico, including numerous horses. Tonti, in 1690, observed horses in the Caddo country that bore Spanish brands (Swanton 1942:39, 44). In 1719, also, La Harpe indicated that the Caddo tribes themselves raised very fine horses (Margry 1875–86, VI:294).

Spanish reaction to La Salle's presence on the lower Mississippi resulted in attempts to establish Franciscan missions among the "Texas" Indians. In 1691 Father Casañas, a firsthand observer, listed the "Aseney" or "Texas" tribes, including among the names that of the "Caynigua" (Kiowa?), and noting that one of the group was not Aseney, but only allied with them (Swanton 1942:250–51).

This first missionary effort failed, but Fray Francisco Hidalgo later attempted to reestablish missions among the Caddo tribes of east Texas, and the indifference of Spanish officials led him to consort with the French (Swanton 1942:52–54, 265–71). From these rivals of Spain he obtained information concerning the "upper" Missouri. In 1716 he wrote the viceroy of Mexico that on the greater part of the "upper" Missouri that had been explored, the French carried on trade with the "Yndios Caynigua, Panni." The context of this second reference to the "Caynigua" suggests that they may have been the Kiowa. (It is possible that the spelling in the original manuscripts was actually "Cayhigua" since the handwritten Spanish *h* and *n* looked very much alike at that time.) Father Hidalgo also learned that some of the "Pannis" (probably those near the junction of the Loup and Platte rivers) bordered on the Apaches, with whom they had great wars, and the Pannis, who were better warriors, took many Apache captives, whom they sold to the French for slaves (Swanton 1942:269–70). Here, before the expedition of Valverde in 1719, is almost certainly an account of the conflicts that led the Paloma Apaches to abandon their lands. The statement that the French were trading with the Caynigua (Kiowa?) *and* the "Panni" suggests that they had put into effect La Salle's plan to trade for horses with western tribes.

In addition to these comments of the Spanish friars, there is another relevant observation of La Harpe, who included a group of "Quataquois" (phonetically "Katakwa," a version of Gattacka) in a list of nine tribes represented at the Wichita village he visited in 1719, although he held a council with only eight of the nine (Margry 1875–86, VI:289–90). The Indians at this village were allies of the Arikaras. In a footnote to La Harpe's list, moreover, Beaurain says that all the tribes named by La Harpe were allies of the "paniouassa" (Wichita) (see Wedel 1959:27); that they had knowledge of the Arikaras, but that they carried on cruel war with the "canecy," the "padoucas" and with some villages of the "Panis" (Margry 1875–86, VI:289–90). In connection with La Harpe's "Quataquois," it is interesting that, although the Wichita in the late 1800s usually called the Kiowa Apache "Gïnä?s," they sometimes called them "Ga?taqkä" (Mooney 1898:1081).

If the Caynigua were the Kiowa and the Quataquois the Kiowa Apaches, as seems probable, we surmise that they were getting horses from the Wichitas and Caddos through trade and later selling them to the French via the Arikara. Such an orientation toward the French could have created or intensified hostilities between the Kiowa Apaches and those Apaches friendly with the Spaniards. It is not surprising that the Caddo-Wichita alliance with the Arikara excluded the Pawnee, since the Pawnee and Arikara were on bad terms at intervals.

Actually, the horses traded by the Kiowas and Kiowa Apaches seem later to have come from a variety of sources. They were undoubtedly taken from enemy tribes such as the Comanches, and the herds were probably also augmented by capture of wild horses and natural increase. However, if the primary procurement route lay east of the High Plains in the 1700s, the fact would be compatible with various other aspects of the total picture of the Plains and their margins in that period, including the scarcity of information on the Kiowas and Kiowa Apaches in the New Mexico archives.

The presence of friendly Apaches on the Central Plains and in the Sangre de Cristo Mountains probably served to some extent as a buffer for the Spanish settlements. The Jicarillas, for example, were explicitly enemies of the Kiowa Apaches (Opler 1938:381–83), making it likely that the Cuartelejos and Palomas were also. The Comanches, who challenged the Apaches on the western Plains in the early 1700s, were bitter enemies of the Kiowa and Kiowa Apaches (Mooney 1898:162) and hence probably also served to divert them to the east.

The first and only reference we have found to the Kiowa Apaches as such in a Spanish document occurs in 1746. It has to do with a "native of the Apache Kiowa tribe" purchased when about

twelve years old "from the barbarous Apaches who brought him as has been the custom in this kingdom" (listed as doc. 183 *in* Twitchell 1914, I:73). This reference indicates that the Kiowa-Kiowa Apache alliance had taken place by 1746, and the fact that the captive involved was brought in by other Apaches shows that there was already hostility between the Kiowa Apaches and those friendly to the Spaniards.

As a tribe, the Kiowas seem not to have had direct contact with the Spaniards of New Mexico until about 1800. But individual Kiowas were brought in as captives of other tribes and purchased by Spaniards as slaves or "servants" much earlier. The first known record of a Kiowa (Caigua) in New Mexico is reported by Brugge (1965), who presents information on Plains Indians recorded in New Mexico church records. A Christianized Kiowa woman fifty to sixty years old was buried at Isleta Pueblo in 1727, and between 1730 and 1790 thirty-five baptisms of Kiowas are recorded. There could have been others, since many Indians were not identified by tribe, but only by such terms as *gentile* or *barbarian*. Among the New Mexico archives in the Bancroft Library is the record of the trial, in 1738, of Santiago Crizaval, a "Caigua" Indian (see Chavez 1950:249).

In 1748, at Santa Fe, officials questioned a Christian Indian "of the Caigua nation" who had been bought from the Comanche Indians in barter by a Spaniard when he was about eight years old. He had a brother living at Taos (SANM No. 494). And in 1752, there is reference to a Kiowa woman who had been bought from the Utes, who in turn had captured her from the Comanches in a battle "to the Northeast." The Comanches had captured the woman directly from the Kiowas (Thomas 1940:114–17).

There is a secondary source, Villaseñor (1746–48, II:412), that lists the "Cayguas" as enemies of the inhabitants of the "Kingdom" of New Mexico. However, this list is a hodgepodge that includes names that were no longer in use when Villaseñor wrote, such as "Hachos" (Acho Apaches), as well as names of tribes that were never hostile, such as the Jicarillas and Sierra Blancas (Carlanas), so it has to be considered unreliable. Actually, there is no evidence of Kiowa attacks on New Mexico settlements until the early 1800s (e.g., Brugge 1965).

By the early 1800s, if not before, the Kiowas actually were reaching the borders of New Mexico, although the relevant sources suggest that for several years they still had no formal relations with the officials in Santa Fe. Rather, the Spaniards had to go to considerable effort to make contact with them on the Plains, sometimes without success, because the Kiowas were traveling back and forth between New Mexico and the upper part of the Missouri River.

The Kiowas apparently raided in New Mexico in 1803 (Brugge 1965:188). Late in 1805 a Spanish emissary ("carabineer") named Juan Lucero was sent out from Santa Fe to make peace with them (Loomis and Nasatir 1967:449). He visited the Kiowas again in July of 1806, but, when he tried to find them in September of that year, he failed because they were on their way to the Missouri River (Loomis and Nasatir 1967:449–51; see also Carroll and Haggard 1942:134, 135).

The records of Lewis and Clark and the account of the French trader Tabeau indicate that the Kiowas and Kiowa Apaches were still trading actively with Arikaras ("Ricares") in the early 1800s.

In 1804, under the heading "Names of the nations who come to the Ricares to trafick and bring horses and robes," Clark listed, among other tribes, the Cat-tar-kah and Ki-e-wah, and commented below that all these tribes lived on the prairies from southwest by south to west of the Ricares (near present-day Sioux City), that all spoke different languages, were numerous, that all followed the buffalo and wintered near the mountains (Thwaites 1959, I:190). (The "r" in Cat-tar-kah may reflect Clark's dialect, since he spells "squaw" as "squar," e.g. Thwaites, 1959 I:185; but see Tabeau *in* Abel 1939:154.)

In another place Clark says of the Cay-au-wah (Kiowas) that they "*raise* [italics ours] a great number of horses, which they barter to the Ricaras, Mandans, etc. for articles of European manufacture" and adds that they "again barter a considerable proportion of the articles" thus obtained to other tribes. It was also recorded that they had a defensive war with the Sioux, that they roved on

the "Paducar" (north) fork of the Platte, and from the Loup River to near the mouth of the Chien (Cheyenne) River. Curiously enough, considering their long history of trade on the Upper Missouri, Clark says they were little known.

As for the "Cataka," he said they were friends of the Mandans and Arikaras, sometimes visited the Arikara, and were, like the Kiowas, at war with the Sioux. They moved on the headwaters of the Loup, the headwaters of the southeast branches of the Yellowstone, and between the Black Hills and the Rocky Mountains. They did not cultivate the soil (Thwaites 1959, VI:101–2).

Tabeau, also writing in 1804, indicates that even before that year the trade of the Arikaras with the Kiowas, Gattackas, and other tribes was being carried on at a rendezvous at the foot of the Black Hills (Abel 1939:154). If these tribes were no longer coming into the Arikara villages, it was probably for fear of the Sioux, who were inundating the village tribes of the upper Missouri.

Although the records of Spanish visits to the Kiowas in 1805 and 1806 contain no recognizable references to the Kiowa Apaches, a diary of events that took place in Santa Fe between November 25, 1808, and March 5, 1809, mentions Indian chiefs, including a Kiowa chief and a chief of the "Apaches del Norte" named "Cola de Aguila" or "Eagle Tail" (Twitchell 1914, II:531–32; document now missing). The letter of transmittal that accompanied this diary reveals that these chiefs had visited Santa Fe (SANM No. 2210). The "Apaches del Norte" were undoubtedly the Kiowa Apaches, who received, however, little further notice as such in the Spanish documents.

We have mentioned the possibility that the Kiowa Apaches were a connecting link between Northern and Southern Athapaskans geographically, if not culturally. Of interest in this connection are Mooney's (1898:160) statements concerning friendship and intermarriage between the Kiowa and Sarsi:

It is somewhat remarkable that they [the Kiowa] knew also the small tribe of Sarsi, living on the Canadian side of the line at the source of the North Saskatchewan, whom they describe accurately as a tribe living with the Blackfeet and speaking a language resembling that of the Apache.

Mooney said that the Kiowa and Sarsi interchanged friendly visits, and that several prominent Kiowa men then living were of Sarsi descent. He added: "By reason of this Athapascan blood, those of Sarsi descent . . . consider themselves in a measure related to the Kiowa Apache."

As usual, Mooney gives no details on this situation from the Kiowa Apache point of view, only implying that the friendships and enmities of the Kiowa were shared by the Kiowa Apaches throughout their association.

Of interest in connection with the geographical proximity of the Sarsi and the Apacheans within historic times is Krauss' opinion that the Sarsi language is closer to Apachean "in certain important phonological respects (especially tone) than are the other Northern Athapaskan languages" and that Apachean and Sarsi may have come from the same sector of the north (Michael E. Krauss, letter, Jan. 22, 1970).

The traditional, historical, and archaeological data taken together suggest (1) that the Kiowa Apaches were, as Mooney thought, always a northern group—namely, the northernmost of the Southern Athapaskans (2) that in archaeological terms they were Dismal River people who lived around, and seasonally in, the Black Hills, and (3) that they did not become associated with the Kiowa until after the Kiowa left the Rocky Mountains and parted from the Crow. If the third part of this hypothesis is valid, and if Mooney's (1898: 155) guess that the Kiowa moved out of the mountains "about or before 1700" is at all accurate, then the Kiowa reached the Plains at about the time the Kiowa Apaches emerged into history well east of the Yellowstone River under their Pawnee-Arikara name of Gattacka, variously spelled in the French and Anglo records, and apparently never used by the Spaniards.

As for Apaches of the Southern Plains, among Caddoan-speaking tribes of east Texas, the French, by 1700, were collecting and recording in various ways the term "Kántsi," "the Caddo collective name for the Apache tribes, signifying 'liars'"

(Mooney 1898:245). Bienville recorded this name as "Canchy" in 1700, and the "Connessi," whom he also describes, may have been the same tribe (Margry 1875–86, IV:442). Later, circa 1717, at any rate, he rendered the name as "Cannecy" (Swanton 1942:55).

Du Rivage, sent out from the Nassonite post established by La Harpe in 1719 (see Swanton 1942:58, 67, Map, Fig. 1; Beauvilliers' map in Wheat 1957 op. 70) to make contact with some nomadic tribes, (probably including Caddoan-speakers), learned from them of a nation of "Cancy," who were their enemies. According to these wandering tribes, the Cancys had a large village on the banks of the Red River (that forming the boundary between Oklahoma and Texas). This Cancy village was said to be about 130 French leagues (circa 350 miles) from the Nassonite post, which would place the Cancy near the southeast corner of the Texas Panhandle. Beaurain states that the Cancy had eleven villages "toward the source of the Red River." And on La Harpe's map, as on that of Beauvilliers, copied in part from it (Wheat 1957: op. 66, 70) several villages of the "Nation des Canci" are placed on the headwaters of the Red, in what would now be the Texas Panhandle. This area, from the Spanish point of view, was Faraon Apache country, and we have already cited Spanish sources that locate substantial Faraon farming villages in that general region.

Du Rivage was told that the Cancys were allied with the Spaniards in New Mexico. They had sabers and European clothing, but no guns, because of the Spanish policy of not bartering guns to Indians. The Cancy had an advantage over their enemies in that they had good horses, in spite of which, however, they carried their tents on the backs of dogs. Beaurain says that at one of the principal villages of the "Cannecy," called Quirireches, they had fine horses (Margry 1875–86, VI:277, 279).

The "Cancys" of the French certainly included the "Apaches" mentioned by the Spanish Franciscans Casañas and Espinosa as enemies of the Caddos (Swanton 1942:251, 277), and because of their location, some of them must have been

Apaches known in New Mexico as Faraons. The Faraons were indeed friendly with the Spaniards just after the reccnquest, in the late 1690s, but were alternately trading and raiding in New Mexico in the early 1700s.

It is probably impossible to ascertain now whether the name *kántsi* as used by the Caddo included the Central Plains Apaches, that is the Cuartelejos and Palomas, in the early 1700s. Confusing the situation is the fact that by 1717 the French were also collecting and applying a Siouan name commonly represented as *Padouca* to the Apaches (e.g., Secoy 1951:530 ff.). Although we cannot indulge in a discussion of the Padouca problem here, it should be pointed out that the French did, explicitly, apply the name *Padouca* to Apaches. The Vermale map of 1717 (Wheat 1957: op. 63), for example, labels the western border of the Central Plains "Pais des Appaches ou Padoucas orientaux."

An anonymous document by a Frenchman, entitled "Memoire sur les Natchitoches," written after 1718 but probably not long after, states that the "Apaches" would stand in the way of commerce between the French of Natchitoches and the Spaniards of Mexico. Most important, in speaking of the problems that the Spanish would face in attempting to open a direct route between San Antonio and New Mexico, he said that the only barrier was "the savages, whom they call Apaches, and we, Padoucas" (Margry 1875–86, VI:230, 232, 236). Here is a clear statement that some of the French knew that at least some of the Padoucas were Apaches. In French usage, at any rate, the term Padouca seems to have finally replaced all other terms for Apacheans.

The Lipan Apaches seem to be first specifically recorded as such in 1732, probably on the San Saba River in Texas. Whether this particular group was there earlier among the undifferentiated "Apaches" whom the Texas Spaniards had been fighting since 1723 is not clear, especially since the Apaches called *Ypandis* or *Lipans* by the Spaniards in 1732 were at that time in the company of three other Apache groups (Tunnell and Newcomb 1969: 154–56). It has been suggested that the Lipans, who are culturally and linguistically close to the Jicaril-

las, may have come from the Sangre de Cristo Mountains (Sjoberg 1953:76), but as yet no verification of this idea has been found in the documents.

In this connection, however, it may be of interest that only half of the Carlana or Sierra Blanca Apaches took refuge with the Jicarillas circa 1719. Chief Carlana told Valverde that the "rest of his people . . . had gone for protection farther into a land of Apaches whom Chief Flaco ["the lean one"] governed" (Thomas 1935:114). There was a Chief Flacco among the Lipan during the early 1800s (Winfrey 1959:164). While he would obviously not have been one who was alive in 1719, there seems to have been a sort of hereditary chieftainship among the Lipan (Sjoberg 1953:94), and in spite of the well-known Apachean aversion to using names of the dead, such names may have been revived after a time. For instance, Mooney records one case in which a Kiowa Apache subchief had inherited his name from his grandfather (Mooney 1898:445, pl. LXXIV).

One of the chiefs killed by the Spanish in their first battle with the Lipans had a silver-headed cane (Dunn 1911:232), the symbol of authority which Spanish officials gave principal Indian leaders. The chief's cane may be an indication that he and his people had been among those Apaches previously well known to the Spaniards in Santa Fe.

Also, Tunnell, who excavated the Lipan mission of San Lorenzo de la Santa Cruz, states that some of the potsherds attributed to the Lipan bear faint impressions suggestive of fine cord marking (Tunnell and Newcomb 1969:79–80). Since this is a good description of the marks left by corncob striating, these sherds may be comparable to Apache pottery from the Sangre de Cristo Mountains.

On the other hand, the Caddo have a specific name for the Lipan: "Sow-a-to," meaning "neighbors" (Swanton: 1942:7). Thus the Lipans may have been the Apaches living closest to the Caddos circa 1700. If so, they were also known then under the generic name *Cancy*, a definite possibility, since the Lipans are the only modern Apacheans known to have cannibalized captives taken in war (Sjoberg 1953:95–96), and the Cancys of the early 1700s also had this practice. La Harpe, in 1719, says, concerning warfare between Caddoan tribes and the Cancy, that these bore so much animosity toward one another that the victors ate the vanquished, not even sparing women and children (Margry 1875–86, VI:278–79). In March 1733, a few months after the Texas Spaniards had defeated the Lipans and their allies on the San Saba, two soldiers were killed by Apaches and their bodies stripped of flesh only a short distance from the San Antonio presidio (Tunnell and Newcomb 1969: 156). This episode is compatible with Sjoberg's description of Lipan cannibalism, and it is noteworthy that it occurred so soon after the appearance of the Lipans in the area.

The archaeology of the Apaches who lived west of the Pecos and the Rio Grande is virtually unknown, but a number of thin-walled pots with pointed bottoms, found by chance at various places in southern New Mexico and Arizona, can probably be attributed to various Western Apachean tribes. There are several pots of this type in the Arizona State Museum in Tucson, where some were identified as Apache by Grenville Goodwin, although the basis for his identification is not stated on the catalog cards. Another vessel, presumably from near Silver City, is at Western New Mexico University in Silver City. Sherds of this or a similar ware came from the upper level of a cave near Point of Pines in Arizona (Gifford 1957), and exceedingly thin sherds were found near Tonto National Monument (Ron Ice, personal communication 1967). The possible Apachean pots from southern New Mexico and Arizona are striated, but the tool used to make the marks cannot be specifically identified.

Since much has been written on Navajo archaeology, it will not be described here, but it is probably significant that Navajo utility vessels of the 1600s, like those attributed to other Western Apacheans and to the Jicarillas, are markedly thin walled (Dittert 1958:20; Brugge 1963). Navajo utility ware, early and modern, shows the distinctive corncob striation characteristic of Jicarilla, Taos, and Picuris pottery. Early Navajo pots, like those attributed to other Western Apacheans, have pointed bottoms, although the Navajo vessels seem

to be larger and taller. We surmise that the pottery of the Western Apacheans, like that of the Eastern Apacheans already discussed, is related to that of non-Athapaskan peoples of the Southwest with whom the Western Apacheans early came into contact. Since the shape of Western Apachean vessels has not yet been successfully traced to any of the Pueblos, we wonder if we should not consider instead influence from less culturally advanced, but still horticultural peoples, such as Yuman-speakers and perhaps even the Paiutes.

*   *   *

So far this study has been concerned with the diversification of early sixteenth-century Apachean material culture brought about as individual Apache bands adopted semisedentary life through association with a variety of non-Apachean groups. It has also considered the identification of some of these bands in terms of modern Apachean tribes.

All the Plains Apaches had adopted horticulture by 1700, and it is possible to demonstrate, by means of tribal traditions, historical documents, and archaeological remains, that at about that date Apacheans formed a continuous bloc from at least the Black Hills of South Dakota to central Texas. At the northern extremity of this continuum, the Kiowa Apache were probably ranging as far north as the headwaters of the Yellowstone, and, along with the Kiowa, exchanging visits with the Northern Athapaskan Sarsi, thus maintaining what was perhaps formerly a less tenuous link with the Northern Athapaskans. South of and contiguous to the Kiowa Apaches were the Palomas, and below the Platte River were the Cuartelejos.

Southwest of these Dismal River people, in the mountains and broken country of southeastern Colorado and northeastern New Mexico, were Carlanas and Jicarillas, who utilized the Plains to the east for buffalo hunting.

Southeast of the Jicarillas were the Faraons, whose farming villages were apparently in the Texas Panhandle and western Oklahoma, but who ranged widely in all directions.

In spite of the immense area dominated by these Eastern Apacheans and the diversity of certain aspects of their material culture, they maintained among themselves, and in common with the Western Apacheans, mutually intelligible dialects of a single language, and transmitted to their modern descendants what Opler (1936a:202) has described as "a round of beliefs and traits which the Southern Athapaskan-speaking tribes share with one another."

This remarkable unity in nonmaterial culture was undoubtedly preserved by means of constant communication, to which there were no barriers until the Comanches created one. The fact that the Kiowa Apaches are now the most divergent of all the Southern Athapaskans is very probably a result of their isolation from their closest linguistic relatives after circa 1719 when their immediate Apache neighbors, the Palomas, deserted their lands in western Nebraska, and in eastern Colorado and Wyoming.

Communication between the other Apacheans, on the contrary, was increased as they were gradually compressed into the Spanish Southwest. Instances of rapid communication in the first half of the eighteenth century are documented by Thomas (1935; 1940), and Cordero (Matson and Schroeder 1957) describes the various alliances formed by Apachean groups in the late 1700s.

This compression may even have resulted in the kind of blurring of dialect differences noted by Lesser and Weltfish (1932:3–4, 13) for Pawnee and Caddo bands brought into close contact on reservations. The Faraons, for example, might originally have spoken an Eastern Apachean dialect, but if they finally merged with the Mescalero, as seems likely, there is apparently no evidence of this addition in the Mescaleros' Western dialect.

The relative ease with which displaced or threatened Eastern Apachean groups were able to find shelter or ally themselves with other Apach-

eans is well explained by a general principle offered by Dumond (1969:862) in connection with Northern Athapaskans, namely that "[r]elated and relatively nomadic hunters who occupy a similar ecological niche in a continuous geographic area experience periodic shifts in population throughout that area." These movements, he points out, "may represent migrations to join people regarded as relatives. In such a situation, where languages are related, out and out language capture would be comparatively easy; at the least, both linguistic and general cultural differences would tend to be leveled."

Some shifting doubtless took place among the Eastern Apacheans before the almost simultaneous advent of pressure from other tribes and from Europeans. As the eighteenth century progressed, these movements were intensified, so that some bands just achieving historical identity were, through displacement, again lost in obscurity, while one, the Lipan, achieved identity for perhaps the first time.

It is certain that, as a result of constant shifting, and because of faulty communication among Spanish officials, Apachean groups known in Texas by one name were known in New Mexico by another. Therefore, clarification of Eastern Apachean culture history in the eighteenth century will require a careful comparison of Spanish archives originating in Texas and New Mexico, as well as in administrative centers in Mexico. It will also require careful comparison of Spanish records with those of the French. The results of the ethnohistorical work will need to be complemented with ethnographic and archaeological data. The result should be a fascinating study in cultural unity and diversity as exhibited simultaneously by widely scattered members of a single linguistic group.

REFERENCES

ABEL, A. H., EDITOR

1939   Tabeau's Narrative of Loisel's Expedition to the Upper Missouri. University of Oklahoma Press, Norman.

ADAMS, E. B.

1953   Notes and Documents Concerning Bishop Crespo's Visitation, 1730. New Mexico Historical Review 28:222–33.

BANDELIER, A. F.

1890   Contributions to the History of the Southwestern Portion of the United States. Papers of the Archaeological Institute of America, American Series 5. Cambridge, Massachusetts.

BRANT, C. S.

1949   The Cultural Position of the Kiowa Apache. Southwestern Journal of Anthropology 5:56–61.

1953   Kiowa Apache Culture History. Southwestern Journal of Anthropology 9:195–202.

BRUGGE, D. M.

1963   Navajo Pottery and Ethnohistory. Navajoland Publications. Series 2. Window Rock, Arizona.

1965   Some Plains Indians in the Church Records of New Mexico. Plains Anthropologist 10:181–89.

CARROLL, H. B. AND J. V. HAGGARD

1942   Three New Mexico Chronicles. Quivira Society Publications 11. Albuquerque.

CHAMPE, J. L.

1946   Ash Hollow Cave. A Study of Stratigraphic Sequences in the Central Great Plains. University of Nebraska Studies, n.s., 1. Lincoln.

1949   White Cat Village. American Antiquity 14, No. 4, Part 1:285–92.

CHAVEZ, FR. ANGELICO

1950   Some Original New Mexico Documents in California Libraries. New Mexico Historical Review 25: 244–53.

CLARK, W. P.

1885   The Indian Sign Language. L. R. Hamersly & Company, Philadelphia.

DITTERT, A. E., JR.

1958   Preliminary Archaeological Investigations in the Navajo Project Area of Northwestern New Mexico. Museum of New Mexico Papers in Anthropology 1. Santa Fe.

DUMOND, D. E.

1969   Toward a Prehistory of the Na-Dene, with a General Comment on Population Movements among Nomadic Hunters. American Anthropologist 71:857–63.

DUNLEVY, M. L.

1936   A Comparison of the Cultural Manifestations of the Burkett (Nance County) and Gray-Wolfe (Colfax County) Sites. Chapters in Nebraska Archaeology, E. H. Bell, editor: 147–247. University of Nebraska, Lincoln.

DUNN, W. E.
  1911   Apache Relations in Texas, 1718–1750. Southwestern Historical Quarterly 14: 198–274.

ELLIS, F. H. AND J. J. BRODY
  1964   Ceramic Stratigraphy and Tribal History at Taos Pueblo. American Antiquity 29: 316–27.

ESPINOSA, J.
  1942   Crusaders of the Rio Grande. Institute of Jesuit History Publications, Chicago.

FORBES, J. D.
  1960   Apache, Navaho, and Spaniard. University of Oklahoma Press, Norman.

GIFFORD, E. W.
  1940   Culture Element Distributions: XII Apache-Pueblo. University of California Anthropological Records 4, No. 1. Berkeley.

GIFFORD, J. C.
  1957   Archaeological Explorations in Caves of the Point of Pines Region. Unpublished M.A. thesis. University of Arizona, Tucson.

GODDARD, P. E.
  1911   Jicarilla Apache Texts. Anthropological Papers of the American Museum of Natural History 8. New York.

GUNNERSON, D. A.
  1956   The Southern Athabascans: Their Arrival in the Southwest. El Palacio 63: 346–65.

GUNNERSON, J. H.
  1959   Archaeological Survey in Northeastern New Mexico. El Palacio 66: 145–54.
  1960   An Introduction to Plains Apache Archeology—The Dismal River Aspect. Bulletin of the Bureau of American Ethnology 173: 131–260, pls. 1–38. Smithsonian Institution, Washington, D.C.
  1968   Plains Apache Archaeology: A Review. Plains Anthropologist 13: 167–89.
  1969   Apache Archaeology in Northeastern New Mexico. American Antiquity 34: 23–39.

GUNNERSON, J. H. and D. A. GUNNERSON
  1970   Evidence of Apaches at Pecos. El Palacio 76, No. 3: 1–6.

HACKETT, C. W.
  1937   Historical Documents Relating to New Mexico, Nueva Vizcaya, and Approaches Thereto, to 1773. Carnegie Institution of Washington Publication 330, Vol. 3. Washington, D.C.

HAMMOND, G. P. AND A. REY
  1940   Narratives of the Coronado Expedition 1540–1542. University of New Mexico Press, Albuquerque.

HARRINGTON, J. P.
  1910   On Phonetic and Lexical Resemblances between Kiowa and Tanoan. American Anthropologist, n.s., 12: 119–23.

HODGE, F. W., EDITOR
  1907–10   Handbook of American Indians North of Mexico. Bulletin of the Bureau of American Ethnol-

ogy 30, Parts 1–2. Smithsonian Institution, Washington, D.C.

1929   French Intrusion Toward New Mexico in 1695. New Mexico Historical Review 4:72–76.

HODGE, F. W., G. P. HAMMOND AND A. REY

1945   Fray Alonso de Benavides' Revised Memorial of 1634. University of New Mexico Press, Albuquerque.

HOIJER, H.

1938   The Southern Athapascan Languages. American Anthropologist 40:75–87.

1948   The Structure of the Noun in Apachean Languages. Proceedings of the International Congress of Americanists 28:173–84.

1956   The Chronology of the Athapaskan Languages. International Journal of American Linguistics 22:219–32.

1958   Athapaskan Kinship Systems. American Anthropologist 68:309–33.

HUGHES, J. T.

1949   Investigations in Western South Dakota and Northeastern Wyoming. American Antiquity 14:266–77.

JELINEK, A.

1967   A Prehistoric Sequence in the Middle Pecos Valley, New Mexico. University of Michigan Museum of Anthropology Anthropological Papers 31. Ann Arbor.

KEIM, DE B. R.

1885   Sheridan's Troopers on the Borders: A Winter Campaign on the Plains. D. McKay, Philadelphia.

KIDDER, A. V.

1932   The Artifacts of Pecos. Papers of the Phillips Academy Southwestern Expedition 6. New Haven, Connecticut.

1958   Pecos, New Mexico: Archaeological Notes. Papers of the Robert S. Peabody Foundation for Archaeology 5. Phillips Academy, Andover, Massachusetts.

KROEBER, A. L.

1947   Cultural and Natural Areas of Native North America. University of California Publications in American Archaeology and Ethnology 38:1–242. Berkeley and Los Angeles.

LEHMER, D. J.

1954   Archeological Investigations in the Oahe Dam Area, South Dakota, 1950–51. Bulletin of the Bureau of American Ethnology 168. Smithsonian Institution, Washington, D.C.

LESSER, A. AND G. WELTFISH

1932   Composition of the Caddoan Linguistic Stock. *Smithsonisan Miscellaneous Collections* 87, No. 6. Washington, D.C.

LOOMIS, N. M. AND A. P. NASATIR

1967   Pedro Vial and the Roads to Santa Fe. University of Oklahoma Press, Norman.

LUMMIS, C. F.

1898   A New Mexican Episode in 1748. Land of Sunshine 8:74–78.

McALLISTER, J. G.

    1937   Kiowa-Apache Social Organization. *In* Social Anthropology of North American Tribes, F. Eggan, editor: 96–169. University of Chicago Press, Chicago.

MARGRY, P.

    1875–86   Découvertes et Establissements des Français Dans l'Ouest et Dans le Sud de l'Amerique Septentrionale (1614–1754). Memoires et Documents Originaux. Parties 1–6. Paris.

MATSON, D. S. AND A. H. SCHROEDER

    1957   Cordero's Description of the Apache—1796. New Mexico Historical Review 32:335–56.

MOONEY, J.

    1896   The Ghost-Dance Religion. Bureau of American Ethnology Annual Report 14, Part 2:653–1,136. Smithsonian Institution, Washington, D.C.

    1898   Calendar History of the Kiowa Indians. Bureau of American Ethnology Annual Report 17:129–445. Smithsonian Institution, Washington, D.C.

OPLER, M. E.

    1936a   A Summary of Jicarilla Apache Culture. American Anthropologist 38:202–23.

    1936b   The Kinship Systems of the Southern Athabaskan-speaking Tribes. American Anthropologist 38:620–33.

    1938   Myths and Tales of the Jicarilla Apache Indians. Memoirs of the American Folklore Society 31: New York.

SANM

    Spanish Archives of New Mexico. State of New Mexico Records Center, Santa Fe.

SECOY, F. R.

    1951   The Identity of the "Padouca": An Ethnohistorical Analysis. American Anthropologist 53, No. 4, Part 1:525–42.

SJOBERG, A. F.

    1953   Lipan Apache Culture in Historical Perspective. Southwestern Journal of Anthropology 9:76–98.

STRONG, W. D.

    1935   An Introduction to Nebraska Archeology. Smithsonian Miscellaneous Collections 93, No. 10. Washington, D.C.

SWANTON, J. R.

    1942   Source Material on the History and Ethnology of the Caddo Indians. Bulletin of the Bureau of American Ethnology 132. Smithsonian Institution, Washington, D.C.

THOMAS, A. B.

    1935   After Coronado. University of Oklahoma Press, Norman.

    1940   The Plains Indians and New Mexico, 1751–1778. University of New Mexico Press, Albuquerque.

THWAITES, R. G., EDITOR

    1959   Original Journals of the Lewis and Clark Expedition, 1804–1806. 7 vols. Antiquarian Press, New York.

TRAGER, G. L. AND E. C. TRAGER
  1959   Kiowa and Tanoan. American Anthropologist 61:1,078–83.

TUCKER, S. J.
  1942   Indian Villages of the Illinois Country, Part I, Atlas. Illinois State Museum Scientific Papers 2. Springfield.

TUNNELL, C. D. AND W. W. NEWCOMB, JR.
  1969   A Lipan Apache Mission. Texas Memorial Museum Bulletin 14. The University of Texas, Austin.

TWITCHELL, R. E.
  1914   The Spanish Archives of New Mexico. 2 vols. The Torch Press, Cedar Rapids, Iowa.

TYLER, S. AND H. D. TAYLOR
  1958   The Report of Fray Alonso De Posada in Relation to Quivira and Teguayo. New Mexico Historical Review 33:285–314.

VILLASEÑOR Y SANCHEZ, J. A. DE
  1748   Theatro Americano. Mexico City, Mexico.

WEDEL, W. R.
  1959   An Introduction to Kansas Archeology. Bulletin of the Bureau of American Ethnology 174. The Smithsonian Institution, Washington, D.C.

WHEAT, C. I.
  1957   Mapping the Transmississippi West, Vol. 1. Institute of Historical Cartography, San Francisco.

WINFREY, D. H., EDITOR
  1959   Texas Indian Papers, Vol. 1. Archives Division, Texas State Library, Austin.

WISSLER, C.
  1967   Indians of the United States. Revised edition. Doubleday and Company, Garden City, New York.

Chapter 3

POTS, APACHE, AND
THE DISMAL RIVER CULTURE ASPECT

Morris E. Opler

MORRIS E. OPLER, professor of anthropology at the University of Oklahoma, first visited the Apache in the summer of 1929 and has been devoted to the study of their culture and interrelationships. Among his numerous publications, his book *Apache Odyssey* (Holt, Rinehart and Winston, Inc., 1969), deals essentially with Mescalero Apache culture. He has continued study of Lipan Apache ethnography. During the course of his long academic career, Dr. Opler has taught at Reed College, Claremont Colleges, Harvard University, and Cornell University.

Over sixteen years have passed since Waldo Wedel called for "a thorough-going ethnographical and ethnohistoric synthesis and interpretation of western Plains Indian culture" to supplement and extend information that archaeological work in the area was yielding (Wedel 1953:511–12). One of the problems which he hoped that coordinated research would illuminate was the interrelations of the archaeologically known Dismal River culture aspect, the Apache, and the "17th century puebloan fugitives from the upper Rio Grande" (Wedel 1953:508).

Since the time when Wedel called for a co-operative effort, a good deal of archaeological work at Dismal River sites and at locations thought to have been inhabited by Apache of the high Plains and its peripheries has been carried out, mainly as a result of the energetic efforts of James Gunnerson (1959; 1960; 1968; 1969). Yet such syntheses as have been attempted have been the pooling of archaeological and ethnohistorical intelligence, as witness the work of Dolores Gunnerson (1956) and James Gunnerson (1969) and the report of Tunnell and Newcomb (1969) on the excavation of San Lorenzo de la Santa Cruz, the mission established in 1762 in south-central Texas for the Lipan Apache. Ethnographic materials have

been little utilized, in part because they are sparse. Nevertheless, even where they exist they are often ignored. For instance, the authors mull over the data relating to the ethnic identity of certain skeletons found buried at San Lorenzo with heads arranged to the west and decide they must be Lipan. Yet a paper on Lipan death customs published in 1945 describes an easterly orientation of the head in burial (Opler 1945:124). This does not mean that the skeletons cannot be Lipan, for the Indians at the mission may have had little to say about the mode of burial, but, in reaching a judgment, all facts, including ethnographic facts, should surely be considered.

In the same study, which is in many ways a rounded and admirable one, sherds, all apparently pieces of one pot, are said to be probably of local Lipan manufacture largely on the basis of their strong resemblance to Dismal River ceramic materials (79–81). A single pot may indicate trade rather than an industry, and Tunnell and Newcomb (168, 170) themselves supply documentary evidence that Indian groups other than the Lipan came and went at San Lorenzo. Their tentative identification rests on two assumptions: first, that Apache were responsible for Dismal River culture, and, second, that Apachean ceramics are uniform throughout their range.

This study will be generally addressed to the first proposition. As to the second, we know that Navajo and Western Apache pottery differ in shape and other particulars from Jicarilla pottery, and a glance at the relevant pages of *An Apache Life-Way* will indicate that Chiricahua pottery differed from all of these (Opler 1941:382–84). The Mescalero Apache supply still another variant (Opler 1969:

50–51). I hope, before too long, to have something to say about Lipan Apache pottery-making from the ethnographic point of view, too. Intriguing as such a comparative treatment may be, because of limitations of space and because the Jicarilla are considered by many to be associated with the Dismal River culture of approximately 1700, I shall content myself with presenting some ethnographic material on Jicarilla ceramics.

Material has already been published that indicates that the making of pots was generally practiced among Jicarilla women, for instruction in the craft was a normal part of the training of the girl. In the process, in which the maternal grandmother took a prominent part, the manufacture of a number of vessels of different shapes and sizes was taught. The girl also learned to make clay pipes such as women smoke (tubular) and also the kind smoked by men (elbow type). Some of the ritual aids and precautions which accompany work in ceramics are discussed in this account (Opler 1946: 93–97).

In a volume of Jicarilla myths and tales (Opler 1938), a legend of the origin of clay pots and of clay pipes used by men and women for ceremonial purposes is found. A powerful supernatural leads a Jicarilla man and woman to a mountain containing precious materials. He shows them gold and silver but tells them these are reserved for foreigners who will eventually appear. He then leads them to the other side of the mountain and shows them a cave from which they can obtain clay for pottery. The supernatural next instructs the woman in the manufacture of various pots and in a dream informs her of how they are to be used and what names to give them. In another dream the woman learns how ceremonial pipes of clay are to be made, and later she guides her granddaughter in this art (Opler 1938:238–42). Thus there has been published material available for some time that suggests an important place for Jicarilla ceramics both in ritual matters and in practical affairs. To expand information about Jicarilla pottery, I should like to summarize information which I gathered in the field in 1934 and 1935.

Clay for pots and pipes was obtained by the Jicarilla from a spot in the mountains approximately eighteen miles southeast of Taos. Members

of both bands were free to gather their supplies of clay from the same place, which had the status of one of the important Jicarilla holy spots. Before undertaking a journey to the shrine, those who needed clay prayed and used a clay pipe in ceremonial smoking. Anyone who "does not believe the pipe" (that is, who omits this ritual gesture) is likely to fail to find the hole and return empty-handed. Men accompany women on the journey in order to help with the load on the return trip, "for the clay is heavy." When the travelers arrive at the holy spot, they sprinkle pollen toward it from the east and then from the other directions in clockwise order, saying: "I have come here because I want to use you. I want to live on you." Weapons or artifacts of flint have to be kept at a distance, or the pots made from the clay will break, for flint, representing male undertakings, is incompatible with clay, symbolic of the woman's world. The clay is dug with pointed sticks of mountain mahogany. Offerings of specular ore and pollen are left; otherwise the clay obtained will prove to be rocky and of poor quality.

During the period when a woman is making pots she must observe continence. If this restriction is not heeded, the pots will break and the marriage "will go like that too; it will go all to pieces." Before she starts to work the clay, the potter ties her hair at the top of the head on the sides in two bunches. The only explanation it was possible to get for this custom was that she does this "because she believes." Before she begins to work the clay, the woman goes out to urinate and defecate, for she is not supposed to answer the call of nature once she has begun to shape the pot. Two food restrictions come into force as soon as the work begins. Salted dishes may not be eaten, for salt explodes in fire and the pots, too, will break if this injunction is not honored. Boiled food is avoided; otherwise the "necklace," or design at the top, will be defective. While the work is in progress, the men must keep their flint-tipped arrows at a distance; if they are careless in this respect, holes will soon appear in the pots. The untipped arrows of children can be left nearby with impunity.

The clay is malleable and immediately usable if the return journey has not taken too long, and the work is begun at once. What is left is rolled in a ball and stored. Later on what is needed is broken off, reduced to smaller pieces, pounded, mixed with water, and worked with the hands. Nothing is added to the clay; "the shining particles [mica] are right in it as it comes." It is believed that if anything were added, the pots would break during the firing process.

In the making of a vessel the potter first works the clay to the right consistency, locating the impurities with her fingers and removing them. Bowl-shaped forms are modeled from the mass; "the thumbs are used to push in the clay and form the inside while the hand meanwhile is shaping it from the outside." The work is done on the right thigh, over which a hide or cloth has been laid.

If the potter intends to make a vessel of olla shape, she prepares clay coils and lays them on sunwise, building up the pot. When it has reached the right size and approximate shape, she begins to smooth it, first using a straight corncob for the outside and a corncob that has been bent and tied for the inside. A curved implement fashioned from a pine branch sometimes replaces the curved corncob. The corncob is dipped in water as the smoothing continues. A round stone is sometimes used for the smoothing, too. The potter tries to make the body of the pot as smooth as possible, for "it doesn't look nice otherwise." After the interior is properly smoothed, the "necklace" of the pot is placed along the upper rim if the pot is to be decorated. The "necklace" consists of rounded bits of clay that are pressed on or a fillet of clay that is attached. In either case there should be a "road" or a break in the "necklace" or decoration. As one informant said:

If he is going along a rocky ledge a man will find a way out, though it looks impossible, providing his wife, when she makes a basket or pot, doesn't enclose the whole object with the design but leaves a "road" open. As long as his relatives make a "road" on their baskets and pots, a man will be able to find his way out of a difficult place. If he is chased to a deep arroyo, he'll find a way to cross. His pursuers won't be able to pass the barrier. He'll be the only one who has a road.

After the pot is decorated, it is put out in the sun. If the sun is strong, it does not take too long

to dry. At this time the potter watches to make sure that the rim does not sag or become uneven. As soon as the clay is quite dry and firm, the potter builds a fire and places the pot at the edge of it, turning it at intervals. At first the pot is kept upright; then it is laid with the open end to the fire. When it is quite black, the potter rubs it with a rag soaked in water.

For the final firing, the bark of the Western yellow pine and the needles, too, are employed, for "it makes a big smoke and the pot comes out nice and black." In gathering the materials the woman must be careful to eliminate bark from trees that have been hit by lightning, "for they [the trees] are broken already and the pots will be that way" if she uses something from them. The pot is placed upside down and is covered with needles and bark, and then the fire is kindled. At this point the potter must be alone. As an informant put it:

When the fire of bark is built over the top of the pot, no one is allowed to be around. Before that it is all right to have others around; just while the bark is on she must be alone. At this time a woman would send away her own daughter. When the bark is burned to ashes she calls her daughter again, for she wants help in putting the pitch on while the pots are still warm.

The hot pots are pulled out with sticks and pushed to a level place. Lumps of pine and piñon pitch have been gathered, often by men, and melted in a pot. This pitch is applied to the outside of the pot with a grass brush or with a brush made from the coarse leg hair of the buffalo. This is considered to give the exterior a pleasing gloss and is also believed to harden the vessel.

What is the significance of such ethnographic materials for Plains and Southwest protohistory and prehistory? For one thing, they suggest that the Jicarilla pottery complex has considerable time depth. The antagonistic dichotomy between flint-tipped artifacts and pottery suggests this. The rather thorough integration of pottery-making into Jicarilla culture—its determinate place in ritual, child-training, the relation between the sexes, and other facets of life—points in the same direction. The elaboration of the complex—the fact that both coiling and modeling from the mass were employed and that a variety of shapes and sizes were made for specific foods and purposes—also supports this view.

Another noteworthy feature of Jicarilla ceramics is its strong association with the region around Taos and Picuris, a circumstance that takes on added significance because of the close resemblance of Jicarilla pottery to that made at Taos and Picuris since the late seventeenth century. The favorite place from which the desired micaceous clay comes is considered to be one of the important Jicarilla shrines and must be approached only after ritual preparations and with ritual safeguards. It will be remembered that in an account already published one of the reasons assigned for raiding to the east was the acquisition of horses for the easier transportation of clay from the Taos area stronghold (Opler 1938:247). That the center of gravity of the Jicarilla pottery complex was west rather than east emerges in testimony from informants such as this:

> The Jicarilla never used buffalo chips for firing pots. They always used pine bark. Pots were never made when they were out on the plains where there was no wood. They just went to the plains for hunting, raiding, and fighting. They used the chips then for cooking and warmth but not for pottery-making. They didn't stay out in the plains long enough to make pots. They were afraid of the Plains people, and the Plains people were afraid of them.

In reviewing the evidence I have summarized and also in considering other data which I have not had space to introduce, such as the virtual identity of Taos, Picuris, and Jicarilla methods of pottery manufacture, it is difficult to escape the conclusion that the Jicarilla pottery complex had its origin in the Taos-Picuris area and was essentially inspired and influenced by eastern Pueblo examples. Of course, the elements of the pottery complex are not the only debts the Jicarilla owe to the region and their Pueblo neighbors. The

shrine places from which red and yellow ochre were obtained are to be found in the same general area. We have historical records of the brisk trade between the Jicarilla and the eastern Pueblos. The mythology of the Jicarilla contains many references to these peoples (Opler 1938:22, 26, 44, 73, 100, 104, 113, 246, 336). The contributions of Taos, Picuris, and San Juan to Jicarilla ritual have been indicated in another published account (Opler 1944). Jicarilla agricultural practices developed in the proximity of the upper Rio Grande Pueblos and show many elements that are linked to Pueblo examples. This is a subject which I hope to continue to pursue.

As what I have said indicates, I think we must look to the Pueblo Southwest rather than to the village Indians at the eastern periphery of the Plains for the impulses that resulted in the Jicarilla Apache ceramic and agricultural complexes. If this is true, it raises anew the question of the identity of those responsible for the Dismal River sites of the short fifty-year period in the late seventeenth and early eighteenth centuries. We know that eastern Pueblo resistance and revolt against the Spaniards sharpened after 1640, peaked in 1680, and sent a flow and then a flood of refugees into the Plains. The period of their desperate resolve is essentially the time span ascribed to the Dismal River manifestations. Apache, too, fled to the Plains or further into the Plains to avoid Spanish wrath, just as they were to do to avoid American soldiery later on, and we have documentary evidence that fugitives from the Pueblos and Apache not infrequently made common cause. Yet, in my opinion, to consider Dismal River culture mainly a progressive stage in Apache development rather than a Pueblo retrenchment is to ignore historical knowledge and an array of ethnographic fact. In 1953 Wedel speculated about the relationship of the seventeenth-century Puebloan fugitives from the upper Rio Grande to the Dismal River cultural horizon. I believe that we have to entertain the possibility that this relationship is a very substantial one.

REFERENCES

GUNNERSON, DOLORES A.

1956   The Southern Athabascans: Their Arrival in the Southwest. El Palacio 63, Nos. 11–12:346–65.

GUNNERSON, JAMES H.

1959   Archaeological Survey in Northeastern New Mexico. El Palacio 66, No. 5:1–10.

1960   An Introduction to Plains Apache Archeology—The Dismal River Aspect. Anthropological Paper 58. *In* Bulletin of the Bureau of American Ethnology 173:131–260. Smithsonian Institution, Washington, D.C.

1968   Plains Apache Archaeology: A Review. Plains Anthropologist 13, No. 41:167–89.

1969   Apache Archaeology in Northeastern New Mexico. American Antiquity 34, No. 1:23–39.

OPLER, MORRIS E.

1934–35   Unpublished Jicarilla Apache field notes. University of Oklahoma, Norman.

1938   Myths and Tales of the Jicarilla Apache Indians. Memoirs of the American Folklore Society 31. New York.

1941   An Apache Life-Way. The University of Chicago Press, Chicago.

1944   The Jicarilla Apache Ceremonial Relay Race. American Anthropologist 46, No. 1:75–97.

1945   The Lipan Apache Death Complex and Its Extensions. Southwestern Journal of Anthropology 1, No. 1:122–41.

1946   Childhood and Youth in Jicarilla Apache Society. The Southwest Museum, Los Angeles.

1969   Apache Odyssey: A Journey between Two Worlds. Holt, Rinehart and Winston, New York.

TUNNELL, CURTIS D. AND W. W. NEWCOMB, JR.

1969   A Lipan Apache Mission: San Lorenzo de la Santa Cruz, 1762–1771. Texas Memorial Museum Bulletin 14. The University of Texas, Austin.

WEDEL, WALDO R.

1953   Some Aspects of Human Ecology in the Central Plains. American Anthropologist 55, No. 4: 499–514.

Chapter 4

MESCALERO APACHE BAND ORGANIZATION AND LEADERSHIP

Harry W. Basehart

HARRY W. BASEHART, professor of anthropology at the University of New Mexico, and editor, *Southwestern Journal of Anthropology*, has conducted ethnographic research among the Iroquois (Oneida), the Apache tribes of the American Southwest, and the Matengo of Tanzania, Africa. Dr. Basehart is the author of a number of articles dealing with problems of social organization in African and American Indian tribes.

The problem examined in this study constitutes a kind of paradox: how is it that in a society with a markedly egalitarian ideology, where the right of the individual to make and carry out his own decisions has unchallenged priority, the role of the leader is the crucial feature in the constitution of political units? To place the paradox in perspective, it should be noted that in the society under study the leader lacks coercive authority and plays no key role in economic redistribution. The characteristics of the small groups centering on leaders among the Mescalero Apache of the mid-nineteenth century and of leadership as it pertains to these groups are the central themes which will be explored in attempting to resolve the paradox.

From a more general perspective, the study is concerned with the analysis of one of the structurally significant levels of social integration—the political dimension—in this society of equestrian hunters, gatherers, and predators. Groups comprising leaders and their followers, which I have chosen to term "bands" for simplicity of reference,

NOTE: Research among the Mescalero Apache was supported by the Apache Tribe of the Mescalero Reservation in connection with their land claims and by National Institute of Mental Health Grant M-3088. L. Bryce Boyer, M. D., and the author were co-principal investigators for the latter project. I wish to thank Stanley Newman and L. Bryce Boyer for comments on the preliminary draft. This article appeared in the *Southwestern Journal of Anthropology*, Volume 26, No. 1, 1970.

were the major units with political functions among Mescalero. Decisions with respect to a variety of problems—economic, political, solidary, and ritual—were effected in the context of the band. The political complexion of these units was colored by processes initiated in the course of adaptation to internal and external problems; the latter involved relationships among similar units and links with the larger, non-Mescalero political field. The band leader was particularly important in connection with these problems; his role can be thought of as a homeostatic mechanism regulating (or failing to regulate) these varied political pressures.

Although political integration was a function of the segmental band organization, the maximal level of social integration was represented by the predominantly economically oriented resource-holding corporation. Comprising all those recognized as Mescalero, the corporation was not a corporate group; nevertheless, it was characterized by perpetuity and by a single jural personality (Basehart 1967).

Fundamentally, the Mescalero social system was predicated upon kinship: cognatic consanguineal bonds and affinal ties were the essential anchoring points for the extensive network of social relations. The kinship dimension is treated only incidentally in this study, since primary emphasis is placed on the organization and operation of political units. Membership in these units was not determined exclusively by kinship criteria; neither genealogically demonstrated connection nor stipulated kinship were requisites for affiliation with any particular band.

This examination of Mescalero band organization and leadership is an exercise in historical reconstruction. Typically, an enterprise of this kind is hazardous and, hence, I have used historical resources, particularly those concerning the relations between agents of the United States Government and the Mescalero during the latter part of the nineteenth century, in an effort to supplement and document materials secured through field research. The emphasis of the study is on a systematic synchronic description of one aspect of social structure, although I have attempted to place this description in a historical context wherever possible. Finally, there is the question of the extent to which the analysis is informed by the point of view of the Mescalero actors who have provided the basic information. In my judgment, the fit between informants' constructs and the synthetic and analytic statements in the following discussion is reasonably good; there is not isomorphism, but there is congruence.

BACKGROUND

In 1848, when the United States assumed sovereignty over New Mexico, the Mescalero Apache utilized an extensive territory east of the Rio Grande in southern New Mexico, western Texas, and northern Mexico. Their subsistence, based upon hunting, gathering, and predation, required a high degree of mobility to exploit the variable resources of different ecological zones. Equality of rights of access to the animal and plant resources assured to all Mescalero by virtue of membership in what I have termed the "resource-holding corporation" (Basehart 1967), together with the plunder secured through raiding, provided a margin of subsistence security. The degree of dependence upon a particular economic activity was not only a function of the productivity of natural resources in relation to technology, but of the wider political field in which Mescalero were involved, particularly by virtue of predation. For example, during some portions of the eighteenth century the booty acquired by raiding the Spanish frontier settlements formed a major contribution to the Indian economy, but at other times punitive expeditions and past treaties necessitated recourse to nonpredatory modes of adaptation (cf., e.g., Thomas 1932:10–11; Thomas 1941:125–29).

As heir to the Mexican territories of the Southwest, the United States succeeded as well to the series of problems associated with the Apache presence in the region. The opposition and conflict which had marked the relations of the Mescalero and previous foreign powers continued during the American regime until the reservation confinement of the tribe in 1873.

Historical documents for the period of U.S. control suggest that military and civil authorities were potent agents of change for the Mescalero, but it is not evident that the political forms remarked by informants and sketched in early reports were altered radically. It is true, of course, that the establishment of Fort Stanton, New Mexico, in the heart of the northern mountains in 1855 resulted in the concentration of a portion of the tribe in the vicinity of the fort. Officials recognized a "principal chief" through whom communications were channeled and regarded this spokesman as the leader of a "peace" party. But those army officers who acquired even limited familiarity with the Indians realized that the office of principal chief was an imposed legal fiction. The effective political units continued to be small groups centering on leaders, as the repeated references to the names of various "captains" in the documents suggest.

The concentration of groups near Fort Stanton was important in underlining for outside observers the extent to which Mescalero subsistence depended upon mobility. Fort commanders not only proscribed raiding, but for a time attempted to confine Indian movements to the narrow limits defined by an agreement made at Dog Canyon in 1855 (Pee 1855). The application of the policy quickly led to destitution and starvation for the Indians. To cite only two reports in illustration, Captain Van Horne in 1856 noted that "the people are miserably poor and very badly clad. They avidly devour a dead mule and eat up the leavings of dogs" (Van Horne 1856). Lieutenant Colonel Reeve in 1858 remarked on the destitute condition of the Mescaleros, who were then receiving small rations of corn and beef (Reeve 1858).

In assessing the impact of American power on Mescalero social organization it is important to bear in mind that the Apache had faced similar pressures over a lengthy period of time. Spanish policy for the control of the northern frontier had involved military expeditions, defensive bastions, and attempts to settle the Indians through the provision of rations, the introduction of farming, and the construction of special communities in the vicinity of presidios. Conflict with the Comanche also assumed increasing importance by the latter portion of the eighteenth century; Cordero (Matson and Schroeder 1957:354) claimed that by 1796 the group he referred to as "Mescalero" had been reduced to a small number of families as a result of the Comanche struggle. It is reasonable to suggest, then, that the features of political organization to be discussed below do not represent adaptation to a novel repertoire of problems. At a minimum, the form of Mescalero political units could not be inconsistent with the requirements of the continual emergency war situation engendered by the features of the wider political field in which the tribe was enmeshed.

MESCALERO BAND ORGANIZATION

The maximal level of integration among Mescalero, as I have pointed out elsewhere (Basehart 1967:277), did not comprehend a political nexus; there was no tribal chief, no council of leaders, and no device for decision-making which could implicate the tribe as a whole. It might be argued that all Mescalero acknowledged at least one general norm—the right of freedom of access to resources—and that tribesmen therefore were bound together under a common rule of law, but there was no superordinate authority empowered to administer this "law," as there was no single office for dealing with pressing questions of offense and defense. Bands did act in concert on particular occasions, but there is little evidence to support Major Carleton's informant's 1853 assertion that "When they are engaged in war, or upon any other enterprise of importance, these bands become united . . . [and] choose a head-man to direct affairs for the time being" (Carleton 1855:315). Indeed, this view is contradicted by the statements of two "captains or chiefs" (Palanco and Santos) who visited Lieutenant Colonel Miles at Fort Fillmore

in 1854: ". . . they replied, their nation was broken up into bands, there was no head captain or chief, but each acted independently and as he thought proper" (Miles 1854).

While the tribe was not a political entity, the wider integration of the resource-holding corporation had a significant implication for political behavior in that decisions by bands in relation to public goals did not lead to conflict over subsistence. Thus, one potential source of tension among these units was minimized, and the principle of mobility was maximized.

With this background it is possible to turn to a more detailed examination of salient features of the band. The following topics will be discussed: number of bands; band size; territoriality; membership composition; production and distribution; interband relations; and offense and defense.

Number of Bands and Band Size

Despite many limitations, documentary sources provide the most definitive evidence as to the number and size of Mescalero bands during the early period of American contact. Informants' statements with respect to prereservation group size were clouded by their conviction that there were very large numbers of Mescalero at that time and by the viewpoint exemplified by one very old man's comment that "there never was any reason to count the number of tipis."

I have examined historical materials (primarily letters from military officers and Indian agents) for reference to leaders during the years 1849 through 1861. For purposes of discussion, I have grouped the names of "chiefs and captains" into two time periods: (1) from 1849 to 1854, when American officials sought to deal with an undifferentiated Apache entity, and no treaties signed exclusively by Mescaleros appear in the records; (2) from 1855 to 1861, a period marked initially and finally by treaties involving only Mescalero leaders. The names of nineteen different leaders were recorded between 1849–54 for an area ranging from Manzano and Anton Chico, in New Mexico, on the north, to Presidio del Norte, in Texas, on the south. The most extensive lists for this time period were provided by Carleton's 1853 diary with seven names (Carleton 1855:315), and by a letter from Lieutenant Colonel Miles at Fort Fillmore which noted the names of nine band leaders (Miles 1854). The number of names increased markedly for the seven-year period 1855–61, with references to thirty-one leaders; five of these were reported to have died or been killed by 1857. The largest registers of names are those of the 1855 Fort Thorn Treaty, where sixteen signatures appear, and a treaty revision of 1861 with fourteen names (Roberts 1861). Sixteen names appear also in the minutes of a talk between Lieutenant Colonel Miles and leaders at Dog Canyon (Pee 1855). To summarize, historical reports indicate that United States authorities recognized as many as twenty-six leaders at a given time among Mescalero during the years 1855–61.

It is possible that the estimation of the number of bands by the enumeration of leaders' names exaggerates the segmented character of Mescalero political organization. But I do not think so. Some names mentioned in the documents may be those of fledgling leaders who may not have been able to maintain their positions over time but, as later materials will suggest, this is an expectable feature of the political process. Further, the available documents do not provide comprehensive coverage for the southern part of the Mescalero range; for example, the names of only six leaders who favored the territory beginning with the southern portion of the Guadalupe Mountains were noted. Since there is no evidence indicating that groups in this region differed from those in the north, who were better known to American officials, it is not likely that estimates based upon historical data are inflated.

Historical materials provide only a few references pertinent to the question of band size. The most significant general account is that of Carleton's informant, based upon eight months' residence as a Mescalero captive. He reported the strength of seven bands in terms of "fighting men" as follows: forty, nine, nineteen, twenty, fifteen, thirteen, nineteen. In addition, two chiefs in the Sacramento Mountains were said to have fifty warriors (Carleton 1855:315). Information complementing Carleton's record is sparse. Venancio and

Mateo visited Apache Agency in 1859 with fifteen men and boys and forty-five women and children (Steck 1859b), and Manuelito was said to have "about" thirty warriors when attacked by Captain Graydon in 1862 (Carson 1862). An anonymous memorandum of 1857 includes figures juxtaposed to four leaders' names; presumably, these refer to group size. The figures are 120, 140, 150, 160. Other indications of band size are provided by estimates of the number of "lodges": Cigarito's camp in 1849 had twenty-five lodges (Whiting 1938: 276); "Jose Cito" was said to head about twenty lodges in 1851 (although Carleton credited him with but nine warriors in 1853); late in 1869 Lieutenant Cushing destroyed a Mescalero rancheria consisting of "40 to 50 wigwams," and another of "about 25 wigwams" (Hennisee 1870).

I have used these and similar sources (Basehart 1967:282) to offer "an informed guess as to band size . . . [estimating] that numbers ranged from about 45 to 300 men, women, and children. The majority of bands at this time [in the 1850s] were intermediate in size, with a population of about 90 or 100 persons."

Informants' accounts corroborate the documentary materials in a general way. A few older Mescalero were familiar with the names of pre-Fort Stanton leaders such as Cadete, but the majority of references were to chiefs of the early reservation period—Natsile, San Juan, Roman, Tobacco. In addition, a number of less widely known men were designated as leaders by different informants and as "prominent men," but not leaders, by others. If those two categories are considered together, the number of leaders would approximate that reported for the 1850s. Further, groups with prominent men as their focus were small in size, suggesting a range in variation in band size consistent with the available evidence from the historical records.

Territoriality

The spatial aspect of Mescalero band organization needs careful statement if an adequate description is to be achieved. It is important to emphasize that bands were not local groups; they were not resource-holding units, and they exercised no control over a specific portion of land. At the same time, as I have noted (Basehart 1967:68), Mescalero recognized large, named geographical regions, which certain bands tended to frequent and within which particular leaders and their groups had favored camping places. But the exercise of these preferences was always subject to the subsistence pressures which were the critical determinant of Mescalero location at a particular time.

American officials were primarily interested in classifying the Indians as peaceful or hostile, but they also tended to seek information linking leaders with particular territories. For example, in 1854 Lieutenant Colonel Miles wrote that two chiefs of bands ranging west of the Sacramento Mountains to Manzano had reported on the localities occupied by seven other groups. A hostile leader, Santa Ana, ranged from the Sacramentos to the Guadalupes; three bands were east of the Sacramentos; and three others were located south of these latter mountains (Miles 1854). The geographical references are highly general, but even so, the statement tends to overformalize the bonds between leader and territory. When the names and locations of leaders recorded during the early portion of U.S. control are plotted on maps, the historical documents lend support to the emphasis placed here on band mobility. Leaders' names are duplicated in varied locales extending from Agua Nueva in Mexico in the south to the White Mountains and as far north as Anton Chico, New Mexico.[1]

The polarization of Mescalero into northern and southern divisions delineated by Agent Steck receives only slight support from ethnographic and historical sources. Steck considered that the northern portion of the tribe constituted the "peace party" and asserted that "at least ¾ of the robberies committed by Mescaleros have been committed by Agua Nuevo Apaches . . ." (Steck 1856). These Apaches, he wrote, "who belong to the dept. of Texas live in the southern portion of the Guadalupe and in the Limpia Mts. from there into the mts. between the City of Chihuihui and the Rio Grande . . ." (Steck 1857b). Nevertheless, "southern" leaders also frequented the Sacramentos (Steck 1859a), and northerners appeared in the southern

Guadalupes and elsewhere in the south. The patterns of movement of leaders and their groups reported by informants covered a geographical range from north to south; in the course of time most leaders visited the "network foci" and sacred places located in both northern and southern reaches of Mescalero territory (Basehart 1960: 106–10; 1967:279–81, 284).

When the Mescalero as a whole are considered, group movements were conditioned by environmental factors, including climate and seasonal developments affecting plant and animal life, so that there was a tendency for peoples living in the north to shift gradually southward with the approach of winter. Similarly, southern groups were likely to move to the northern mountains during the summer. These general patterns should not be overformalized, however; there were many exceptions, and decisions about actual group movements at any particular time depended upon the assessment of the relative importance of multiple variables.

In summary, then, Mescalero statements exalting their one-time freedom to roam as they pleased appear something more than nostalgic constructs developed to counter the boundedness of contemporary reservation life. Leaders and their groups did manifest long-term preferences for particular localities, other factors being equal. I do not know that groups with favorite spots in the same general area considered themselves as sharing a larger territorial communion, although these regions were recognized by Mescalero names. Commitment, ideologically and in terms of resource utilization, was to mobility as opposed to geographical entrenchment.

Band Membership

Band composition, like band size, was variable, subject to fluctuation over time, and determined primarily by the character of the leader. Kinsmen of the leader comprised the nucleus of the unit and ordinarily were its persisting feature as well. However, kinship was not a defining attribute for recruitment to the band; a close relative of the leader could choose to affiliate with another group, and even small bands were not composed exclusively of kinsmen. The constitution of the band was influenced by the options open to its members, who were free to align themselves with another group, or with no group at all, as they chose. A specific band might persist over time, but it need not do so. As bands grew, lost members, and disappeared, and as new groups developed, there was a continual but gradual redistribution of the population. In this state of flux the fixed reference point was provided by the leader, for whatever the fortunes of a particular group, the system of leaders and followers was the perduring feature of the political scheme among Mescalero.

Detailed information on band composition during the 1850s could hardly be expected, but it is possible to reconstruct the general features of one leader's group for a later period on the basis of informants' accounts. In the 1880s this band occupied a relatively remote area of the reservation some thirty-five miles from agency headquarters, and members had little contact with government officials.

At various times the band included three different groups, whose members were unrelated or linked by genealogical ties so remote that kinship was not considered a binding element for the group as a whole. Two of the groups occupied camp sites situated about a mile apart; the third group was less strongly attached and might camp in the area for several years, move to another part of the reservation, and return again to the band.

The leader's camp, referred to as the Lower Group, was composed of a small cluster of consanguineal and affinal kinsmen, including the leader and his wife; the latter's mother; two sons, one of whom was married but had no children; and two married daughters with their husbands, children, and the mother of one of the husbands.

The camp of the Upper Group was of more heterogeneous composition. In the kinship nucleus of the elder and his wife were two married sons and their children; the brother of one of the daughters-in-law, his wife, wife's mother, and wife's sister; two married daughters and their husbands; and one unmarried daughter. In the same camp, but unrelated to the elder, were two brothers, their wives, and children.

Information with respect to the membership of the third group associated with this leader is muddled as well as deficient. Most informants considered that the elder was a prominent man who had attracted a few people other than kinsmen to himself, but they were unable to specify the composition of the group. Others linked the elder with another man who, with his brother, had achieved some renown through raiding. The two elders were said to be married to sisters, with the combined families roaming in the Staked Plains region. The data are frequently contradictory, but it seems clear that the elder, his family, and allies did camp for extended periods in the remote corner of the reservation favored by the band under discussion.

The variation in informants' statements with respect to the composition of this band may be taken as representative of the flexibility of bands in general. Thus, two brothers who were kinsmen of an in-married female of the Upper Band segment lived in the area for a time; both were suspected of witchcraft and moved elsewhere. The taint of witchcraft remained with the group, however, and was the basis for the strained relationships between the segments. Eventually a quarrel developed during a drinking party, the leader was killed, and the band was dissolved.

The extent to which similar events led to band fission or breakdown in earlier days is difficult to determine. Fights accompanying drinking are reported in ethnographic and historical accounts, but their effect on group organization is unclear. Vengeance was likely immediately to follow an act of violence, but if the guilty party escaped and remained away from the band for a year or so, he could regain membership in his original group. The minimal role of ascription in defining band membership made it easy for individuals and larger units to become followers of another leader, and it might be expected that this option would be elected when friction became evident. The instance of band dissolution remarked above occurred in late reservation days, when band mobility was restricted and pressures for a sedentary mode of life had become effective. Thus, tensions which might have been contained by the flexible band organization apparently became explosive when constrained in a bounded field of social relations.

The inclusion of both married sons and daughters in the membership of Upper and Lower segments of the band may appear to conflict with Mescalero norms stressing matrilocal residence after marriage, the strong bonds between mother and daughter, the perception of the son-in-law as an economic asset, and the great importance attached to respect in defining relations between an in-marrying male and his affines. However, it is not evident that the presence of married offspring of both sexes represents a departure from earlier custom. Informants did emphasize that a young married couple should reside initially in the wife's mother's camp, but they placed equal stress on the prerogative of the couple to decide for themselves their later residential arrangements. If the son-in-law was a good husband and provider, the girl's parents preferred that the couple continue residence with them, but it does not seem that they had a jural right to demand conformity to their desires. Matrilocal residence may have been statistically predominant, but exceptions would not violate expressed norms. Further, political factors possibly exerted pressure for the retention of married sons and daughters in the core kinship clusters of leaders and elders. Documents from the 1850s and later years occasionally report sons succeeding fathers as "chiefs," and imply that the former had been active members of their fathers' groups. This pattern, of course, would be consistent with the organization of the Upper and Lower segments of the group which has been described as illustrating the principles of Mescalero band composition.

Production and Distribution

The majority of productive activities were carried out in the context of the band, although the extent to which the group constituted a single foraging unit depended upon its size. In addition, larger groups were considered advantageous for certain tasks such as bison hunting, so that several bands or segments might unite for hunting on the plains. In general, hunting and gathering activities were organized informally, with participation in a particular activity open to all members of the band but required of none.[2] For a band of average size— perhaps one hundred persons—foraging parties of men and women at any given time were likely to include only a portion of the group's membership. Hunting or collecting by solitary individuals was condemned as representing stinginess; this was particularly true for hunting, since every member of the hunting party was entitled to share the meat and other products of animals killed. According to informants, the male membership of a band did not form a distinctive unit for raiding. Any warrior, in theory, could propose a raid, drawing upon volunteers from his own band as well as others who became acquainted with the plan and were enticed by the prospect of booty.

Subsistence activities, then, centered about the band, although cooperative task groups were rarely composed of all the able-bodied members of the unit. Nevertheless, from another perspective, the band can be considered as a unitary production group, since the membership of various task groups fluctuated over brief periods of time. Individuals who hunted or collected together on one occasion were likely to associate with others at another time, whether for the same or different tasks. The shifting alliances of kinsmen and neighbors in productive activities resulted in an intricate cooperative network of a flexible character focusing on the band but capable of extension beyond it to adapt to exigencies of the subsistence quest.

Patterns of reciprocity ensured the circulation of subsistence products throughout the band. Successful hunters, upon their return to camp, could expect to receive visits from relatives, friends, and neighbors; the visitors were considered entitled to gifts of meat and could not be turned away empty-handed. Thus, in addition to the sharing of game among members of the hunting party, further distribution brought the majority of the family units in the camp into the exchange system. Livestock secured as booty in raids were eventually slaughtered (except for horses) and the meat distributed in the same way as game.[3] If a number of horses were captured, they were divided among members of the raiding party; warriors with excess horses might present one to in-laws or other kinsmen, or to an elderly man or woman without transportation. Wild plant foods likewise were widely disseminated by means of transactions initiated by visits after women returned from gathering expeditions. It is worth noting, incidentally, that the more reliable subsistence pursuit of gathering was not characterized by the sharing of the collected products among the women of the task group, in contrast to the obligatory distribution of meat among those participating in a hunt. Small game and wild plant foods in excess of immediate needs were preserved and stored for future use by individual family units.

Although the band was a focus for production and distribution, it was not a wholly independent economic entity. Not only might members of other bands be included in particular task groups and visitors share in the distribution of foodstuffs, but the band ultimately was dependent upon freedom of access to the varied resources available in the total tribal territory.

Interband Relations

Mescalero bands were autonomous and equivalent political units despite the considerable variation in the number of members comprising the groups. The bands constituted a segmentary organization in that structurally similar units were replicated throughout Mescalero territory. In a very broad sense bands also may be thought of as segmentally opposed, if it is remembered that the groups were open rather than closed and that, over time, groups were continually forming and re-forming. Bands competed with one another for members and opposed one another in attempting to maintain their identities.

Intergroup relationships were not characterized by conflict. Common membership in the resource-holding corporation eliminated a potential major source of conflict over access to subsistence resources. Bands were not vengeance units; no band member was required to "take up the fight" for an injured party simply because of shared group membership. Informants recalled numerous instances of intragroup violence, but only one example of conflict between bands was reported. In this case, both groups were reputed to be quarrelsome and "tough"; there was mutual dislike between the leaders. Eventually, the bands engaged in an open fight during a ceremonial in the Guadalupe Mountains, several persons were killed, and one group left Mescalero country to live among the Jicarilla for a number of years.

The character of intergroup relations also was influenced by a widely ramified network of consanguineal and affinal ties. As noted earlier, band membership was not defined exclusively by kinship, and, while the group was not exogamous, cognatic kin restrictions channeled the majority of marriages outside the band. It is unlikely that every Mescalero leader's group could claim to have kinsmen in every other group, but kinship links were very extensive.[4]

Opportunities for social interaction, in addition to encounters in the course of the subsistence quest, were furthered by the presence of network foci and by ceremonies, especially by the puberty ritual for girls, which attracted large numbers of visitors.

Finally, the flexibility of band membership contributed to solidary ties among these units. Individuals could and frequently did shift their band affiliations for a number of reasons: to escape conflict or vengeance; to observe a period of mourning; to relieve fear of witchcraft; to attach themselves to a particularly successful leader. These shifting allegiances aligned persons in different oppositions at various times, restricted the development of exclusive solidarities, and reduced the possibility of intergroup conflict.

Offense and Defense

Informants conceived of the band as the major locus for personal security and cited its role in defense as the most important function performed by the unit. The mountains, although offering some protection, were not a secure haven, and the plains were even more hazardous. Mescalero thought of themselves as constantly exposed to enemy attack; thus, camp sites commonly were selected for their defensive potential rather than for convenience. The disposition of lodges in the camp reflected Mescalero conceptions of tactical advantages in different ecological zones: in the mountains lodges tended to be scattered, while they were grouped together more closely on the plains.

The band acted as a unit for defense rather than offense. The hit-and-run raid was the characteristic offensive tactic; as noted above, members of a raiding party might be drawn from a single band or from several groups. Offensive and defensive tactics were opportunistic. If a raiding objective was strongly defended, the warriors sought another target, and a camp usually would be actively defended only when the attacking force was weak. The major advantage of the band for defense was that it provided sufficient manpower for guarding the camp and for engaging in delaying action in the event of an attack, while the group was small enough to permit rapid escape when necessary.

Although Mescalero generally avoided large-scale confrontations with an enemy, historical sources and informants' accounts indicate the possibility of concerted action on occasion. In engagements with United States Army units in 1855, according to Steck, the military strength of northern groups was greatly augmented by "Mos-caleros belonging to the state of Texas and Chihui-hui [who] were fighting and acting with them" (Steck 1856). Lieutenant Lazelle's account of his pursuit of raiders who stole stock from San Elizario offers another example of Mescalero ability to bring together larger forces under propitious cir-cumstances. Lazelle, with thirty men, followed the trail of the raiding party for several days and eventually encountered thirty armed warriors in the Dog Canyon area of the Sacramentos. The troops advanced to the raiders' camp—the lodges were temporary structures of boughs and leaves, and women and children were absent—but did not attack because their position was unfavorable. When Lazelle and his command engaged the Indians on the following day, the latter's force had been reinforced and numbered fifty to sixty war-riors. The soldiers suffered casualties in the skir-mish that followed and were forced to retreat (Lazelle 1859). Two Mescalero leaders and their people were charged with responsibility for the fight in informants' reports to Steck (Steck 1859b). At the same time it should be emphasized that there was no organization for regularly assuring collec-tive action by a number of bands under a single "headman" for warfare or other "enterprises of importance" as Carleton's guide had maintained (Carleton 1855:315).

Documentary materials affirm informants' per-ceptions of their situation as one requiring constant vigilance in the face of persistent danger of enemy attack. Lax security could lead to disaster, as when Lieutenant Cushing's forces surprised a rancheria of forty to fifty lodges late in 1869 in the southern Guadalupes. The Indians fought a delaying action which permitted residents of the camp to escape, but a number of warriors were killed, and a large store of provisions and equipment was abandoned (Cushing 1870).

LEADERS AND LEADERSHIP

Mescalero leaders were men of influence rather than wielders of power. To state this is not to imply that leaders were ineffective; on the contrary, they were the embodiment as well as the symbol of Mescalero polity. In discussions of decision-making, the counterpoise to the rugged individual-ism of the ordinary Mescalero was the model of the "good-thinking man"—the leader. In the metaphor of one informant, "Only the leader has a swivel in his neck, so he can turn; the others have a stiff neck, so he guides them, commands them." In fact, the leader did not command; he could not order his followers to take any specific course of action, however reasonable. He could exhort and persuade, and his effectiveness was in large measure a func-tion of his ability to "preach to the people," as Mescalero say. "Good thinking" and "good talk-ing" were inseparably linked attributes of the leader. Other qualities, such as renown as a warrior, were decidedly secondary in importance. An inarticulate man, however great his knowledge and experience, would be unable to assume the role of leader. But in spite of the emphasis placed on verbal facility as a prerequisite for leadership, the Mescalero leader was not described as gregarious. He was expected to offer food and drink to his followers after the customary morning discussion of problems, as he was expected to be generous and aware of the needs of his people. I have the impression (though the evidence, admittedly, is slight) that leaders tended to maintain a degree of social distance from ordinary members of their bands, preserving a demeanor of dignity and, perhaps, of aloofness.[5]

Reciprocal respect governed relationships between leaders and members of their bands. Respect was the major prestation extended to the leader, and in return he was expected to have respect for his people; failure to conform to this expectation could result in the dissolution of the band. According to some informants, a leader occasionally might be offered gifts of subsistence products or other items, but these were presented neither regularly nor in large amounts. The leader, then, did not serve as a focus for the collection and redistribution of subsistence or other products.

There was not a one-for-one correspondence between leadership and prowess in warfare and raiding. Some mid-nineteenth-century leaders were noted as raiders, but others were not. Informants disagreed as to whether leaders ought to accompany raiding parties, but achievement in this domain was not considered an essential quality for a leader. Whether, as some Mescalero claimed, leaders essentially were peaceful men who discouraged raids is doubtful; probably these statements reflect the altered role of leaders in the reservation period.

Leadership was not linked to the possession of supernatural power, even though it is likely that leaders, like other Mescalero, had access to some source of power. The role of seer, in particular, was considered distinct from that of leader, and accounts of the acquisition of supernatural blessings do not feature leaders as recipients.

Consistent with the emphasis on wisdom and experience as attributes of leadership, informants considered that full adult status was a prerequisite for assumption of the leader's role. A youth in his twenties who had for years participated in raids might arouse sufficient support to form and lead a raiding party, but his authority was limited to that specific task. Experience, ordinarily gained through maturity, constituted the most heavily weighted criterion for the leadership of various task groups. The historical materials rarely specify

the ages of leaders, but it is a reasonable inference that in most cases American agents dealt with mature men. Several chiefs were elderly men: Cigarito, in 1849, was an "old and portly man" (Whiting 1938:270); Barranquito was reported to be a "feeble old man" (Miles 1855); Pluma was listed as the "old chief" in a document of 1857 (Anonymous 1857). At the same time, some leaders must have been considerably younger: Whiting estimated that Gómez was thirty or thirty-five years old; Barranquito died in 1856 and was succeeded by his son, Cadete (Van Horne 1856); by 1857 José Pino had succeeded his father, Pluma, as leader, although the latter was still alive (Anonymous 1857).

Equality of access to resources and reciprocal gift-giving limited the development of differences in wealth among members of a band but did not prevent some individuals from acquiring a greater store of valued items, especially horses. The leader, however, was not a wealthy man; the demands upon his generosity were too great to permit accumulation. Through diligent industry the leader was expected to be able to procure goods sufficient for the requirements of hospitality. By example and exhortation he sought to ensure that his less-fortunate followers received at least a minimal share in whatever good fortune the band might have.

Mescalero offer a clear conceptual distinction between individuals categorized as "chiefs" and others whom they class as "prominent men," but not as leaders or chiefs. Earlier, I referred to the latter as "elders," and the term is not altogether inapt, since longevity was valued and the long-lived person was accorded special recognition. The incumbents of a variety of roles (some of which were open to women as well as men) might be considered prominent—for example, warriors, seers, hunters, and shamans. However, I am concerned primarily with those persons whom Mescalero regard as filling a leadership role, in addition to whatever other roles they may have occupied. There was considerable disagreement among informants as to the proper classification of "elders" (i.e., "prominent men"); some considered them to be leaders—albeit with a small number of followers—while others regarded them as equivalent to family heads within the band. The conceptual distinction between prominent men and leaders evoked greater informant consistency than did judgments about the positions of particular individuals, which appear to reflect the reference-group orientations of the informants. It is possible that the dichotomy attained importance after the 1850s, as Anglo officials attempted to impose a "head chief" upon the Mescalero. As noted earlier, group size varied considerably in the 1850s, but it is not evident that the leaders of smaller groups were subordinate to chiefs with larger followings. In general, then, it seems probable that the category of prominent man, with the connotation of relatively permanent subordination to a leader, was a development of the reservation situation. And the uncertainty manifested by Mescalero as to who was or was not a leader again suggests that the partitioning of the role of leader had greater conceptual than practical significance.

Thus far I have examined leadership in terms of various qualities which have relevance for the role of leader. Now I propose to review aspects of leadership which depict the leader as a man of action in relation to internal and external problems of the band. I will discuss, first, his role in decision-making and affect management within the band and, second, his relation to outsiders as representative of the band.

A critical feature of leadership emerged in the process of decision-making, where the mettle of the leader was constantly tested. The leader exercised no power, but his contribution as catalyst in the development of decisions was of major importance. Typically, members of the band gathered at the leader's lodge in the early morning, and the leader initiated a discussion of current problems. An exchange of views followed, with the leader proffering a suggested solution for the question at issue. Often the leader's proposal was accepted without debate; if opposition developed, a compromise might be attempted. When consensus could not be reached, the gathering simply dissolved. The leader's judgment and skill in persuasion was severely tested under these conditions, as failure to assess adequately the disposition of his followers could result in the fragmentation of

the band. Particularly in large bands, the leader's conception of a program adaptive to public goals might conflict with the interests of segments of the group, so that it would be necessary for the leader to weigh the importance of a proposed course of action for the group as a whole against the possibility of loss of members.

In addition to the group perspective which the leader brought to bear on his program formulations, he had the advantage of greater access to information and, probably, a more profound understanding of the range of alternatives open to the band. Visitors, including his peers, sought the lodge of the leader and provided reports on current conditions in other parts of Mescalero territory. Although a leader probably had no more detailed knowledge of ecology than other members of the band, his assessment of the multiple variables involved in decisions with respect to major subsistence movements often reflected his "good thinking." An illustration is provided by informants' accounts of the selection of a site for a permanent reservation settlement when the tribe was removed from Fort Stanton. Several leaders proposed different locations but neglected to consider one or another ecological factor. The "good-thinking" leader—variously identified by different informants—argued for the advantages of the modern agency area, pointing to the abundance of game, firewood, and water for irrigation.

A successful leader needed to be aware of tensions within the band, which could pose problems requiring the utmost in resourcefulness. On some occasions he served as a mediator in disputes, but more than a modicum of delicacy and skill was essential, since an inept move by the leader could result in accusations of meddling or favoritism. At the same time, the leader's attempts to reduce tension were buttressed by his reputation for "good talk," or "preaching." Mescalero evidence a strong distaste for people who "talk too much" and are wary of gossip, which may lead to charges and counter-charges of witchcraft. In a solidary group, this "bad talk" was countered by the "good talk" of the leader, emphasizing the major values crucial to community solidarity. The leader was the exemplar of the moral order, stressing by behavior and word the values of sharing, generosity (especially to the poor and solitary aged), industriousness, cooperation, and vigilance. It is not an exaggeration, I think, to view this expressive aspect of leadership as the critical bonding element in group solidarity. The post of leader was the major fixed point in the flux of the social landscape, apart from kinship; most Mescalero sought to orient themselves by this persisting symbol of sociability. Strong commitment to leaders was the rule rather than the exception. As one informant remarked: "There's no guidance without the leaders, and that guidance they have to have."

In external relationships the leader represented his band vis-à-vis like units and in relation to foreigners. This aspect of the leader's role became increasingly significant during the period of Anglo-American contact, to judge by the historical records, although it had been important earlier as well. By the 1850s some leaders had become skilled in using their representative role to create images designed to win approval and support from foreigners. Consider the plight of Barranquito, as reported by Lieutenant Colonel Miles in 1855:

> Belanquito [spelling uncertain] has professed entire ignorance of everything tending to rascality in his nation. He says he would be the last to hear of it, and is in daily apprehension of being killed by other bands. His own whipped him this day week. He of course must lie to screen his men, for he sent Indians in when Hayward's horse was stolen to inform me that a man of Francisco's party had taken it. He is a poor feeble old man, with no authority or consideration, troublesome, *and in the way* . . . .

The details provided by Barranquito are dubious, but they constitute a well-designed instance of impression management. To arouse compassion, the leader displayed his weakness; he emphasized his lack of power as a prelude to a disclaimer of responsibility for the actions of his band. But, despite the dubiousness of the particulars of this account, the statements form an impeccable record of the realities of power in the Mescalero band. Historical sources provide numerous instances of leaders acting in representative roles in relation to white officials and, as well, to one another.

The multiple expectations linked with leadership militated against the development of hereditary principles of succession. Nevertheless, a son, brother, or other relative closely associated with a leader occupied a strategic position in that he could familiarize himself with the problems of the post. As noted earlier, sons of two leaders succeeded their fathers in the 1850s, while at least one uncle of Cadete was a leader (Anonymous 1857). Mescalero did not always find the preferred qualities in their leaders, and they recognized that more than one style of leadership was possible. There were limits to permissible variation in role performance, however; a leader who exceeded these limits was faced with the ultimate sanction of desertion. His followers simply left the camp and aligned themselves with other groups. As an example, an informant cited the case of a man who lost his position as "chief" when it was discovered that he was dishonest, unreliable, and a liar. I could not determine the frequency of failed leaders from available data, but informants appear to believe that the conjunction of qualities necessary for effective leadership was relatively uncommon.

In this discussion of leadership I have depended largely upon ethnographic data secured from Mescalero informants whose experiences at best date to the Fort Stanton period preceding the establishment of the present-day reservation. It is reasonable to ask whether informants' reports may represent changes in leadership patterns fostered by the conditions of reservation control. Is the leader whose expressive function embodied band solidarity, the "good-thinking" man, the product of recent social change? A number of lines of evidence, including historical data, could be pursued in attempting to answer this question. However, I will limit myself to two points: (1) there was some continuity of leadership from pre- to postreservation periods, so that characterizations of early postreservation leaders need not be caricatures of earlier leaders; (2) the problems confronting Mescalero in the course of Anglo-American contact were different in degree rather than kind from those faced during the Mexican and Spanish periods. There is no clear evidence that a different type of leadership was immediately required by United States control which, in any event, was not completely effective until about 1880.

CONCLUSION

Mescalero social organization has been depicted in terms of two levels of integration: on the one hand, the tribal resource-holding corporation and, on the other, the small band centered on the leader.[6] At the maximal level of integration the resource-holding corporation linked tribal members through their shared right to exploit a territory common to all. The character of the integration provided by the multifunctional band is perhaps more obvious, in part because anthropologists commonly have examined this process by reference to the political variable, and the band is the effective political unit among Mescalero. At this point I wish to explore briefly the problem of the adaptive-integrative significance of the band and of leadership with particular reference to the variables of mobility and flexibility.

Mescalero subsistence required access to a range of resources which varied geographically, seasonally, and over time. The exploitation of these resources necessitated traversing an extensive territory, as well as lesser movements when animal and plant foods were discovered. With the availability of horses, rapid movement of large groups would have been possible, but in practice subsistence moves were gradual, with members of the band seeking to maximize whatever windfalls they might encounter on their route. In good years the combined resources accessible to Mescalero might have supported aggregations larger than bands for extended periods, but small groups were just as effective under these optimal conditions. When food sources were scarce, bands scattered over the territory provided for maximal utilization, at the same time minimizing problems of distribution and consumption. Further, as noted earlier, the common defensive tactic was based upon the mobility assured by groups of small size.

The external pressures which placed Mescalero on a constant emergency footing contributed to the continuing importance of flexibility for their social organization. The open character of band membership permitted the redistribution of personnel in the event of losses in warfare and raiding. In competition among bands there was selection for the efficient leader; the ineffective chief was deserted by his followers, and his group failed to persist as an independent entity. Flexibility applied to interband relationships also, as both alliance and disjunction were feasible when situationally warranted. Relations among groups were not defined in pyramidal fashion, however, and there was no genealogical or other specified form to order the massing of segments. At the political level the autonomy of the band paralleled the individual's right to independent decision.

In the context of mobility and flexibility, the role of the leader acquires added significance. For all that he was but first among equals, he was the firm reference point in a system lacking fixed membership groups above the level of domestic units. The institution of leadership preserved the options of the individual at the same time that it fostered the processes that maintained a structure of autonomous political segments. It is appropriate that, for Mescalero, the leader rather than a territorial locus was the prime symbol of the band. Whereas the widest integration of Mescalero society was achieved through the resource-holding corporation, in which each individual was a shareholder, the band was the essential intermediate unit, mediating between the shareholder and the maximal extension of solidarity represented by the corporation.

NOTES

[1] The mobility of Mescalero leaders and their groups is evidenced by the migratory patterns described briefly in previous reports (Basehart 1967:279–81; Basehart 1960:106–10).

[2] The extent to which captives were utilized for production aside from labor within the camp is not clear. Whiting (1938:277–78) reported of Cigarito's camp in 1849: "Each lodge also has a

Mexican slave, a boy or girl stolen in infancy and brought up by the blows of the women to very severe labor. Literally do the Mexican race thus become hewers of wood and drawers of water, bondsmen to the Indian." However, some captives became fully assimilated to Mescalero lifeways, and assumed customary male or female roles.

[3] Steck, in 1857, estimated that one-half of the subsistence of nonrationed Apache bands was derived from stealing (Steck 1857a).

[4] Kin ties between bands were noted occasionally in the historical records; as one example, "Binanchio," the leader of a group whose activities tended to center on the southern portion of the Mescalero area, was married to the daughter of Manco, one of the leaders at Fort Stanton (Reeve 1858b).

[5] Leaders did not wear distinctive regalia, although historical records note that a few adopted hats and other articles of Spanish clothing. The leader's lodge, usually a commodious tipi, was situated in the center of the camp; in 1849 Whiting noted that the only tipi in Cigarito's Davis Mountain camp was that of the leader (Whiting 1938: 276).

[6] In addition, I recognize a third level of integration of the Mescalero social system: the domestic level. However, problems of kinship and family organization related to this level of integration have not been explored in this study.

REFERENCES

ANONYMOUS

1857   Names of some of the principal Mezcalero Apaches who have been in at Fort Stanton. March 25, 1857. (Probably a draft memorandum.)

BASEHART, HARRY W.

1960   Mescalero Apache Subsistence Patterns and Socio-Political Organization. Mimeographed paper for the University of New Mexico Mescalero-Chiricahua Land Claims Project. Albuquerque.

1967   The Resource Holding Corporation among the Mescalero Apache. Southwestern Journal of Anthropology 23:277–91.

CARLETON, JAMES HENRY

1855   Diary of an Excursion to the Ruins of Abo, Quarra and Gran Quivira, in New Mexico, under the Command of Major James Henry Carleton, U.S.A. Ninth Annual Report of the Smithsonian Institution. Washington, D.C.

CARSON, COL. C.

1862   Unpublished letter to Lt. B. C. Cutler. Fort Stanton, New Mexico. October 30, 1862. The National Archives, Record Group 98. Washington, D.C.

CUSHING, LT. H. B.

1870   Unpublished report to post adjutant. Fort Stanton, New Mexico. January 8, 1870. The National Archives, Record Group 98. Washington, D.C.

HENNISEE, LT. A. G.

1870   Unpublished letter to Major William Clinton. Fort Stanton, New Mexico. January 31, 1870. The National Archives, Record Group 75. Washington, D.C.

LAZELLE, LT. H. M.

1859   Unpublished letter to Lt. William Jackson. Fort Bliss, Texas. February 18, 1859. The National Archives, Record Group 98. Washington, D.C.

MATSON, DANIEL S. AND ALBERT H. SCHROEDER
1957 Cordero's Description of the Apache—1796. New Mexico Historical Review 32:335–56.

MILES, LT. COL. D. J.
1854 Unpublished letter to W. A. Nichols. Fort Fillmore, New Mexico. September 18, 1854. The National Archives, Record Group 98. Washington, D.C.
1855 Unpublished letter to Dr. M. Steck. Fort Fillmore, New Mexico. August 12, 1855. Steck Papers. University of New Mexico Library, Albuquerque.

PEE, LT. P. E.
1855 Minutes of a "talk" held at Dog Canyon on April 3, 1855. National Archives, Record Group 75. Washington, D.C.

REEVE, LT. COL. G. V. D.
1858a Unpublished letter to Major W. A. Nichols. Fort Stanton, New Mexico. January 6, 1858. The National Archives, Record Group 98. Washington, D.C.
1858b Unpublished letter to Major W. A. Nichols. Fort Stanton, New Mexico. July 15, 1858. The National Archives, Record Group 98. Washington, D.C.

ROBERTS, COL. B. S.
1861 Unpublished letter to Colonel Collins. Fort Stanton, New Mexico. May 24, 1861. The National Archives, Record Group 75. Washington, D.C.

STECK, M.
1856 Unpublished letter to Governor Meriwether. Fort Stanton, New Mexico. November 17, 1856. Steck Papers. University of New Mexico Library, Albuquerque.
1857a Annual Report of Commissioner of Indian Affairs Attached Report No. 123. Washington, D.C.
1857b Unpublished letter to Col. J. L. Collins. Apache Agency, New Mexico. June 8, 1857. Steck Papers. University of New Mexico Library, Albuquerque.
1859a Unpublished letter to Col. James L. Collins. Apache Agency, New Mexico. February 11, 1859. The National Archives, Record Group 75. Washington, D.C.
1859b Unpublished letter to Col. James L. Collins. Apache Agency, New Mexico. February 27, 1859. Steck Papers. University of New Mexico Library, Albuquerque.

STEVENSON, CAPT. O. L.
1861 Unpublished letter to Capt. D. H. Marcy (?). Fort Stanton, New Mexico. February 13, 1861.

THOMAS, A. B.
1932 Forgotten Frontiers: A Study of Spanish-Indian Policy of Don Juan Bautista de Anza, Governor of New Mexico, 1777–1787. University of Oklahoma Press, Norman.
1941 Teodoro de Croix and the Northern Frontier of New Spain, 1776–1783. University of Oklahoma Press, Norman.

VAN HORNE, MAJOR J.
1856 Unpublished letter to M. Steck. Fort Stanton, New Mexico. July 1, 1856. Steck Papers. University of New Mexico Library, Albuquerque.

WHITING, WILLIAM HENRY CHASE
1938 Journal of William Henry Chase Whiting, 1849. *In* Exploring Southwest Trails, 1846–1854, Ralph B. Bieber, editor. The Arthur H. Clark Company, Glendale, California.

Chapter 5

NAVAJO CULTURE CHANGE: 1550 TO 1960 AND BEYOND

James J. Hester

JAMES J. HESTER, associate professor of anthropology at the University of Colorado, published his Ph.D. dissertation, *Early Navajo Migrations and Acculturation in the Southwest*, with the Museum of New Mexico Press in 1962. Dr. Hester's primary area of specialization has been archaeology with emphasis upon culture change and man-environmental relationships. He participated in research in South Dakota, New Mexico, Texas, Mexico, and Egypt, and in 1970 was directing a project in coastal British Columbia.

In an early 1960s monograph (Hester 1962), Navajo culture history was reviewed in some detail. The historical aspects of this study focused on the Pre-Bosque Redondo Period (pre-1868), with only limited attention being devoted to events which occurred after that time. A visual presentation of this description of Navajo culture change appears in Figure 1.

On the basis of these data a set of statements was developed which attempted to describe prominent processes of acculturation. In addition, several predictions were offered as to the direction future changes in Navajo culture were likely to take. Inasmuch as these predictions were developed primarily on the basis of pre-1868 data, it seems appropriate at this time to expand the coverage of events since that date. A second aim of this study is an evaluation of the culture change predictions after an interval of approximately eight years.

We will consider each period of Navajo acculturation as presented in the 1962 monograph before reviewing subsequently published data. For each period we will also attempt to isolate the cultural processes at work.

NOTE: I wish to express my appreciation to William Y. Adams, Bryan P. Michener, Gottfried O. Lang, and Deward Walker for suggestions that have been incorporated into this article.

NAVAJO-PUEBLO ACCULTURATION

Navajo-Pueblo contact was prolonged and varied. At one time or another during the Spanish Period, the Navajo were allied with the peoples of Jemez, Acoma, Taos, Picuris, and Cochiti. They raided Jemez, Acoma, Zia, Hawikuh, Laguna, Santa Clara, Hopi, San Ildefonso, and San Juan. Refugees known to have fled to the Navajo include Hopi and Jemez. Additional contacts took place at Spanish trade fairs. These contacts may best be discussed in terms of two separate periods, the Initial Contact Period and the Pueblo Revolt Period.

During the Period of Initial Contact, approximately 1550–1600, the Navajo obtained agriculture and agricultural ritual from the Pueblos. The conditions under which this contact occurred were intermittent, firsthand, and both friendly and hostile. These complexes seem to have been easily accepted, presumably because they were compatible with the existing culture. The earlier economy, hunting and gathering, was retained with some loss of emphasis, as agriculture performed more adequately the function of supplying ample food in a new environment. Agricultural ritual was only partially integrated, suffering some loss of form and considerable loss of meaning.

Following the Pueblo Revolt, the conditions of contact were radically altered. Pueblo Indians, in large numbers, lived side by side with the Navajo, often in the same settlement (Hester 1962: figures 6, 14a). Much intermarriage must have occurred, as this condition existed for a number of years. The cause of this situation, the need to escape from Spanish domination, was a common theme affecting both ethnic groups and was probably an important factor in acculturation. After 1700, the

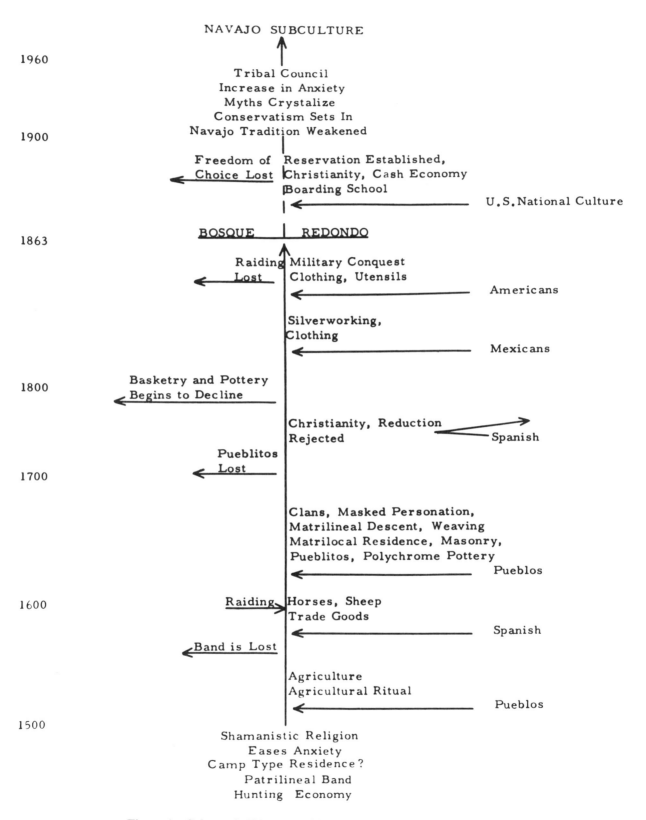

Figure 1   Schematic Diagram of Navajo Culture Change 1500–1960

period of intense acculturation began to draw to a close. Gradually, some of the Pueblos returned to their original homes, and the remainder amalgamated with the Navajo. In terms of rate of acculturation, the results of this contact period were impressive. In the space of a few years the Navajo adopted Puebloan styles of architecture, manufacturing techniques, and religious paraphernalia, plus many elements of nonmaterial culture, such as clans, matrilineal descent, matrilocal residence, the origin myth, and ritual. A detailed analysis of these adoptions in religious paraphernalia and ritual is presented in Parsons (1939:1039–63) and Horner (1931). The economy remained essentially unchanged.

Thus, the first half of the eighteenth century may be described as a period of Navajo-Pueblo fusion in which Pueblo influence dominated, especially in the sphere of material culture. The last half of the eighteenth century saw a simplification of the introduced Puebloan traits with considerable loss in form. This fact may be interpreted as a reassertion of the traditional Navajo cultural focus.

NAVAJO-SPANISH ACCULTURATION

Navajo-Spanish contacts fluctuated in quantity but were essentially the same throughout the Spanish Period. The conditions of contact were intermittent and firsthand, they tended to be hostile, and the Spanish attempted to effect directed culture change through the application of force. Types of contacts included the establishment of trade fairs; missions; encomiendas; and the sending out of exploration, slave-raiding, and punitive expeditions. The Spanish stipulated which areas Navajos might inhabit, established rules of barter, enforced settlement in towns, and forced the Indians into slavery.

The nature of the cultures involved was marked by extreme contrast. The Spanish emphasized absolute political control with power vested in a supreme ruler. The Navajo believed in individual freedom of action with political control allocated in accordance with the kinship system. The Spanish practiced group worship with a belief in a supreme deity. The Navajos practiced a highly individualis-

tic religion with an elaborate pantheon. Christianity stressed conformance in order to achieve rewards in an afterlife. Navajo religion stressed relief from anxiety through curing in the present life, with the afterlife being of relatively little moment. The economies of the two cultures were also in complete contrast. The Spanish practiced a cash economy and looked to the Navajo for resources to exploit, a one-sided attitude unlikely to make the latter accept a cash economy voluntarily.

The results of Spanish-Navajo contact, which stretched over more than two centuries, derive in part from the historical conditions of contact. The Navajos had been able to observe the effects of the Spanish intrusion on the sedentary Pueblos (Scholes 1936:20–21) and, protected somewhat by their isolation, were then able to choose which Spanish traits to accept and reject. Accepted trait complexes included the horse and horse trappings, sheep-herding, metal tools, and ornaments of European manufacture. Rejected complexes were the Spanish political system, Christianity, and forced settlement in towns. This rejection is clearly stated in the following historical reference in which the Navajo make explicit their reasons for abandoning the missions at Cebolleta and Encinal in 1750 (Hackett 1937:433–34).

They [the Indians of Cebolleta] replied that they did not want pueblos now nor did they desire to be Christians, nor had they ever asked for the fathers; and that what they had all said in the beginning to the reverend father commissary, Fray Miguel Menchero, was that they had been raised like deer; that they would give some of the children who were born to have water thrown upon them, and that these, as believers, might perhaps build pueblos and have a father, but that now they did not desire either fathers or pueblos; . . . they themselves would live as they had always lived. Therefore Reverend Father Fray Miguel Menchero had given hoes and picks as payment to those who brought their children to be baptized, but they never told him that they would consent to live in a pueblo, and now all of them said that they did not desire to be Christians. The Indians of Encinal . . . made the same answers . . . as stated above, adding that the said rever-

end father custodian—I should say Menchero
—had not given then all that he had promised
for bringing their children to be baptized. He
said that he would send mares, mules, horses,
cows, clothing, and many sheep; but perhaps
because he did not have them or wish to give
them, they now spoke of it no more. They did
not desire pueblos nor wish to be Christians,
which was what they said at the beginning.

It is apparent that the Navajo selected on an
objective basis those Spanish traits that could
easily be integrated into their existing cultural
system (Spicer 1954a:675; Reed 1944:57–65).
Those elements that were incompatible with
Navajo tradition were rejected. As noted previously, the adoption of sheep-herding resulted in
a considerable reorientation in Navajo culture
which resembles to a striking degree that which
occurred at an earlier date when the Navajos
became agriculturalists. This pattern of selection
and incorporation of Spanish intrusive traits by
the Navajos closely parallels their selection and
incorporation of Puebloan traits.

NAVAJO–ANGLO-AMERICAN ACCULTURATION

The conditions of Navajo–Anglo-American
acculturation may best be described in terms of
three historical periods: the period before the
removal to Bosque Redondo, the Bosque Redondo
Period (1863–68), and Bosque Redondo to the
present.

Prior to 1863, conditions of contact were intermittent, with military conflicts accounting for
almost all relations between the two cultures. As
these military encounters increased in intensity,
the Navajo were forced into retreat and hiding.
This epoch ended with the defeat of the Navajo
and their removal to Bosque Redondo. Other
contacts during this period included a few Anglo
expeditions of exploration and indirect trade which
had little importance as direct acculturative influences.

The nature of the cultures in contact was not
fully known to the participants. The limitation of
contact to military engagements obviously pro-
hibited much cultural exchange. At the time of the

military defeat of the Navajo, pervasive acculturation had not occurred. However, it was to begin
on a large scale during the succeeding epochs.

The Bosque Redondo Period was characterized
by the establishment of new political and economic
relationships. The Navajo were no longer masters
of their own fate, but were a subject people
governed by men of another culture. Directed
culture change was begun immediately, and the
Navajo were given little choice but to comply.
They were given new implements and seed and
told how to farm; they were issued rations of food
and clothing; they were herded together and
counted (Underhill 1953:166–75). These conditions lasted for a brief interval, only five years,
but they must be considered as having profound
acculturative intensity.

The chief results of this period included the
realization by the Navajo that the old, free way of
life was gone forever and that the new way of life
would be dictated by Anglos. Secondary results
included the adoption of Anglo dress and implements, and the beginnings of bilingualism.

In the Reservation Period the conditions of
contact changed again. The Navajo returned to
their homeland and were permitted to resume their
aboriginal way of life as best they could. The
American Government embarked on a program of
directed culture change with the avowed purpose
of integrating the Navajo into American national
culture. Federal programs of health, welfare, and
education were established with which the Navajo
had to comply (Kluckhohn and Leighton 1947:
23–24, 33–36). A final important contact was
established with the induction of Navajos into
military service in both world wars (Underhill 1953:
252–59). Many themes in Anglo culture conflicted
with those in Navajo culture. Christianity, monogamy, a strong centralized political system, a cash
economy and their reinforcing complexes—these
and other Anglo complexes were in direct opposition to Navajo traditional beliefs.

The results of this final period of acculturation
have been: (1) widespread acceptance of elements
of American national culture; (2) an increase in
anxiety brought about by having to choose between
opposing beliefs and the holding of inconsistent

beliefs; (3) the onset of conservatism in Navajo traditional culture; (4) a weakening of the influence of Navajo tradition.

PROCESSES OF ACCULTURATION IDENTIFIED IN NAVAJO CULTURE

Several of the major processes of acculturation which have affected the Navajo through time can be identified. The key factors isolated for consideration here are the compatibility of the cultures in contact, the nature of the contact, and the result of the interaction of the cultures. These variables lend themselves to expression as formulas or equations which, in turn, may be considered as hypotheses to be tested.

1. Compatible cultures + intermittent contact = limited acceptance of elements along lines of preexisting culture + possible reorientations in areas outside the cultural focus (defined in section below). Example: Navajo-Pueblo contact prior to the Pueblo Revolt.

2. Compatible cultures + intensive contact = widespread acceptance and fusion and some alterations extending to the cultural focus. Example: Navajo-Pueblo contact during and after the Revolt Period.

3. Incompatible cultures + intermittent contact = limited change between compatible portions of cultures; incompatible portions are rejected. Example: Navajo-Spanish contact.

4. Incompatible cultures + enforced intensive contact = tendency toward disruption of preexisting cultural tradition of subjugated culture, the development of anxiety, and the long-term result of loss of all elements of traditional culture incompatible with intruding culture. The loss of freedom of choice results in disruption of the cultural focus. Example: Navajo–Anglo-American contact.

HYPOTHESES OF NAVAJO ACCULTURATION

Pre-Bosque Redondo Navajo tradition emphasized a system of beliefs which corresponds to the "cultural focus" as defined by Herskovits (1945: 164–65): "that area of activity or belief where the greatest awareness of form exists, the most dis-cussion of values is heard, the widest difference in structure is to be discerned."

Aspects of this focus in Navajo culture included a ceremonial system concerned with individual curing, taboo as a mechanism for the minimizing of anxiety, political leadership vested in a local headman, and a strong sense of individual political independence. In all probability, these beliefs have been core features since the arrival of the Navajo in the Southwest.

Selection of new cultural traits and complexes by the Navajo was deliberate and of the Navajos' own free will with primary emphasis on the following:

1. Traits incompatible with aspects of the cultural focus were rejected, as they threatened to increase anxiety.

2. Traits or complexes not threatening the stability of the cultural focus were examined objectively in terms of function, and those judged superior were readily adopted.[1] This process of change has been termed "incorporation" by Vogt (1961:328).

3. Reorientation tended to occur in those areas of the culture outside of the cultural focus.

After Bosque Redondo, the following processes went into effect:

1. Loss of political freedom resulted in the disruption of the Navajo cultural focus. As a result, the Navajo were no longer able to act in a traditional manner with respect to intrusive cultural elements, but could only react to them. This meant that the Navajo traditional way of life was no longer successful in reducing anxiety and promoting stability. Indications of this lack of success are: (a) there has been an increase in the number of items that are taboo;[2] (b) aspects of American national culture such as Christianity, monogamy, modern medical practices, and a cash economy have been widely accepted, even though these elements are "inconsistent" or even "incompatible" with Navajo tradition (Spicer 1954:197–202).

2. The enforced acceptance of incompatible cultural elements has weakened the process of "incorporation" of new items. The current process tends to be simply one of replacement.

Predictions as to the direction of future Navajo culture change are discussed in the "Conclusions and Evaluations" section of this study.

THE NAVAJO TRIBAL HISTORY

In commemoration of the one-hundredth anniversary of the signing of the treaty between the United States and the Navajo Nation, June 1, 1868, the Navajo Tribal Museum published "The Historical Calendar of the Navajo People." This document features historical photographs of Navajo leaders, sand paintings from the Shooting Chant, and detailed notations of historical events of importance to the Navajo Tribe. The historical notes are extremely important to the present inquiry, as they range in time from 1583 to 1967 and are numerous, 969 in all. The historical notes seem to me to be of importance in understanding the current official point of view of the tribe with respect to its past.

In any history the selection of events for inclusion is indicative to some degree of the cultural biases of the historian. In the analysis of this material I have proceeded from the hypothesis that in a relatively unstructured situation the historical references would tend to be more common the more recent they are in time. Deviations from this hypothetical situation should reflect a corresponding degree of cultural concern—thus indicating the biases, or reasons for selection, involved. In the present case there are 146 entries dating prior to 1800, 771 dating between 1800 and 1900, and 52 dating after 1900, as shown on Figure 2. These facts suggest that strong cultural selection has indeed taken place.

A second type of selection concerns the nature of the entries included. The kinds of events mentioned frequently can be conceived of as cultural "themes"—areas of major cultural concern. In an attempt to understand this aspect of selectivity I have examined the events on the Historical Calendar and itemized them by subject and by frequency with which each subject is mentioned. Such an approach may be spuriously accurate since there is no guarantee that the most often mentioned theme is the theme of greatest cultural significance. For example, references to the stock reduction

program of the 1930s are relatively few in spite of the strong reaction to and the major consequences of this program.

A second qualifying factor is that it is possible to assign one reference to more than one theme. In this event the bias of the investigator becomes relevant. The approach utilized here is the listing of major and minor themes identified in their assumed order of importance. Major themes isolated are: (1) campaigns or attacks against the Navajo, (2) raids or stealing of livestock by the Navajo, (3) baptism of individual Navajos, (4) specific events at Fort Sumner, (5) the holding of Navajos as slaves, (6) conflicts with other Indian tribes, (7) land transfers or boundary disputes, (8) Indian agents and agencies, (9) treaties, (10) specific chiefs. A prominent feature of these major themes is that many cluster in the Bosque Redondo Period: twenty-one percent of all items on the Historical Calendar fall within the decade 1861–70 (see Figure 2). This is four times the frequency of all citations in the seven decades after 1900. Minor themes (not in order of frequency) include health, alcoholism, tribal cooperation, law enforcement, gambling, weaving, community centers, periods of peace, relief, tribal identity, U.S. Government appropriations, tributes to individual Indians, wage work, recommendations for location of specific Navajo settlements, and stock reduction.

One additional method of evaluation of biases in this tribal history is to compare the themes in it with themes isolated by other ethnohistorians working with Navajo historical data. One such comparison is between the events listed in my 1962 monograph and those on the Historical Calendar. Major differences are as follows: the Navajo tribal history frequently cites references to baptism of individuals rather than conversion of large groups; another feature not cited in the tribal history is the killing of priests and the abandonment of missions in the eighteenth century. These differences suggest to me that the tribal history seeks to demonstrate a long-term adherence to Christianity in a post hoc manner. Another theme not referenced in the tribal history is the widespread practice of the Navajo to incorporate members of other tribes into their numbers. Then, too, many important

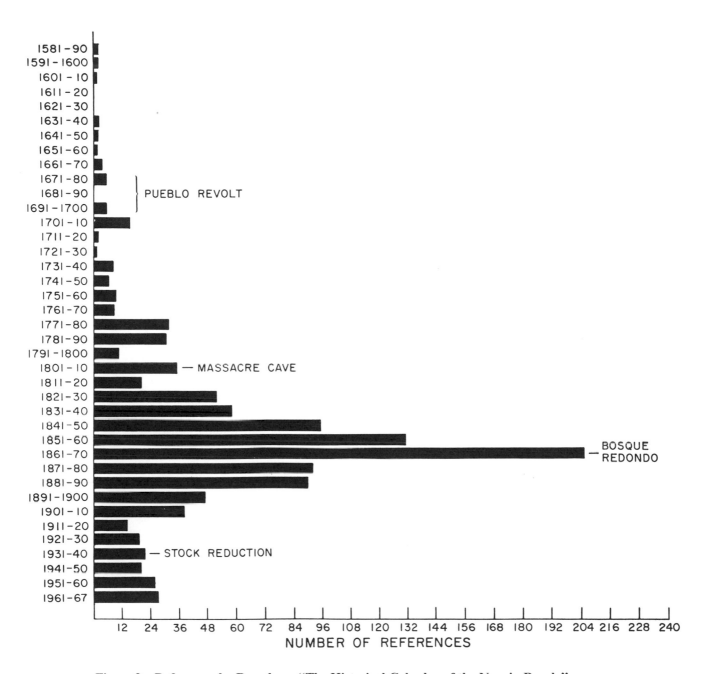

Figure 2   References by Decade on "The Historical Calendar of the Navajo People"

events in recent decades have not been selected or emphasized in the tribal history. As stated above, what *is* emphasized is the Bosque Redondo Period, and this is emphasized to the degree that it forms an almost legendary origin for the formation of the tribe in its present form. Also of interest is the complete separation between the Navajo tribal history and the body of Navajo mythology.

My final use of the tribal history involves the selection of a number of historical events that have occurred since 1868. These events were chosen because of their importance in documenting the acculturative situation which has been in effect since that date. In Table 1 these events are listed and associated with the specific acculturative situation which affected or caused them. Probable long-term effects of these factors are also included.

In my opinion, the series of historical events and acculturative situations itemized in Table 1 can be fitted into a sequence of cultural periods or acculturative stages as follows:

1868–1900
Period of Economic Readjustment and Establishment of New Relationships of Independence and Dependence

Related Cultural Processes:
1. Introduction of directed culture change
2. Introduction of new roles of authority both within Navajo culture and from outside
3. Establishment of new limits of acceptable behavior
4. Introduction of new cultural values
5. Attempted rejection of introduced traits and continuation of banned practices

1900–1941
Period of Fusion and Incorporation of Anglo-American Culture; Establishment of Reservation Navajo Cultural Pattern
Related Cultural Processes:

1. Realization and acceptance of subordinate role of Navajo
2. Economic stabilization of family units
3. Outward acceptance of many introduced traits, e.g. schools, missions, BIA policies, Tribal Council

4. Reassertion of those traditional Navajo beliefs and practices not in direct conflict with Anglo culture, e.g. curing, individual accumulation of livestock as wealth

1941–60
Period of Increased Culture Contact with Assimilation of Introduced Traits and Replacement of Basic Navajo Beliefs

Related Cultural Processes:
1. Acceptance of some full-fledged individual roles in Anglo society, e.g. military service and wage work
2. Assertion of power by Tribal Council
3. Loss of some aspects of ceremonial practice
4. Increase in Peyotism, possibly as an alternative to assimilation
5. Adoption of some Anglo values; approval of education and modern medical practices

1960
Period of Navajo Autonomy and Reassertion of Incorporative Mechanism

Related Cultural Processes:
1. Assumption of legal and political power by Tribal Council with intent to govern the affairs of all Navajo
2. Assumption of manifestations of statehood
3. Establishment of a formalized historical tradition
4. Hiring of Anglos to work for the tribe
5. Establishment of Navajo-directed schools

MAJOR STUDIES OF NAVAJO ACCULTURATION

In a classic study, Adams (1963) has dealt with the complex of acculturative factors affecting a single Navajo community. He views the contact situation as varying in complexity according to the type of local institution involved, e.g. trading post and school. Historical factors play a significant role, as do factors of access, role structure, and communication. Adams' work provides a detailed analysis which is methodologically sound and leaves no doubt as to the complexity of the actual acculturative situation.

By contrast, the present approach is impressionistic, generalizing, and in no way attempts to present a detailed analysis of Navajo acculturation in specific areas.

Another major description of Navajo culture change is that of Vogt (1961). Within the structure of a comparative symposium on culture change, Vogt's article focuses on a description of Navajo history and an analysis of factors influencing change and continuity. In his terms, the major acculturative process identified is "incorporation," i.e. elements from other cultures are incorporated in such a way that the structural framework of the institutional core is maintained and borrowed elements are fitted into place and elaborated upon in terms of the pre-existing patterns (Vogt 1961:327).

Vogt views incorporation as a standard cultural process which has been in effect among the Navajo for over four hundred years. He relates the incorporation of introduced traits to an institutional core made up of a scattered settlement pattern, the matrilocal extended family and matrilineal exogamous clans, a material culture complex composed of a nuclear family hogan, a sweat house, and a sheep corral, political leadership of a local headman, a ceremonial system featuring individual curing and ghost and witchcraft patterns as means of managing hostilities and aggression, values stressing "harmony" and "motion," the Navajo language, and an economy of farming, sheepraising, weaving, and silversmithing (Vogt 1961: 326).

Vogt's approach differs little from that expressed in my 1962 study. The major difference in our views is that in my opinion the incorporative process has been under severe stress since Fort Sumner and the introduction of "directed change" (Spicer 1961). Since 1868, the basic incorporative process has been weakened through the enforced acceptance of incompatible cultural items, with the result that assimilation and replacement are much more frequent than they were prior to 1868.

"THEMES" IN THE *NAVAJO TIMES*

Let us turn now to other sources in an attempt to further document recent acculturative trends and attitudes. One approach to an understanding of current Navajo cultural themes is possible through a review of recent issues of the newspaper, the *Navajo Times*, a weekly publication by the tribe in English. This is an impressionistic approach, as again we rely on the frequency with which themes are mentioned as an indication of their relative importance. The general impression one receives from reading the *Navajo Times* is that the tribe is changing very rapidly in the direction of modernization, with the individual Navajo being exposed to aspects of modern education, medical practices, and industrialization at an ever-increasing rate.

Several themes which commonly occur in the *Navajo Times* are as follows:

1. The heritage of the Navajo ancestors. This theme is especially reinforced with references to the Long Walk and events at Fort Sumner.

2. Progress. This is an oft-stated goal, with major achievements including the establishment of tribal industries, the building of schools—especially the Navajo Community College—and numerous items indicative of the establishment of tribal autonomy.

3. Nationalism. The establishment of a tribal flag, a bill of rights, a draft of a constitution, a tribal history, the incorporation of Navajo history into the schools, the celebration of a centennial as a "nation," references to Window Rock as a "capital," the election of beauty queens, and legal tests of Navajo autonomy all suggest the emergence of nationalism.

4. Conflicts between the traditional Navajo culture and the "new ways of life."

5. Education as essential but without BIA paternalism.

6. Health. The need for more health facilities and training is emphasized, with a major subarea being the problems of alcoholism.

7. Status roles. Statuses emphasized include those of sports heros, beauty queens, policemen, Tribal Council members, and members of the U.S. Armed Forces.

TABLE 1 Historical Events and Navajo Culture Change After Bosque Redondo

Date	Historical Event	Acculturative Situation	Long-Term Effect
1966	Rough Rock School—Navajo-directed secondary education	Anglo-initiated but with provision for cooperative leadership	Not yet determined; possibly compartmentalized biculturalism
1960s	Acts of tribal autonomy—flag, tribal park, etc.	Permissive Anglo attitude	
1958	Building of chapter houses; Navajo industries established	Formalization of outside-imposed political structure; permissive Anglo atmosphere allows some initiative	Navajo nationalism; increase in community cohesion, increased autonomy
1945–present	Increasing off-reservation contacts	Opportunity to increase wage income with concomitant opportunity to observe Anglo culture	Continued segregation in economic role; greater comprehension of Anglo culture
1948	Indians given right to vote	Outside-imposed status of equality	Increased inculcation of Anglo values
1947	Tribal Council resolution for compulsory schooling	Response to felt need for better communication	Increased inculcation of Anglo values
1941–45	Military service and war industries on reservation	In part Navajo-initiated contact	Increased communication and greater integration into Anglo culture
1935–46	Mission high schools opened	Religiously sanctioned attendance	Greater integration into Anglo culture
1934	Stock reduction	Enforced compliance	Crushing of opposition to outside introductions
1934	Indian reorganization act rejected	Opportunity to vote to accept or reject an outside idea	Little change in overall acculturative trend
1932	Introduction of modern methods of sheep care	Part of overall plans of an outside paternalistic agency	Increase in productivity

Date	Event	Mechanism	Consequence
1928	Tribal Council organized	Outside introduction by dominant culture	Addition of higher level of political organization
1924	All Navajos given U.S. citizenship	Outside introduction by dominant culture	
1927	Beginnings of chapter organization (Williams 1970)	Outside introduction by dominant culture	
1876–1946	Land allotments and requests for land	Continuing changes in U.S. legal procedures	Acquisition of lands; continuation of squatting; land claims case
1877–1883	Gradual end of slavery	Dominant Anglo culture anti-slavery concepts legally forbid the practice	Former Spanish-Navajo dominant-subordinant relationship is replaced by other forms of subjugation
1882	Completion of railroad	Provides method of direct contact with outside world, especially with manufactured goods	Partially responsible for loss of most native manufacturing technologies
1870–99	Limited continuation of stock raiding	Intermittent contacts both with legal officers and vengeance-seeking private Anglos	Loss of raiding as an economic activity
1875–80	Conflicts with Indian agents	Enforced contacts with representatives of "outside" power agencies	Loss of individual freedom of action
1875–1900	Introduction of better quality sheep; start of rug and silver industries; establishment of trading posts	Initial dependence on rations at Fort Sumner leading to trade of wool for outside manufactured goods	Restructuring of economy; economic dependence
1869–99	Introduction of schools	Forced attendance	Loss of freedom of choice; bilingualism; loss of traditional knowledge
1870–1903	Introduction of missions	Enclaves of national organizations	Acquisition of incompatible beliefs
1868	Signing of treaty at Fort Sumner	Military conquest	Legal subjugation

Quotations from the *Navajo Times* which appear to me to develop some of the themes itemized above are as follows:

Centennial Proclamation
To The People:

WHEREAS, Our Navajo People have for more than a century struggled for the right to live according to our ways, it is appropriate that we, at this the 100th year since the Long Walk, pause to mark our lives, being thankful for the blessings of our heritage, our land, and our progress.

We are fortunate to be a People with a strong heritage founded on our beliefs.

We are fortunate that we have been returned some of our beloved land secure within the four sacred mountains guarding us and our ways.

We are fortunate that today we can see about us the progress resulting from past and present efforts, knowing that we must continue to fulfill and realize the established goals of our People.

We are fortunate that we are strong and determined to be free to charter our course for the future and our progress for the betterment of our People; with particular strength in our youth who today dedicate themselves to securing a better education and opportunity that they may lead our People in the future. Therefore, we do hereby designate and set apart The Year 1968 as a year dedicated to renewing ourselves with our heritage, our land and our People, giving thanks for that with which we have been so generously blessed; recognizing our progress; and pledging to our People a continuing effort to bring greater progress in the future for all the People—that each Navajo may live his life in our ways—a life bountiful with the blessings sacred to us.

> Done at Window Rock, this
> twenty-fourth day of January,
> One Thousand Nine Hundred and
> Sixty-eight

Raymond Nakai
Chairman, Navajo Tribe
(*Navajo Times*, Centennial Issue, 1968)

*   *   *

Ft. Sumner, N.M. The reenactment of the signing of the Treaty of Peace of June 1, 1868, between the U.S. Government and the Navajo Tribe, was carried out in an open field here Sunday. The following day, about 165 Navajos, who made the trip to Fort Sumner Saturday in four air-conditioned buses, had an early breakfast Sunday, followed by a rehearsal of the treaty signing. A noon barbecue was provided by the community of Fort Sumner, a town of about 3,000 population, on the actual site of the old fort southeast of the town. (*Navajo Times*, July 4, 1968, p. 1)

*   *   *

From an advertisement:

A proud record: 100 years of continuing Progress by the Navajo Tribe in the Enlightened Development of a Priceless Natural Resource—NAVAJO PINE . . . in this centennial year that resource is harvested on a scientific, sustained yield basis; processed in one of the nation's most advanced sawmill complexes, and marketed to a large and growing number of customers . . . in this centennial year, the Navajo people take pride in Navajo Forest Products Industries, the largest single, profit-making enterprise of the Navajo Tribe. (*Navajo Times*, Centennial Issue, 1968, p. B20)

*   *   *

From "The Future of the Navajo People," first place award in centennial literary contest:

The homogenous nature of the federal administrations and their methods of dealing with the Indians following the American Civil War, presents basically the same problems to all other existing Indian tribes in the United States. These other Indian tribes have focused their attentions on development on the Navajo reservation because what the future holds for the Navajo Tribe, it also holds for the other tribes. (*Navajo Times*, Centennial Issue, 1968, p. B1)

*   *   *

From "Hope," an article by Elizabeth Benally:

Another problem that confronts the so-called leaders of tomorrow is their parents. Although the parents mean well when they stress that their children must be proud of their heritage, this conflicts with what the children have been taught earlier in school. They emphasize that their children are their only hope for a better tomorrow.

As the young Navajo adult proceeds to a higher education, he is confronted with many new ideas from a different culture. Trying to be modern he feels he must drop the old ways for the new. Many times, for example, he must choose between Catholicism and the Navajo religion. He finds it very difficult to make a choice. He is taught that the new religion (whatever it may be) is better than the old. Thus again, he feels ashamed of what he is. (*Navajo Times*, Centennial Issue, 1968, p. B9)

* * *

From "The Navajo Today and Tomorrow," an article by Lucinda A. Yelloman:
The older generation still yearns for the old way of life in which they were born and raised, but the trend of the younger generation is toward new horizons. With our knowledge of the newer things we must help close the gap between tradition and progress. We must remember we are no longer the "Vanishing American" but proportionately increasing in numbers. With the desire to better our tribe's present state and with more education, we shall excel. The road ahead is unknown; our further progress may be slow, but we face our next forward movement in the second hundred years with courage and eagerness. (*Navajo Times*, Centennial Issue, 1968, p. B18)

* * *

From proposed tribal constitution:
The Navajo Tribal Council shall be vested with all legislative powers of the Navajo Tribe, and shall exercise such powers subject only to applicable laws of the United States, regulations of the Secretary of the Interior pursuant thereto, and this Constitution. Specific powers to:
1. protect wildlife
2. lease and manage lands
3. approve plans of any industry
4. use tribal funds for loans and grants to tribal associations
5. negotiate contracts and leases
6. acquire any individual interests in tribal lands
7. borrow funds for tribal use
8. expend funds for public use of the tribe
9. administer charity
10. make loans to tribal members
11. enact ordinances
12. administer oaths

(*Navajo Times*, Nov. 21, 1968, pp. 3 and 4)

From "Community Development: What Does It Mean?," an article by Kent Fitzgerald:
The tribal council . . . is something that was created by the Secretary of the Interior and has grown rapidly without any serious planning on the part of the council.

The council, faced increasingly with all the new programs offered it, seems as though it never has time to stop and look at the direction it is going and whether this is really what the people want.

There are many complaints from people at the chapter level that the council members are voting on issues without much discussion with their constituents.

I think in a way the council is kind of helpless in this situation. . . . They are under tremendous pressure all the time and are frequently being told, There isn't any time! You've got to make this decision now! . . .

I think there are many able people in the tribal council who are also concerned with this problem of communication with people at the grass-roots level. (*Navajo Times,* Feb. 6, 1969, p. 13)

* * *

From *Navajo Times* reprint of "Report of the Indian Studies Project of the Far West Laboratory for Education and Research Development," Berkeley, California:
Many things need to be, and can be, undertaken to improve the schools serving Indian children. The curriculum needs to be reformed, particularly in the lower grades, to take into account what the Indian child knows when he comes to school. His language, his home, his surroundings, his cultural background should all be taken into account. Any effective educational program starts with what the individual knows and builds on that base; education for Indian children has not. The curriculum also needs to be modified to include more material on the history, culture, and values of Indian people to help perpetuate knowledge of the special culture of the people the school serves and thus to develop a sense of pride in the individual Indian as to who he is and who his people are.

* * *

The relationship we are speaking of between the white people and the Indian people is essentially paternalistic. The government officials, etc.—have not laid down their burden. The paternalism is often carried out as official policy without kindness and often with considerable expressions of overt prejudice, although with good intentions. The effects are the same, however: a loss of self esteem, a sense of powerlessness, an inability to cope with everyday problems, and a distrust of the white man and his system. (*Navajo Times*, Dec. 12, 1968, p. 29)

"THEMES" AND THE ROUGH ROCK SCHOOL

The opening of the Rough Rock Experimental School provides still another opportunity for cultural change in a Navajo setting. The success of this endeavor is assessed by an OEO-sponsored report by Broderick Johnson (1968). I have attempted to summarize my major impressions of this report in the following comments:

1. There is a strong OEO bias that the school should succeed to justify the investment.
2. The total community involvement in the school's function is in contrast to prior BIA schools and their effect.
3. School board "control" reveals that Navajo methods of operation are quite different from those typical of Anglo society. According to Johnson (1968: chap. 13), Navajo methods applied in context were more successful.

Themes identified in school board members' comments are as follows:

1. We are on the right path.
2. The school gives Navajos a chance to learn both Anglo and Navajo cultures and languages, which is a necessity.
3. I am proud to serve.
4. It is good for our community.
5. The school strengthens kinship ties.
6. Children must realize their strength comes from traditional Navajo culture.
7. Adult education is important and could be more successful.
8. Children respect their parents more as the parents become important in the school.
9. We would like to see other schools like the Rough Rock School.
10. Course areas include Navajo mythology, kinship, methods of economic livelihood, Navajo medicine and medicine men, as well as the do's and don'ts of Navajo society and language.
11. Complaints center around selection of employees.

The major theme of Tribal Chairman Nakai's talk delivered at "Tribal Chairman's Day" at the Rough Rock School, June 9, 1967, was that "the preservation of Navajo culture, history, legends, and language is important."

CONCLUSIONS AND EVALUATIONS

My 1962 monograph listed three predictions as to the direction of the future Navajo culture change. These predictions were:

1. The level of sociocultural integration will change from a "folk level" to a "national level" (Steward 1955: 43–77).
2. The Navajos will become a subculture of American national culture distinguished by race, language, a diminishing native tradition, and the holding of community property in a corporation.
3. The stresses developed as a result of the lack of success of the traditional way of life will lead to the intensification of two individual roles, the traditionalist and the liberal, with the liberals being typified by the Tribal Council. If the liberals accept American national culture too rapidly, the traditionalists may be stimulated to develop some sort of nativistic movement (Hester 1962: 87–94).

After a consideration of a number of different kinds of sources published since the above predictions were developed, we are in a position to evaluate their accuracy.

Prediction No. 1. The overt, vocal, and legally empowered segments of the Navajo Tribe would certainly indicate by their words and actions that a change to a "national level of sociocultural integration" is not only a goal but has in many respects been achieved.

Prediction No. 2. Subculture status seems warranted. Racially most Navajos (fully ninety-five percent) consider themselves fullbloods. More people speak Navajo today than at any time in the past, although the degree of fluency has decreased. The Navajo language is being introduced into the curricula of schools on the reservation. However, native traditions are diminishing, and here we can perceive a dichotomy. There is official emphasis on the *preservation* of traditional tribal knowledge but not on its *transmission* through the educational system. In this area the Rough Rock experiment may lead to mechanisms for the achievement of the ambiguous goal of presenting traditional knowledge through an Anglo-dominated educational system. On a broad front, changes in the traditional patterns would suggest that the native tradition is indeed being reduced. For example, fewer ceremonies are being held, and the Squaw Dance is becoming increasingly secularized (Bryan Michener, personal communication, 1969).

Prediction No. 3. This is the most difficult prediction to evaluate. Certainly there has been no overt movement resulting from the intensification of the "traditionalist versus liberal roles." However, the true nature of the problem cannot be ascertained from the sources consulted, as these tend to be the efforts of vocal liberals or of anthropologists. The "traditionalists" have not been as vocal. Probably the liberal-traditionalist dichotomy is too simplistic, since the "traditional" Navajo pattern has been one of eclecticism and incorporation. Therefore the "traditional" has always been changing, and it is possible that the Rough Rock type of adult involvement may lead to an orderly development into compartmentalized biculturalism.

Some of the quotations given above indicate that conflicts are present between the new and old ways of life. However, at this time it seems that resolution of these differences may be less dramatic than it appeared to me in 1962. With the reassertion of Navajo autonomy, it is possible that the "incorporative" process may again be successfully applied. If so, then the kind of overt nativistic movement I predicted in 1962 may never develop.

In conclusion, although we cannot predict the specific details of the stresses of cultural change and their resolution by the Navajo, we can at least comprehend their general nature as perceived by an individual Navajo, E. B. B. Mitchell, in his poem "The New Direction."

> The vanishing old road,
>   Through hail like dust storm,
> It stings and scratches,
>   Stuffy, I cannot breathe.
> Here once walked my ancestors,
>   I was told by the old ones,
> One can dig at the very spot
>   And find forgotten implements.
> Wasting no time I urged on.
>   Where I'd stop I knew not,
> Started, I listened to the wind,
>   It whistled, screamed, cried,
> "You! Go back, not this path!"
>   Then I recalled this trail.
> Swept away by the north wind,
>   It wasn't for me to follow.
> The trail of the Long Walk,
>   Deciding between two cultures,
> I gave a second thought,
>   Reluctantly I took the new one,
> The paved rainbow highway.
>   I had found a new direction.

(*Navajo Times*, Centennial Issue, 1968, p. B8)

NOTES

[1] The concept of function in Navajo culture has been examined by Reichard (1950:7–12). Cultural elements considered "alike" by the Navajos are freely substituted. These items perform a similar function but differ in form.

[2] An item becomes taboo if it can be identified by an *individual* as producing anxiety (Newcomb 1940:15–16).

REFERENCES

ADAMS, W. Y.
   1963   Shonto: A Study of the Role of the Trader in a Modern Navajo Community. Bulletin of the Bureau of American Ethnology 188. Smithsonian Institution, Washington, D.C.

CORRELL, J. LEE
   1968   Historical Calendar of the Navajo People. The Navajo Tribal Museum, Window Rock, Arizona.

HACKETT, C.
   1937   Historical Documents Relating to New Mexico, Nueva Vizcaya, and Approaches Thereto, to 1773. Carnegie Institution of Washington Publication 330, Vol. 3. Washington, D.C.

HERSKOVITS, M. J.
   1945   The Processes of Cultural Change. *In* The Science of Man in the World Crisis, Ralph Linton, editor. Columbia University Press, New York.

HESTER, J. J.
   1962   Early Navajo Migrations and Acculturation in the Southwest. Museum of New Mexico Publications 6. Santa Fe.

HORNER, E. M.
   1931   Masked Gods of the Navajos and Their Occurrence among the Pueblos and Apaches. Unpublished M.A. thesis. University of Chicago.

HRDLIČKA, A.
   1900   Physical and Physiological Observations on the Navajo. American Anthropologist 2, No. 2: 339–45.

JOHNSON, B. H.
   1968   Navajo Education at Rough Rock. Rough Rock Demonstration School. DNA [Navajo Legal Aid Society], Rough Rock, Arizona.

KLUCKHOHN, C. AND D. LEIGHTON
   1947   The Navajo. Harvard University Press, Cambridge, Massachusetts.

NAVAJO TIMES
          The official newspaper of the Navajo Tribe. Window Rock, Arizona.

NEWCOMB, F. J.
   1940   Navajo Omens and Taboos. Rydal Press, Santa Fe, New Mexico.

PARSONS, E. C.
   1939   Pueblo Indian Religion. 2 Vols. University of Chicago Press, Chicago.

RAPOPORT, R. N.
   1954   Changing Navajo Religious Values. Papers of the Peabody Museum 41, No. 2. Harvard University, Cambridge, Massachusetts.

REICHARD, G.
   1950   Navajo Religion, A Study of Symbolism. 2 Vols. Pantheon Books, New York.

SASAKI, T. T.

  1960   Fruitland, New Mexico: A Navajo Community in Transition. Cornell University Press, Ithaca, New York.

SCHOLES, F. V.

  1936   Church and State in New Mexico. New Mexico Historical Review 11, No. 1:9–76.

SPENCER, K.

  1947   Reflection of Social Life in the Navajo Origin Myth. University of New Mexico Publications in Anthropology 3. Albuquerque.

SPICER, E. H.

  1954a Spanish-Indian Acculturation in the Southwest. American Anthropologist 56, No. 4:663–84.

  1954b Potam: A Yaqui Village in Sonora. Memoirs of the American Anthropological Association 77. Menasha, Wisconsin.

  1961   Perspectives in American Indian Culture Change (editor). University of Chicago Press, Chicago.

STEWARD, J. H.

  1955   Theory of Culture Change. University of Illinois Press, Urbana.

THOMPSON, R. H., EDITOR

  1956   An Archaeological Approach to the Study of Cultural Stability. *In* Seminars in Archaeology: 1955, Robert Wauchope, editor. Memoirs of the Society of American Archaeology 11. Salt Lake City, Utah.

UNDERHILL, R.

  1953   Here Come the Navajo! Haskell Institute, Lawrence, Kansas.

VIVIAN, G.

  1960   Navajo Archaeology of the Chacra Mesa, New Mexico. Unpublished M.A. thesis. University of New Mexico, Albuquerque.

VOGT, E.

  1961   Navajo. *In* Perspectives in American Indian Culture Change, E. H. Spicer, editor. University of Chicago Press, Chicago.

WILLIAMS, A. W.

  1970   Navajo Political Process. Smithsonian Contributions to Anthropology, Vol. 9. Smithsonian Institution Press, Washington, D.C.

Chapter 6

WESTERN APACHE ECOLOGY:
FROM HORTICULTURE TO AGRICULTURE

P. Bion Griffin, Mark P. Leone, and Keith H. Basso

KEITH H. BASSO, assistant professor in the Department of Anthropology at the University of Arizona, has conducted ethnographic research in Australia, Canada, and the American Southwest. Dr. Basso's publications include a monograph on Western Apache ceremonialism, another on Western Apache witchcraft, a short ethnography entitled *The Cibecue Apache* (Holt, Rinehart and Winston, Inc., 1970), and several articles on language and culture.

P. BION GRIFFIN, assistant professor in the Department of Anthropology at the University of Hawaii, has carried out archaeological fieldwork in the American Southwest; Oaxaca, Mexico; and Hawaii as well as ethnographic research in Arizona.

MARK P. LEONE, assistant professor in the program in anthropology, Princeton University, has carried on archaeological fieldwork including investigations of the Classic Maya of the Peten (Guatemala) and prehistoric societies of the American Southwest. Dr. Leone's subsequent work focused on the Mormon settlement of the Southwest in the late nineteenth century and modern Mormon religion.

In an interesting and provocative paper entitled "Culture as Adaptation," Yehudi Cohen (1968:46) states that "the adoption of a new source of energy by a society is invariably followed by changes in the institutional configurations of its culture." We interpret this to mean that Cohen conceives of institutions as being dynamically related to the exploitation of energy potentials and, on this basis, anticipates that the adoption of a new energy source will result in changes in social organization.

The Western Apache of the Canyon Creek band, Cibecue subtribal group, have changed from a horticultural adaptation to agriculture and, finally, to participation in the mechanized Anglo-American culture all within the last century, thus providing a splendid source for evaluating Cohen's proposition. In what follows, attention will be directed toward historical changes in Western Apache subsistence activities whose scheduling and structure we shall describe as "procurement systems." These, in turn, will be divided into "energy units" and "social units." The latter are simply those task groups that engage in the acquisition of energy units.

Information concerning the horticultural adaptation is derived from published and unpublished sources, notably from the work of Goodwin (1935, 1937, 1942), Basso (n.d.), and Buskirk (1949). Data on the more recent agricultural adaptation were obtained from investigations conducted at Chediskai Farms, an old farm site located near Canyon Creek on the Fort Apache Indian Reservation in east-central Arizona, and from protracted interviews with several Apache informants who lived at Chediskai Farms before it was abandoned in the late 1940s.

The Horticultural Adaptation

The horticultural adaptation began well before A.D. 1870 and lasted until approximately A.D. 1900. During this time Apaches of the Cibecue subtribal group ranged seasonally through several different biotic zones, but concentrated dwelling sites in only two: winter camps below the Gila and Salt Rivers in the Lower and Upper Sonoran biotic

NOTE: The research on which this study is based was funded by the Doris Duke Oral History Project at the Arizona State Museum. We are pleased to acknowledge this support. We would also like to thank William A. Longacre and David Tuggle for their valuable comments on an earlier draft.

zones, and summer farm sites in the Transitional biotic zone in the broken uplands south of the Mogollon Rim. Winter camps were moved regularly every few days, but communication between members of different local groups was frequent, since food resources were rich enough to permit the close clustering of camps.[1]

The horticultural adaptation involved several procurement systems. These were as follows:

Procurement System No. 1: Wild Floral Resources. Energy units included the fruit and body of a variety of cacti, the seeds of desert shrubs, and grass seeds. The social units that collected these resources were composed of women and girls drawn from a single local group and, more specifically, from matrilocal extended families.

Procurement System No. 2: Large Game. The energy units in this system were mule and whitetail deer, javelina, and, occasionally, antelope. Small social units, generally composed of from two to five adult males, operated during the late fall and winter when hunting was at its best.

Procurement System No. 3: Small Game. Energy units included jack and cottontail rabbits, squirrels, prairie dogs, woodrats, quail, doves, owls, wild turkeys, and jays. Youths hunted this lesser game on a regular basis, while adults sought it only incidentally or when they were unsuccessful in procuring larger game. The social units were composed of small teams of adult males and somewhat larger parties of boys.

Procurement System No. 4: Plunder. Especially during the fall and winter months, raids to secure livestock and grains were directed against Mexican settlements in Sonora and Chihuahua and against Indian populations closer to home (e.g., Navajo, Yavapai, Pima, and Papago). Members of raiding parties were recruited almost exclusively on the basis of residence, the men of a local group (or several adjacent local groups) uniting under the leadership of a single "war chief."

Procurement System No. 5: Horticulture. In late spring, the members of local groups left their winter camps and traveled to farm sites on Canyon and Oak creeks, which were situated at elevations of between 4,500 and 6,000 feet. Local groups varied in size according to the amount of land they controlled, and it is noteworthy that not all families owned or worked fields. Landless families, which were occasionally called upon to cultivate and harvest in exchange for small amounts of corn, attached themselves to families having land-use rights according to lineage, clan, and phratry ties (Goodwin 1942).

Fields were small, often less than a half-acre in size, and those located immediately adjacent to streams were irrigated. At Chediskai Farms, a farm site on Canyon Creek, half the fields were irrigated. One dry-farming site is known, this on the slopes of Blue House Mountain near the present settlement of Cibecue; it was abandoned around A.D. 1885.

Energy units in the horticultural procurement system were corn, beans, and squash, with an increasing number of introduced crops as the year A.D. 1900 approached. Although it has been estimated that domesticates provided only one-fourth of the total energy intake of the Western Apache, the easy storability of these crops and their concentrated nutritive value greatly enhanced their importance (Goodwin 1935).

Prior to A.D. 1900, social units participating in horticultural activities included sizable groups of men, women, and children who, working collectively, refurbished irrigation systems and broke up soil for planting with dibble sticks. Men and women alike joined in planting and harvesting, but cultivation was primarily the responsibility of women, adolescent boys and girls, and the elderly.

It should be emphasized that, throughout the horticultural phase of Western Apache adaptation, procurement systems 1–4 were not neglected during the summer months. Women continued to collect cacti, for example, and trips of several days duration were made to collect maguey and acorns. Youths continued to hunt small game and, since mule deer concentrate at higher elevations during periods of warm temperatures, men were able to secure game in the late spring, summer, and early fall. Raiding, it appears, was limited to brief forays against the Navajo to the north and Yavapai to the west (Basso n.d.).

Agricultural Adaptation: Draft Animals and Plows

Between 1890 and 1900, the transition was made on Canyon Creek from dibble sticks to hoes and shovels, and then to the use of harnessed mules and horses to pull plows. Harnesses, plows, and wagons were issued to the Western Apache by the U.S. Government at various times after 1885, and we are interested here in describing any changes in Apache culture that can be directly attributed to their introduction.

According to Apache informants now residing in the settlement of Cibecue, approximately fifty people, including children, lived at Chediskai Farms at the beginning of this century. There were ten married couples grouped into four matrilocal extended families. Wickiup clusters, located close to cultivated fields, were arranged along Canyon Creek for a distance of about a half mile.

Adjustment of procurement systems to horse-and-plow agriculture can be summarized as follows:

Procurement System No. 1: Wild Floral Resources. After A.D. 1900, the practice of "wintering below"—i.e., leaving farm sites in the mountains and establishing camps at lower elevations—began to cease owing to the government's firm insistence that Apaches remain close to schools, missions, and trading posts. Despite this change, however, the exploitation of floral resources remained basically unaltered. Energy units were the same as those characteristic of the horticultural adaptation except that fewer types of cactus species were gathered. The composition of the social units which collected wild plant foods also remained unchanged.

Procurement System No. 2: Large Game. The cessation of "wintering below" resulted in minor scheduling shifts in the hunting of large game. Less hunting was done in the winter, and hunting trips, which probably covered greater distances, may have become longer in duration. However, the social units in this procurement system remained identical to their pre-1900 equivalents, and the same set of energy units continued to be exploited.

Procurement System No. 3: Small Game. No changes in the hunting of small game can be attributed to the adoption of horse-and-plow agriculture. Wild turkey, rabbit, and lesser game, which continued to be hunted, were very plentiful in the Canyon Creek area and provided a fairly substantial dietary supplement during all but the months of heavy snows.

Procurement System No. 4: The Trading Post. After A.D. 1900, two new procurement systems began to supply energy units that had been formerly obtained through plunder. One of these systems was the trading post, which provided a few canned products, sugar, salt, and coffee. These goods were acquired either through trade or by cash purchase. It should be emphasized, however, that cash was very scarce, and that due to its geographical isolation—the nearest trading post was at Cibecue some miles away—the local group at Chediskai Farms was only minimally involved in the emerging Anglo economy.

Procurement System No. 5: Beef Cattle. Beef cattle became a new source of energy after 1900, when several large herds were introduced onto the Fort Apache Reservation by the U.S. Government. Although cattle were never numerous along Canyon Creek, the new procurement system may be viewed as a substitute for raiding, replacing as a source of meat the livestock previously captured in Mexico. The social units involved in cattle-raising were composed of young adults who, depending on the specific task at hand, worked either singly or together under the supervision of an Anglo stockman.

Procurement System No. 6: Agriculture. Energy units did not change markedly with the adoption of draft horses, the plow, and wagons. Several introduced crops, including tomatoes, potatoes, and one or two types of vegetables, were grown in small amounts. While a precise specification of the nutrients that the new domesticates replaced is not possible at present, we suggest that several acted as substitutes for desert flora not significantly exploited after 1900–1910.

The social units involved in agricultural activities shifted slightly, and since this bears sharply on our evaluation of Cohen's proposition we shall describe the units and their associated activities in some detail. As horses and single plows replaced hoes and dibble sticks, adult males replaced females in the task of ground-breaking. Normally, one or two males plowed with harnessed singles and teams of horses, preparing the land of their wife's family and frequently that of their own sisters. When plowing began, so did the reconstruction of the irrigation system. Dams and head gates were built, and the main ditches—over a mile in length—were repaired and cleared of debris. Dam construction involved groups of adult males and youths, who placed large logs across Canyon Creek and secured them with piles of small boulders. Brush and earth were then packed between the boulders by adult females and adolescent girls.

The traditional horticultural social unit that cultivated and harvested crops—women, children, and the elderly—remained unchanged after A.D. 1900. As before, sets of sisters and their children tended to work together.

CONCLUSIONS

The adjustment of procurement systems to horse-and-plow agriculture produced few significant changes in Western Apache culture. While several shifts in energy units took place, these functioned primarily as replacements for sources that had become unavailable when the practice of "wintering below" came to an end. The only significant change, it appears, took place with respect to the sexual division of labor and involved the exclusive assumption by men of ground-breaking tasks. With this one exception, there is no evidence to indicate that the use of draft animals resulted in the reorganization of either work groups or other types of social units at Chediskai Farms. Of course, major changes did take place during the period of agricultural adaptation—the most striking being the cessation of seasonal movements by local groups—but these were stimulated by different sources, especially by the increasingly dominant Anglo culture, and cannot be positively correlated with the basic shift to draft animals.[2] We conclude, therefore, that Cohen's assertion that institutional changes *invariably* follow upon such shifts is not supported.[3]

NOTES

[1] For a thorough description of prereservation Western Apache social organization, see Goodwin 1942.

[2] A partial analysis of these Anglo-stimulated changes may be found in Basso 1970.

[3] It can be said that, as a statement of general evolution, Cohen's hypothesis is well substantiated, but presented as specific evolution it is not necessarily true. This study provides what we consider an important qualification to Cohen's rather incautiously worded hypothesis, but we are aware that it may not constitute a fully acceptable negative test, for, as David Tuggle has reminded us,

". . . significant changes in social organization or levels of adaptation may not come about unless the circumstances both select for and allow the *full utilization* of a new source of energy. It is possible, in the Western Apache case, that draft animals produced little real increase in energy use because they may have been exploited to only a fraction of their potential" (1969). In other words, if energy use involving draft animals was not significantly greater than that involving hand cultivation, major institutional changes would not be expected to occur.

REFERENCES

BASSO, KEITH H.

1970 The Cibecue Apache. Case Studies in Cultural Anthropology. Holt, Rinehart and Winston, Inc., New York.

n.d. Western Apache Raiding and Warfare: From the Notes of Grenville Goodwin. University of Arizona Press, Tucson. In press.

BUSKIRK, WINFRED

1949 Western Apache Subsistence Economy. Unpublished Ph.D. dissertation. University of New Mexico, Albuquerque.

COHEN, YEHUDI

1968 Culture as Adaptation. *In* Man in Adaptation: The Cultural Present, Yehudi Cohen, editor. Aldine Publishing Company, Chicago.

GOODWIN, GRENVILLE

1935 The Social Divisions and Economic Life of the Western Apache. American Anthropologist 37:55–64.

1937 The Characteristics and Function of Clan in a Southern Athapascan Culture. American Anthropologist 39:394–407.

1942 The Social Organization of the Western Apache. University of Chicago Press, Chicago. Reprinted 1969 by the University of Arizona Press, Tucson.

TUGGLE, DAVID

1969 Personal Communication.

PART TWO

Apachean Ethnography
and Ethnology

Chapter 7

NAVAJO ECOLOGY AND ECONOMY: A PROBLEM IN CULTURAL VALUES

William Y. Adams

WILLIAM Y. ADAMS, associate professor in the Department of Anthropology at the University of Kentucky, grew up on the Navajo Indian Reservation and was employed there as a trader before he began systematic studies of Navajo culture. These experiences served as background for his major published work, *Shonto: A Study of the Role of the Trader in a Modern Navaho Community* (Bureau of American Ethnology Bulletin 188). Dr. Adams has also done anthropological fieldwork with other Southwestern tribes, as well as extensive archaeological work both in the Southwest and in the Republic of the Sudan, Africa.

Everyone studies Navajo culture change, but nobody measures it. The difficulty, of course, is to find a meaningful starting point from which change can be plotted. However naive the idea may be, our studies of most aboriginal peoples proceed from the notion of a relatively stable precontact cultural configuration, which we try to reconstruct through the classic techniques of ethnography. Upon this hypothetical pristine condition we measure the impact of industrial civilization in terms of adaptation or disintegration.

Such a simplistic model of analysis has never been appropriate to the Navajo, or, for that matter, to any southern Athapaskan people. As far back as history and archaeology will allow us to peer into the Apachean past, we seem to see nothing but a continuing process of adaptation to new peoples and new environments. Western man is only the latest in a long succession of alien peoples who have left their impress on the Apachean cultures.

Navajo culture, it would seem, never settled down long enough to achieve that degree of integration and internal consistency which we profess to find in other aboriginal cultural systems.

Indeed, the term "system," with its static connotations, seems somehow inappropriate to Navajo culture. What we see is not so much a cultural framework as a cluster of core values which hold together a set of seemingly disparate parts. The individual parts have changed considerably through the ups and downs of history, and yet on the whole they have held together remarkably well. Despite centuries of cultural contact, no one could mistake Navajos for Pueblos, Utes, Paiutes, Mexicans, Mormons, or Gentiles—in fact, they could be nothing but Navajos.

Whatever the unyielding core of Navajo culture may be, it seems to be far removed from the material sphere. Making a living has not been a matter of traditional and collective concern to the Navajos. From the reminiscences of Left Handed, Son of Old Man Hat, we learn how the family periodically "ran out of grub," as a result of improvidence and bad management. Apparently Navajo society as such provided no dependable relief in these straits: the standard recourse of Old Man Hat's family was to go to the Pueblos (Dyk 1938: 49–55). Whether they would trade or raid would depend upon the condition in which they found their hosts; apparently the Navajos were always prepared for either (See Hill 1948:382–84).

An important truth is observable here: the Navajo economy has never been, in the recorded past, an entirely closed and self-sufficient system. Long before they became dependent upon industrial civilization, the Navajos, either as traders or as raiders, were semidependent upon their wealthier and more provident Indian neighbors, to whom they looked at the very least for emergency relief in hard times. This participation in a larger, though highly unstructured, economic network may help to explain the Navajos' failure to develop a very coherent or distinctive set of economic values. The parallel between this Southwestern situation and the agricultural-pastoral symbiosis of the Near East was long ago pointed out by Kroeber (1928:386–87), but has, I think, received too little critical attention from other anthropologists.

What stands out historically about the Navajo economy is its utter lack of specialization. In classic evolutionist terms, this lack of specialization can be equated with adaptability, and in fact will go a long way to explain why the Navajos, more than any other Indian tribe, have been successful not only in maintaining themselves as a society but in increasing their numbers and influence throughout the period of contact with Western civilization.

In their quest for a living within their present habitat, the Navajos have been by turns hunters and gatherers, subsistence farmers, raiders, subsistence pastoralists, commercial wool and rug producers, commercial farmers, and wage workers. More often than not they have engaged in two or three of these activities simultaneously. Although a certain seasonal pattern of alternation might be observed, the very diversity of the Navajo economic base precluded specialization and at the same time inhibited the development of an integrated economic system. This in turn is reflected in the lack of articulated economic values in Navajo culture.

The situation which I have been describing certainly persisted as late as 1955, when I undertook the studies of Shonto community from which most of my data here are drawn (Adams 1963). In 1955, one hundred Navajo families living in the vicinity of Shonto Trading Post derived their collective income as shown in table at right (Adams 1963:137).

This scale of remuneration could not be discovered through the normal techniques of anthropological inquiry—neither by direct questioning nor by observing the Navajos' investment of time, energy, and interest among the different pursuits. It came to light only through the very detailed records of income and expenditure which we were

able to keep in the course of operating Shonto Trading Post (Adams 1963:137).

Queried about the source of their livelihood, most Shonto Navajo would and probably still will unhesitatingly describe themselves as farmers and stockmen—activities which together contribute about one-sixth of their actual income. Wage work, like relief, would be regarded as supplementary to the basic subsistence complex—something to fall back on when native productive resources were insufficient. This seemingly unrealistic evaluation was in fact accurately reflected in the economic behavior of Shonto Navajos. They would never take a job off the reservation in preference to one on the reservation, no matter how much greater the reward, and they would seldom take a job at all so long as they could wrest any kind of reasonable living from more traditional pursuits. Thus one could predict with certainty that every Shonto family would engage in farming and stock-rearing activity, however minimal the economic rewards. One could not predict with the same certainty that members of every family would engage in wage work, although statistically one could be certain that in any given year ninety percent of Shonto families would have to supplement their income from traditional sources in one way or another. Off-reservation wage work offered the most widespread and the most remunerative form of supplementation, but Welfare and unemployment compensation were always preferred, even when the actual rewards were considerably less.

The effect of an unexpected economic windfall, such as a death benefit or an insurance settlement, would clearly reveal the scale of Navajo economic values. Such a dividend, no matter how large,

Type of Work	Percent of Income
Off-reservation wage work (primarily railroad)	55
Livestock-raising (including value of products consumed at home)	16
On-reservation wage work	12
Welfare	8
Native crafts and specialties	4
Farming	1
Other sources	4

would have no effect upon what the Navajos consider "necessary" economic activity, i.e. farming and stock-raising. On the other hand, so long as the money held out there would be an immediate and predictable end to wage work by members of the family receiving the benefit.

In sum, the preferential value accorded to various economic activities by Shonto Navajos bore no relation to their actual material rewards. What, then, were the economic values which influenced Navajo preference for one form of activity over another? Since they were not, in general, overtly expressed, it is necessary to discover them in another way, by considering the relationship of economics to other areas of Navajo culture.

A special case must be made at the outset for a few traditional esoteric skills—primarily singing by men and weaving by women. These by virtue of their very exclusiveness enjoyed higher prestige than did any economic activities common to the whole community. Their prestige, however, had nothing to do with remunerative rewards, for neither singers nor weavers derived an appreciable part of their income from these activities, though both devoted the bulk of their time to them. The poverty of Shonto's singers was a subject of frequent remark and considerable amusement; it did not, however, detract unduly from their standing in the community.

Setting aside the prestigious specialties of singing and weaving, we can range the preferential value of economic activities common to all Shonto families as follows (Adams 1963:148):

Basic complex
   1. Farming
   2. Stock-raising
Supplementary complex
   3. Relief and unemployment compensation
   4. Reservation wage work
   5. Off-reservation wage work

Generally speaking, we may note that the actual cash return from these various activities was almost in inverse order to their preferential value.

The central position of farming in the Navajo world view has not been adequately acknowledged by anthropologists, although Hill long ago observed that Navajos consider themselves primarily farmers (Hill 1938:18). The overriding importance of agriculture can be seen most immediately in the traditional and persisting Navajo settlement pattern, which is intelligible in no other terms except in relation to a sedentary farming economy. Navajo summer hogans are situated not with regard for grazing land, for roads and other conveniences, or even for water, but explicitly in relation to cornfields, though the latter seldom exceed two or three acres in extent. Winter hogans are located primarily with regard for available firewood, but are seldom more than a mile or two from the summer hogans. It may be that families do not wish to stray too far from their fields in the winter, lest they be preempted by other families in the following spring. It has been estimated that disputes over cornfield ownership are the largest single source of social dissension between Navajo families. Certainly the frequency and bitterness of these quarrels is out of all proportion to the economic issues at stake.

Navajo settlement, determined as it is largely by agricultural considerations, has reached almost exactly the same point as had Pueblo Indian settlement in the same area a thousand years earlier. There is in fact a very close association between modern Navajo camps and archaeological remains of the Pueblo II horizon, before the process of Puebloan nucleation began.

This sedentary pattern of life has had an important and an inhibiting effect upon the development of Navajo livestock practice. Although range experts for years have complained of overgrazing on the Navajo Reservation, in many areas grazing is not so much overdeveloped as it is inefficient. Areas close to camps and water sources are virtually denuded, while substantial tracts, particularly at higher elevations, are very inconsistently utilized. Animals are corralled all night and for part of every day, and as a result they eat voraciously and unselectively during their hours of liberty. The practice of herding primarily by small children makes for limited and unchanging grazing territories. In short, Navajo pastoralism has always had to adapt as best it could to a sedentary base—a sure sign of the higher priority accorded to farming activity in the Navajo scheme of things.

A second measure of the importance of agriculture, relative to all other economic pursuits, may be seen simply in the amount of time and energy devoted to clearing, fencing, planting, weeding, and harvesting during the summer season. If we take all Navajo adults of both sexes and all ages together, the amount of time devoted by them to the various phases of farming activity probably exceeds the time spent in any other productive pursuit. By contrast we may note that the main tasks of livestock-rearing, outside of the lambing and shearing seasons, are relegated largely to children. Other forms of productive activity, such as craft specialties or wage work, are even more narrowly limited by age or by sex.

Agricultural activity thus provides an important unifying experience in Navajo life; it is the only sphere of economic activity which involves both sexes and all ages. It is also, significantly, the only field of activity which consistently engenders interaction and cooperation between extended family groups. At Shonto in 1955, the rather nebulous kin groupings which are sometimes called "outfits" had almost no functional significance and no visible identity except at the beginning and the end of the farming season, when they often joined together either to subjugate new land or to harvest the corn crop. Because it is most closely integrated with other aspects of culture, farming is the one area of Navajo productive activity which comes closest to realizing its full economic potential, minuscule though that is. Nearly every acre of the Navajo Reservation which should be farmed is in fact under cultivation, as are very considerable areas which quite obviously should not be farmed.

Although livestock-rearing is popularly regarded as the most basic of Navajo economic pursuits, we have already observed that at least in the Navajo mind it takes a back seat to farming. There can be no doubt, however, that it is accorded more importance than any nonagricultural activity, and it is certainly developed to the maximum extent possible within the framework of a sedentary life. Other and not strictly economic factors enter into this picture. Fresh mutton is considered an absolute necessity in the Navajo diet; in addition, large livestock holdings are a prime source of prestige, even though their actual capital value is slight.

The one other source of Navajo income which we may speak of as fully and efficiently developed is public Welfare. Although its introduction dates back only twenty years, Welfare payments are anticipated as a universal right by all Navajos over sixty-five and by all dependent mothers. Navajos can usually count on the assistance of traders in disposing of or concealing their assets in such a way as to make sure that they are eligible for assistance at the appropriate time, and in fact at Shonto in 1955 all but six of the twenty individuals over sixty-five years of age were receiving some form of public assistance. Receiving Welfare, of course, did not interfere with traditional subsistence activities, since the minimal cash income derived from farming and sheep-raising did not affect eligibility.

Other forms of supplementary income production necessarily compete to some extent with traditional subsistence activities, since jobs take the individual away from his fields and flocks. Generally speaking, the preference which Navajos show for different kinds of paid employment depends primarily on how little they interfere with more traditional activities. On-reservation jobs are always preferred to off-reservation jobs, even at considerably higher pay. Although they usually require residence away from the home camp, they at least permit frequent visits and intermittent participation in home activities. Among off-reservation jobs, preference goes to temporary and seasonal work and particularly to those jobs which fall during the midsummer and midwinter months —the seasons of slack activity at home. Least valued, although most highly paid, are permanent off-reservation jobs. Shonto Navajos periodically took such jobs, but seldom held them for longer than two or three years.

The values which govern Navajo economic priorities, if not strictly monetary, are not really unusual or surprising. They parallel many Anglo motivations, once minimum standards of subsistence and comfort have been met. In general, and regardless of actual material rewards, Navajos most value those forms of economic activity which most preserve and reinforce the traditional fabric of their society and least value those activities which threaten or disrupt it.

What is of more particular interest to us is the relatively low level at which Navajo subsistence demands are satisfied, and beyond which social considerations take precedence over material ones. It is clear that the central values of Navajo life are in fact social ones, and they have probably remained unchanged at least since the Navajos' earliest days in the Southwest. To these social values, and the lifemodes which they engendered, successive forms of economic activity have had to adapt themselves as best they could. This precedence of society over economy will explain why economic change per se has never threatened the integrity of Navajo society. Only the destruction of the traditional bases of group interaction, and perhaps most particularly of farming, is likely to do that.

In our efforts to understand the course of Navajo cultural evolution, we are confronted with the same problem of adaptability versus specialization which has lately plagued the students of biological evolution. Shall we call the Navajo economic system successful or unsuccessful? In a purely ecological sense it has never achieved more than a fraction of its productive potential, and yet its very lack of specialization has made possible the survival of Navajo society. May we credit the Navajos with the ultimate economic wisdom and foresight of not overcommitting themselves in an unsettled world? Or shall we simply decide that their deepest concerns are not material ones, and that they don't really care how they make a living so long as it doesn't interfere with more important activities?

For myself, I prefer to offer the Navajo case as one more challenge to those cultural materialists who unhesitatingly identify economy and society as horse and cart respectively. We all acknowledge that up to the point where minimum biological necessities are satisfied we can hardly account for human behavior in other than materialist terms. We should also acknowledge that beyond that point necessity becomes a matter of cultural and not of biological definition. From here on a materialist explanation is really only appropriate to a materialist society; it is in fact as *emic* as any other ideological bias.

REFERENCES

Adams, William Y.

1963   Shonto: A Study of the Role of the Trader in a Modern Navaho Community. Bulletin of the Bureau of American Ethnology 188. Smithsonian Institution, Washington, D.C.

1968   The Role of the Navajo Trader in a Changing Economy. *In* Markets and Marketing in Developing Economies, Reed Moyer and Stanley Hollander, editors. Richard D. Irwin, Inc., Homewood, Ill.

Dyk, Walter

1938   Son of Old Man Hat. Harcourt, Brace, & World, Inc., New York.

Hill, W. W.

1938   The Agricultural and Hunting Methods of the Navaho Indians. Yale University Publications in Anthropology 18. New Haven, Connecticut.

1948   Navajo Trading and Trading Ritual. Southwestern Journal of Anthropology 4: 371–96.

Kroeber, A. L.

1928   Native Culture of the Southwest. University of California Publications in American Archaeology and Ethnology 23, No. 9:375–98. Berkeley.

Chapter 8

NAVAJO FACTIONALISM AND THE
OUTSIDE WORLD

Mary Shepardson

MARY T. SHEPARDSON, associate professor of anthropology at San Francisco State College, carried on research among Navajo Indians both before and after receiving her Ph.D. from the University of California at Berkeley. She is the author of *Navajo Ways in Government* (American Anthropological Association Memoir No. 96) and, with Blodwen Hammond, of the *Navajo Mountain Community* (University of California Press, 1970). She also has published articles on political behavior, persistence and change, inheritance patterns, and kinship terminology in a number of professional journals.

In recent years the anthropological study of factionalism has, so to speak, precipitated a "factionalist" struggle among the faction definers. This scholarly conflict was stimulated by the efforts of Bernard Siegel and Alan Beals to clarify the catchall concepts by distinguishing between "pervasive" and "schismatic" factionalism (1960). Reactions ran the gamut from approbation to dissent to abuse. Each writer on factionalism either gives his own definition, lists his own diagnostic traits for the phenomenon, or both. My contribution to the fray will be the analysis of one form of factionalism, *schismatic*, as I have studied it in four conflicts in the Navajo Nation, formerly known as the Navajo Reservation.

Siegel and Beals define schismatic factionalism as "overt, unregulated (unresolved) conflict within a group which interferes with the achievement of the goals of a group" (1960:108). They say further that external stresses will affect the group in a manner determined by internal strains or potential cleavages existing within the group; in an acculturative situation factionalism arises when traditional methods for handling disputes fail.

I shall try to press this analysis further and extract the elements I consider to be crucial for discriminating between schismatic factionalism and other forms of intragroup conflict. First, the conflict occurs within a bounded group, which may or may not have subgroups, where there is consensus on the value of preserving the group and working together for its goals. Splitting the group may be a *result* of the struggle, but it is not the *aim*. Second, an issue arises, either from within or from without, to precipitate an overt struggle. This is invariably an issue to which any immediate solution is blocked. Third, two cohesive but noninstitutionalized quasimembership groups are formed in mutual opposition, each one of which demands the loyalty of its adherents. Fourth, the conflict is of long duration. Fifth, and finally, the conflict is so bitter that cooperation between factions is impossible. Schismatic factionalism has a paralyzing effect as each side tries to bring the other down.

There are a number of elements that may or may not be present. Additional issues may accrete to the original base for contention and crystallize into a "line" for each opposing faction. They serve to attract further support for the core antagonists. Noninstitutionalized methods of strife will supplement institutionalized methods. Schismatic factionalism may or may not take place within an acculturative situation. Although some type of leadership is inherent in the formation of all enduring groups, it need not be that of a charismatic leader pressing for personal power and inspiring

NOTE: This study of factionalism was made between 1960 and 1969 during the course of investigations into problems of law, politics, and social structure on the Navajo Reservation. The work was variously financed by the National Science Foundation, the National Institute of Mental Health, and the American Philosophical Society.

intense loyalty among a band of followers. A factionalist struggle, organized around an issue, may well survive changes in leadership. The ingredient of ambiguity, that is, lack of clarity as to alternate means or ends so that factions are, in French's words (1962), "talking past each other" may be present. The struggle may be realistic or unrealistic. What begins as factionalism on one structural level may shift to another level as from community to nation. Covert as well as overt conflict may characterize the dispute. Factionalism within the group may penetrate to subgroups and even disrupt intrafamilial relations.

The solution of a schismatic factionalist dispute takes one of three forms: some change in the situation removes the original block, one side becomes powerful enough to force the other to capitulate, or a split takes place and one of the irreconcilable factions may withdraw or be expelled from the group. This leads us to consider the following specific instances.

Navajo conflict number one. This is a historical conflict which took place in the 1930s and early 1940s over stock reduction. It was fought on an all-tribal level but most bitterly within the fledgling Navajo Tribal Council. Overgrazing of the range with consequent soil depletion and the silting up of Hoover Dam impelled the U.S. Government to install a permit system for the purpose of drastically reducing the numbers of livestock that an Indian could graze within an arbitrarily established land-management district. Resolution of the dispute was blocked when neither side would compromise. Navajos saw this move as a threat to destroy their basis of livelihood; they refused to reduce their herds voluntarily. The government refused to abandon the conservation policy and rescind its punitive orders against "trespass." Navajos who cooperated with the Bureau of Indian Affairs were opposed by the resisters, who were much stronger numerically but did not have the power of the federal government behind them. Resistance leaders sprang up all over the reservation. Institutionalized means of combat included protest petitions and delegations to Washington, and efforts to vote resisters *in* and cooperators *out* of the Navajo Tribal Council.

Noninstitutionalized methods of struggle included the kidnapping of a district supervisor and threatening range riders and cooperators with witchcraft and/or death.

For more than ten years this struggle disrupted all efforts to form a strong tribal government. Resister councilmen refused to vote power to an executive committee (the old one had endorsed the grazing regulations), so there was little continuity to Tribal Council leadership between quarterly sessions of the council. (Even today the "executive committee" is called "advisory committee" and the "president" has the title of "chairman.") A proposed tribal constitution was defeated. The Indian Reorganization Act, which authorized the promulgation of the hated grazing regulations, was defeated in a plebiscite. Cooperation was at a standstill.

At this point we should note that traditional methods for handling disputes were no longer available. In the past when groups, usually extended families, had strong differences, one or the other of the families would simply move away with their flocks. No formally bounded political organization or formally delimited territory or formally defined use-rights to land prevented this type of solution. I have found no record in early documents or life stories of major, long-enduring factionalist confrontations between Navajo groups. There are, however, many instances of disgruntled families "pulling out." Today Navajos are hemmed in, bounded by the limits of their reservation, subagencies, land-management districts, and communities. They are politically controlled by the federal government, the Navajo Tribal Council, and the local chapters of the council. The population increase has left little or no unused land to which dissenters can withdraw.

Overt factionalism concerning stock reduction slowly subsided as the resisters realized that they were powerless to change federal policy through open resistance. Even the strongest leader, Jacob Morgan of the Shiprock area, found that when he was elected chairman of the tribe he could not reverse the policy. However, the federal government, which was interested in developing Indian self-government, finally concluded that the price in factionalism and noncooperation that it was forced to pay for stock reduction was much too high. In 1948 the punitive provisions of the Special Grazing Act (arrest, trial, incarceration, and fine for trespass) were relaxed, and by 1956 the federal government had turned over the grazing problem to the Navajo Tribal Council. Since then the council has been granted extension after extension of the time set for compliance with their own stock-reduction plan (Young 1961:155–61). Quietly and covertly, the Navajos are noncomplying, and old sheepherders once again are building up their outsized flocks.

This was factionalism in an acculturative situation with perceived stress coming from outside. It was during this period of despair and disruption, according to David Aberle (1966:199) that Navajos began to adopt the pan-Indian cult which involved the eating of a cactus bud called "peyote" for hallucinatory "religious" purposes. This leads us into consideration of a second conflict.

Navajo conflict number two. The arena for conflict number two was the community of Shiprock, New Mexico, during the late 1950s and the early 1960s. Shiprock, more than any other community in the Navajo Nation, is subject to the stresses of acculturation. As of 1961, some fifteen hundred Navajos and three hundred non-Indians lived in Shiprock proper, a town situated at the junction of two paved highways near the Four Corners where Arizona, Utah, Colorado, and New Mexico meet. The election precinct for the Navajo Tribal Council numbered about three thousand voters, and the subagency of the Bureau of Indian Affairs had jurisdiction over some ten thousand people in all. The San Juan River Basin is rich in oil, natural gas, helium, vanadium, and coal, and it is from this area that most of the income for the Navajo tribal government is derived. The river furnishes permanent water, making large-scale irrigation farming possible. Interest groups of stockmen, irrigation farmers, small businessmen, and wage workers for the Bureau of Indian Affairs, the U.S. Public Health Service, the Navajo Tribal Council, and local enterprises have separated from the traditional pastoral economy.

In 1957, Aberle and Stewart estimated that fifty percent of the residents of Shiprock were peyotists (1957:75). In 1961, my informants gave me a rough estimate of sixty percent. Twenty years before, in 1940, Christian missionaries, through their influence on their Navajo converts, had succeeded in getting a resolution to outlaw the use of peyote on the reservation through the Navajo Tribal Council. During the period of my fieldwork in 1960 and 1961, the Navajo police were raiding secret peyote meetings, confiscating sacred paraphernalia, and imprisoning or fining the participants. This brought the members of the cult (known as the Native American Church) into direct conflict with the leadership of the Navajo Tribal Council. A political struggle in 1959 to elect Raymond Nakai, a candidate who was "soft on peyote," to the chairmanship of the council failed. When the council proposed setting aside an area three miles in radius for a townsite to attract outside industry to Shiprock, the opposition went into action, rallying stockmen who needed the land for grazing, squatters working on construction jobs who had pitched their tents or thrown together huts near the river, and Navajo businessmen who feared outside competition. Advocates of "Shiprock revenue for Shiprock use only" joined forces. The fight came to a head with the attempt to recall the local councilman, a peyotist, for drunkenness and absenteeism. Shiprock was paralyzed. Nothing requiring extensive community cooperation could go forward.

In a paper I read to the Southwestern Anthropological Association in 1962, I predicted that factionalism in Shiprock would only be alleviated if the issue of peyotism was resolved, an issue which Shiprock could not settle because the decision did not lie within its jurisdiction. With the election of Raymond Nakai as chairman of the Navajo Tribal Council in 1963 and the choice of a Shiprock councilman who promised to support freedom of religion, the tribal leadership was no longer the "enemy" to peyotists. The Shiprock councilman made common cause with the peyotist candidate he defeated and appointed him to important local committees. The Navajo Police Department, sensing a changed climate at the top, did not expend much energy in enforcing the peyote resolution. Cooperation was again possible. The community worked together on a community center, a farmers' market, FHA housing, and on the task of attracting an electronics industry to Shiprock to furnish jobs for Indians. However, the election of 1963 leads us into consideration of a third conflict.

Navajo conflict number three. Raymond Nakai's platform in the 1963 election included freedom of religion, a constitution to define more clearly the powers of Navajo government, cooperation with the Bureau of Indian Affairs, and the ousting of Norman Littell, the non-Indian tribal general counsel. Mr. Littell, as chief adviser to the previous tribal leaders, had attacked Nakai, his program, and, at every opportunity, public or private, the Bureau of Indian Affairs (keeping forever green the memory of stock reduction, although he himself had signed some of the punitive orders against trespass when he was in the Department of Justice).

The new chairman refused to conform to the old Navajo ideal which required him to "shake hands and forget all about it." He refused to propose his erstwhile adversaries for any important committees. Frozen out of the leadership that they had so long enjoyed, a faction calling itself the Old Guard formed to fight Raymond Nakai down to the ground. Since the new chairman did not have the majority of the councilmen behind him, two nearly equal contending groups brought cooperation to a grinding halt.

The effort to oust Littell enlisted the support of Secretary of the Interior Stewart Udall, who moved to abrogate Littell's contract with the Navajo Tribe. Littell sued Udall in federal court and obtained an injunction preventing the secretary from firing him. The Old Guard maneuvered to capture the Advisory Committee by voting to increase its size. Only bits and scraps of tribal government business could be conducted, and these in an atmosphere of secrecy, bitterness, and character assassination. Nakai's "New Frontier" program went down the drain.

There was no major change in this conflict-ridden situation until the elections of 1967, when Raymond Nakai won the chairmanship by a clear majority. Softened by sad experience, he agreed to nominate some of the Old Guard for the Advisory Committee, and in this manner he succeeded in partially neutralizing his powerful opposition. A federal judge ruled that the secretary of the interior had the power to terminate Littell's contract for malfeasance, and Nakai's opposition was thus further weakened. A 1967 council resolution calling for freedom of religion legalized the use of peyote in religious ceremonies on the reservation. Talk of a constitution revived. Cooperation was again in order. During this peaceful period the Office of Economic Opportunity was asked by the Tribal Council to grant funds for a legal aid program to furnish advice to individual Navajos, which leads us to the fourth conflict.

Navajo conflict number four. An independent citizens' organization, Dinebeiina Nahiilna Be Agaditahe ("attorneys who contribute to the economic revitalization of the people"), was incorporated under Arizona law in 1967 to administer the OEO legal aid program on the Navajo Reservation. Theodore Mitchell, a young Harvard lawyer, was made director, initially with the blessings of the Navajo Tribal Council. In two years DNA, as the organization is called for short, handled 15,435 cases and in 1969 envisioned handling 10,000 cases for the year 1970 alone. Navajos took advantage of the program for representation both in the Navajo Tribal Courts and in the state courts. DNA initiated a program for Navajo counselors to represent clients in the tribal courts.

Soon the organization's activities became far-ranging—too far-ranging to please the Advisory Committee. A DNA lawyer gave advice to disgruntled parents in the Chinle school fight which eventuated in the defeat of some school board members in a recall election and the resignation of the school superintendent. DNA attacked reservation traders and in so doing angered the Indian Traders' Association. Information about "horrible" conditions on the reservation was fed to CBS for a television broadcast, which angered the council. A power struggle developed between the Advisory Committee and DNA centering on the director, Theodore Mitchell. Various moves were made to oust Mitchell, such as the refusal of the chairman to sign a request for the appropriation of OEO funds for DNA. A complete realignment of old factionalists took place. One of the most articulate members of the Old Guard, Frankie Howard, threw his support to Mitchell, while other erstwhile Old Guard leaders stood with the chairman. Mitchell's board of directors and staff gave him firm support, and the Navajo people, by and large, were "sold" on this new brand of legal aid.

A final skirmish took place at a meeting of the Advisory Committee to discuss the implications of the U.S. Indian Civil Rights Act. Mitchell was accused of guffawing, thereby insulting an eminent councilwoman and proving himself guilty of "contempt of court." The Advisory Committee voted to exclude him from the reservation. He was given a hearing but not allowed to bring counsel or witnesses in his own behalf, and Navajo policemen escorted him off Navajo national territory. Mitchell sued in federal court and obtained an injunction on the grounds that he had not been found guilty of, nor even charged with, any of the sixteen offenses listed as grounds for exclusion in Title 17, Paragraph 1782, of the Navajo Tribal Code. Conflict number four still raged.

When I returned to Window Rock in June of 1969, Theodore Mitchell was busily writing a proposal for the refunding of the OEO legal aid program. This was subsequently granted. Edmund Kahn, assistant general counsel for the Navajo Tribe, was busily writing an appeal from the Mitchell decision on the grounds that the decision threatened Navajo sovereignty, which had been guaranteed by the Treaty of 1868. The Navajo Tribe, according to the argument, is a "homeowner," and as such has the right to expel an unwanted guest.

The question I wish to raise at this point is, will conflict number four take on the color of schismatic factionalism? I think not. Cooperation between the branches of Navajo government and DNA is still the order of the day. Navajo judges told me that they welcomed Navajo DNA counselors in their courts and the advice of the non-Indian lawyers. "They prepare the cases for the clients." "They keep us on our toes." Both the

Tribal Legal Aid Department and the BIA Branch of Law and Order were finding no difficulty in cooperating with DNA.

Some Indian Bureau employees view Mitchell and his cohorts as dangerous radicals who are trying to subvert tribal self-government. This attitude was strengthened by the fact that during the Mitchell exclusion period a few young Navajos who had had radical exposure to new action methods in off-reservation colleges picketed the Navajo Tribal Council in protest against the exclusion. One of their placards read "Sing Along with Mitch." Mitchell and his followers assert that they are committed to Navajo self-government, but they see themselves as crusaders for individual rights and as fighters against the tyrannies that have crept into the council system. They also protect Navajos against the bad judgment of their own councilmen and the bad advice of the Bureau of Indian Affairs in matters such as water rights, traders' leases, and so forth. One of the Navajo judges said to me, "Their quarrel is political. The Council wants to be the only voice. But if they don't protect the legal rights of individuals, where is their sovereignty? What good is it to Navajos?"

In my opinion, conflict number four will not develop into schismatic factionalism as I have defined it. Solution to the dispute is not blocked. It can be decided in a court of law. Support for DNA as a program is too widespread, cutting across too many subgroups within the Navajo Nation and even into the tribal administration itself. I believe that the controversy over one person on a legalistic issue does not have the deep impact of a religious issue like peyote or an economic issue like stock reduction. It cannot inspire the kind of total commitment that builds long-enduring factionalist groups. As one Navajo onlooker said to me, "I don't see how they [the DNA staff] can get so racked up over a white man." (Parenthetically, in the months since I wrote the analysis above, Edmund Kahn has resigned as assistant general counsel to go into private practice, the Navajo Tribal Council has passed a resolution to increase the size of the DNA Board of Directors by adding five Navajo tribal councilmen, and Theodore Mitchell has resigned the directorship of DNA to make way for a Navajo but plans to remain in the program as attorney in the litigation and law reform section.)

In summarizing the implications of these four conflicts, we are faced with the same problem Spiro presents in his analysis of Burmese factionalism (1968) and the one Boissevain wrestles with so profitably in his analysis of conflict in a Maltese village (1964). Do the Navajo cases illustrate generic features of schismatic factionalism, or have we isolated only specifics? I submit that the diagnostic traits—a bounded-group, noninstitutionalized conflict over an issue to which solution is blocked, the formation of two groups that are nearly equal in power, a conflict of long duration, and the resulting halt to normal cooperation within the group—are generic to schismatic factionalism. I believe they could be used in the analysis of the Hopi dispute at Oraibi in 1906 in the pueblo of Santa Clara (Dozier 1966), in Protestant sects and their challenge to the Roman Catholic Church, in the Trotskyite split in the Russian Communist Party, and in the confrontation of administration and striking students adhering around the core of black and brown militants with their nonnegotiable demands at San Francisco State College in 1968–69.

Schismatic factionalism could not be the basis for a "segmentary factionalist political system" as described by Nicholas for India (1966) and by Schwartz for Guatemala (1969); it is the breakdown of a system of cooperation. Nor can it be a regular mechanism for the fission of villages in a

stateless society as discussed by Turner among the Ndembu (1964). The aim in schismatic factionalism is to preserve the group, not, as in some of Turner's cases, a method for promoting fission for the purpose of legitimizing the establishment of a new village under a faction leader (1964). Nor are these conflicts covert as in Burma (Spiro 1968: 401), nor ambiguous as on the Klamath Reservation (French 1962:232).

Other types of factionalism, discussed and defined by Fenton (1955, 1957), Lewis (1958), and Murdock (1949:90), deal with assorted conflict groups, such as institutionalized political parties, dual organizations, and economic interest groups. These are either conflicts which are periodically resolved through established mechanisms, or conflicts in which cooperation is halted in one area but continues in another area of interaction between the factions. Thus, when we disagree on a diagnosis of factionalism, it is because we are talking past each other; we are simply analyzing a different process or a different entity.

It has become fashionable to view factionalism as *eu*functional rather than *dys*functional, but *good* is not inherent in the conflict itself. Good may result from the conflict, depending on how one judges the aftermath. We should ask if there are not less socially costly alternatives to schismatic factionalism. If it is eufunctional, we should ask: when? for whom? For the duration of the long, bitter struggle, and for the group involved, I submit, schismatic factionalism can only be divisive, dysfunctional, and paralyzing.

REFERENCES

ABERLE, DAVID F.
   1966   The Peyote Religion among the Navaho. Wenner-Gren Foundation for Anthropological Research. Viking Fund Publications in Anthropology 42.

ABERLE, DAVID F. AND OMER C. STEWART
   1957   Navajo and Ute Peyotism: a Chronological and Distributional Study. University of Colorado Press, Boulder.

BOISSEVAIN, JEREMY
   1964   Factions, Parties, and Politics in a Maltese Village. American Anthropologist 66:1,275–88.

DNA (NAVAJO LEGAL AID SOCIETY)

1968–69   Law in Action. Window Rock, Arizona.

1969   Application for Refunding. Window Rock, Arizona.

DOZIER, EDWARD P.

1966   Factionalism at Santa Clara Pueblo. Ethnology 5:172–86.

FENTON, WILLIAM N.

1955   Factionalism in American Indian Society. *In* Proceedings of the Fourth International Congress of Anthropology and Ethnology 2:330–40.

1957   Factionalism at Taos Pueblo, New Mexico. Bulletin of the Bureau of American Ethnology 56. Smithsonian Institution, Washington, D.C.

FRENCH, DAVID H.

1962   Ambiguity and Irrelevancy in Factional Conflict. *In* Intergroup Relations and Leadership, Muzafer Sherif, editor. John Wiley Company, New York.

LEWIS, OSCAR

1958   Village Life in Northern India. Random House, New York.

MURDOCK, GEORGE PETER

1949   Social Structure. The Macmillan Company, New York.

NAVAJO TRIBAL COUNCIL

1962   Navajo Tribal Code. Equity Publishing Company, Orford, New Hampshire.

NICHOLAS, RALPH W.

1966   Segmentary Factional Political Systems. *In* Political Anthropology, Marc J. Swartz, Victor W. Turner, and Arthur Tuden, editors. Aldine Publishing Company, Chicago.

SIEGEL, BERNARD J. AND ALAN R. BEALS

1960   Pervasive Factionalism. American Anthropologist 62:394–418.

SPIRO, MELFORD E.

1969   Factionalism and Politics in Village Burma. *In* Local-Level Politics, Marc J. Swartz, editor. Aldine Publishing Company, Chicago.

SCHWARTZ, NORMAN B.

1969   Goal Attainment Through Factionalism: a Guatemalan Case. American Anthropologist 71: 1,088–1,109.

TURNER, VICTOR W.

1957   Schism and Continuity in an African Society. Manchester University Press, Manchester, England.

YOUNG, ROBERT W.

1961   The Navajo Yearbook, Report No. 8. The Navajo Agency, Window Rock, Arizona.

Chapter 9

THE NAVAJO CULTURAL SYSTEM:
AN ANALYSIS OF CONCEPTS OF COOPERATION
AND AUTONOMY AND THEIR RELATION
TO GOSSIP AND WITCHCRAFT

Louise Lamphere

LOUISE LAMPHERE, assistant professor in the Department of Anthropology and Sociology at Brown University, conducted ethnographic research on the eastern Navajo reservation for her Ph.D. dissertation "Social Organization and Cooperation in a Navajo Community" (Harvard University). She has published articles dealing with Navajo social organization and ritual symbolism.

Navajo social structure is based, not on a well-defined system of groups, but on a network of kin ties. This view varies from the interpretation of many anthropologists[1] who describe Navajo social life as based on three groups of increasing size and complexity: (1) the household or nuclear family; (2) the residence group, camp, or extended family; and (3) the "outfit" (Kluckhohn and Leighton 1946), which is similar to Collier's "cooperating unit" (1966), Adams' "resident lineage" (1963), and Kimball and Province's "land use community" (1942).[2]

In proposing an alternative analysis I do not deny the importance of the household and residence group, especially in the organization of daily activities. Rather, I wish to emphasize that these domestic groups are not combined into larger groups such as the "outfit" or "cooperating unit," nor are they linked primarily through matrilineal clanship. Instead, they are tied together through

ego-centered "sets" of potential cooperators composed of primary and secondary kin.[3] Recruitment of participants, especially for ceremonial activities, creates a network of ties which extends throughout an entire Navajo community (Lamphere 1970). Cooperation, even within the household and residence group, and especially between members of several residence groups, is ego centered. "Sets" are unbounded and present the individual with many options. Those who may be recruited by ego for one activity may not participate in another activity organized by the same individual.

Parallel to this social system, which incorporates "open endedness" and flexibility into its very structure, is a cultural system[4] through which Navajos interpret and organize cooperative behavior. It is the purpose of this article to describe and analyze this cultural system. First, I will outline Navajo concepts of cooperation and autonomy which provide a very generalized set of notions about appropriate and inappropriate behavior. Second, I will state the ways in which these concepts are communicated during public occasions and in face-to-face interaction situations. Finally, I will illustrate, using case material, how gossip and witchcraft suspicion, in particular, communicate and define cooperative and uncooperative behavior.[5]

These aspects of the Navajo cultural system are all relevant to actual behavior in social situations. They form a very generalized system of

NOTE: The fieldwork on which this analysis is based was supported by a National Institute of Mental Health Fellowship (1FL MH 24,103–01) with a Research Grant Attachment (MH 11631–91). I am grateful to David Aberle, George Hicks, Nancy Leis, and Terry Reynolds for valuable comments and criticism on various ideas presented in this article.

norms and sanctions to "back up" recruitment based on ego-centered unbounded sets and networks.

THE GREENWATER NAVAJO

Data concerning the cultural system of cooperation have been derived from published literature on the Navajo and from fieldwork carried out between June 1965 and August 1966 in the Navajo community of Greenwater,[6] north of Gallup, New Mexico. A Navajo "community" is an unbounded unit—a vaguely defined area of scattered hogans focused on a set of facilities. The Navajo population within a given area utilizes the same schools, trading post, and missions; those on the periphery may send their children to school in one location and trade at another. Communities are becoming more clearly defined due to the increasing effectiveness of local "chapters" introduced by the Bureau of Indian Affairs and now an important part of the Navajo tribal organization. These local political units have a president, vice-president, and secretary and meet regularly to discuss and organize various Navajo Tribe- and government-sponsored development projects (including Tribal Works Projects, Head Start and Vista programs, and sheep dipping and vaccination programs). Since it is becoming less and less possible to attend chapter meetings and sign up for benefits in two communities, the population of many chapters is increasingly stable.

The community of Greenwater has as its center a chapter meetinghouse, a small trading post and cafe, and a Pentecostal mission; residents live in hogans and cabins scattered throughout a ten-mile-square area. Some children attend a public school ten miles north of the trading post; others attend a Bureau of Indian Affairs boarding school fifteen miles away. In the summer, many Navajo reside in the nearby Chuska Mountains, where there is a summer chapter house which provides a community focus. In determining a delimited population to study, I used the chapter census (collected under the auspices of the Navajo Tribe), adding to this a few nuclear families because of their close spatial or kinship ties with other families in the census.

Greenwater has a population of 1,000 Navajo, 750 of whom reside, at present, within the bounds of the community as I have defined it. The remaining 250 are younger couples and children who have moved to other parts of the reservation or to urban areas off the reservation to take wage jobs. Only fifteen percent of the community income comes from such traditional sources as livestock (the sale of lambs and wool) and weaving, though most residence groups still have a few sheep and cultivate small fields. Welfare provides twenty-five percent of the income, and irregular wage work constitutes fifty percent. The remaining ten percent is provided by the Tribal Works Project, through which community members work on local projects (such as road repair, house-building, and weaving), at one hundred dollars for ten days of labor. Most residence groups have access to a pickup truck or car, some have electricity and even TV sets, and many have transistor radios so they can hear local programs in the Navajo language. Despite the dependency on a wage economy and the obvious signs of "Anglo" material culture, Navajo is the main language of every household. The traditional religion, along with belief in ghosts and witches, flourishes. Kinship continues to play an important role in the organization of daily activities even in the midst of economic modernity, making an analysis of kinship and social structure and the complementary cultural system relevant to an understanding of this present-day Navajo community.

CONCEPTS OF COOPERATION

Navajo dictionaries and published analyses of values and ethics, in addition to data from Greenwater on actual conversations, indicate that Navajos discuss cooperative behavior in terms of a generalized conception of "help" or "aid." This is expressed by using a form of the verb stem -ghoł which means *to run* and which is used in phrases like ʔadeeshghoł (*I'll run out of sight*). To indicate "helping" Navajos use the phrase bíká ʔadeeshghoł which means *I'll help him* or *I'll run after him*. Similarly, shiká ʔanájah means *After me they are running along* or *They are helping me* (Young and Morgan 1943:83; part 1).

Navajos feel very strongly that helping is a good thing, and they live under a diffuse moral obligation to give aid when requested or when it appears to be needed. Another aspect of helping is the importance placed on taking good care of relatives and possessions. This is expressed by the stem *-yaał* which means *to be aware or alert*, or *to take care of* as in *baa ʔáháshyą́*, (Young and Morgan 1943:232, part 1). Thus one Navajo might criticize another by stating *doo hózhǫ́ dibé yaa ʔáhalyą́da* or *He doesn't take very good care of the sheep* (Kluckhohn 1954:145); or *doo bischíinii yaa ʔáhályą́da*, which means *He doesn't take very good care of his parents*. Ladd, in his analysis of Navajo ethics, lists eight positive prescriptions which Navajos say should be followed, several of which deal with *helping* or *taking care of*. He has stated these as follows (1957:253–55):

1. Take care of your possessions.
2. You ought to take good care of your children.
3. Children should take care of their parents.
4. In general, people ought to help the aged.
5. One ought to help a person who is in dire need.
6. There are other people whom it is particularly important to help; one's wife and her family.
7. In general, you ought to help anybody who needs it or requests it.

Though Ladd does not provide the Navajo translations for these statements, they can all be rendered in the native language using forms of *helping* or *running after* and *taking care of*.

It is important to emphasize the uncalculated nature of cooperation which is expressed in these native conceptions. A Navajo does not formulate his expectations in specific terms so that he aids a particular person one day, with the hope of returned aid at a specific time in the future. Rather a Navajo is generally obligated to fill the requests made upon him and expects that he will be able to find someone to fill his own requests. The Navajo notion of cooperation is generalized and diffuse; it is not specific to particular types of situations or

to particular kin roles. The specific individual to be asked for aid or the kind of task for which help is expected are both left unspecified.

In contrast to the generalized positive obligation to help and take care of others (i.e., to be cooperative), there are a number of more specific negative prescriptions which indicate that uncooperative behavior is undesirable. Most Navajo behavior prescriptions are negative in form (Ladd 1957:300–302), and many fit the sentence frames, "One does not do X" or "X is not done" (i.e., "Do not do X"). Examples are *One does not commit adultery (doo ʔazhdiléeh da)*; *One does not beat his wife (doo ʔajiizą́ą da)*; *One does not steal (doo 'izhni'įįda)*; *Lies are not told (doo hoyoch'íída)*; and *Man is not killed (diné doo biłhéeda)* (Haile 1943:85).

Data from interviews with informants and conversations between Greenwater residents indicate that behavior prescriptions which describe uncooperativeness use the Navajo terms for "stingy," "mean," "mad," "jealous," and "lazy." They can be stated as follows:

1. *One is not stingy*	*doo jichį́ʔda*
2. *One is not mean*	*doo bá hachį́ʔda*
3. *One is not mad*	*doo bá hojiłchįįda*
4. *One is not envious or jealous of someone's possessions*[7]	*doo ʔoołchʔįįda*
5. *One is not sexually jealous*	*doołeʔ nizin da*
6. *One is not lazy*	*doo ʔooł hóghééʔda*

I suggest that these statements, taken together, describe the antisocial, uncooperative Navajo, one who is not *helping* or *taking care of* others. Similar notions of uncooperative, "un-Navajo" behavior are part of Navajo beliefs in witchcraft. The various kinds of witchcraft have been discussed in detail by Kluckhohn (1944). The beliefs most relevant to defining uncooperative behavior are those concerning *witchcraft (ʔáńtʔį)* as practiced by *witches (ʔádańtʔį)* and *werewolves (yeenaaldloozhii)*. Both *witches* and *werewolves* are "inverted" Navajos, or creatures who embody all the characteristics opposite to the cooperative, social individual. Werewolves are said to dress in wolf or coyote skins. They become animal rather than human and travel about at night (hence the name *yeenaaldloozhii*, meaning *one who goes around*). They are night creatures rather than day creatures as ordinary humans are. Werewolves are said to participate in sings in a *witchery hogan (ʔáńtʔį báhoghan)*—which is the opposite of a normal hogan. They chant the songs from Navajo ceremonials in reverse, feed on corpses, and rob the graves of the dead.[8]

Witches or *werewolves* practice *beeʔiińziid* or *sorcery*. They are believed to cause sickness by taking a portion of a person's clothing or body offal (hair, nails, feces, urine, or body dirt) and chanting over it so that the victim will become ill (Kluckhohn 1944:31–33). Instead of practicing curing and concentrating on *pleasant conditions (hózhóníí)*, *witches* and *werewolves* are concerned with death and *ugly conditions (hóchǫ́ǫ́nii)*.

Kluckhohn analyzes witchcraft beliefs in terms of their general social and psychological functions rather than in terms of their relation to other cultural concepts. Consequently, the connection between witchcraft and concepts of uncooperative behavior did not occur to me through reading Kluckhohn or other anthropologists but only became clear during conversations with members of the Greenwater community. When asked why some Navajos are *yeenaaldloozhii* and would want to practice witchcraft or sorcery, one Greenwater man replied:

> Maybe that man over there has a big truck and lots of sheep and a good family. Maybe this other fellow over here is jealous *(ooɫchʔįį)* of him, so he gets into a skin and goes around at night. Navajos go to the toilet outside and the *yeenaaldloozhii* can get a little piece of it and put it in a grave and the ghost *(chʔįįdii)* will start working on that man and make him sick.

A young girl gave a similar explanation of her own illness. Her recent headaches and dizziness were diagnosed by a handtrembler[9] as being caused by *beeʔiińziid*. She explained this sorcery as "somebody wanting to make you sick or wish you were dead," which can be expressed in the Navajo phrase *doo hotʔééGo ntsékees (not all-right, it-being, he is thinking,* or *he is wishing harmful or unpleasant conditions).*

Witchcraft is not only associated with jealousy and malevolent thoughts directed against the victim but also with "meanness." When visiting one camp, I was told by a young girl riding in the car with me that the wife of the household "looked real mean at us." She maintained that we should be careful or we might get "witch powder" on us. Someone who is designated "mean" or "jealous" on the basis of quarrels or refusal of aid is also likely to be suspected of "thinking against someone" or engaging in witchcraft and sorcery, presumably to enhance his own well-being at the expense of others.

It is important to note that witchcraft is an explanation for illness and is thus part of a post hoc system of causation. As Evans-Pritchard has pointed out (1937, chapter 4), witchcraft explains unfortunate events rather than actual malevolent behavior, which may not occur at all, but is presumed to occur. From the observer's point of view, witchcraft is not practiced by individuals in order to cause illness at some future time. Rather the illness or unfortunate event occurs first and then is explained in terms of presumed witchcraft practiced at some time in the past. The purpose of witchcraft suspicion among the Navajo is not to punish any one individual but to explain the illness and prescribe the correct ceremonial cure which will counteract it. Thus, a living individual need not be accused; a dead relative may be seen as the cause or no specific person is named. When a living individual *is* suspected of witchcraft practices, it is not because he has actually engaged in them. Rather the whispered suspicion that "X is a witch" is offered as an explanation for his "mean" or uncooperative behavior displayed in various social contexts, whether or not his alleged witchcraft is used as an explanation of a particular illness. There are two aspects here: the folk explanation of an illness in terms of witchcraft beliefs and the explanation of antisocial behavior in terms of the same beliefs. The two need not be connected in any one instance; illness can be explained by witchcraft without a specific accusation and an individual can be labeled a *witch* or *werewolf* in contexts where there is no illness to be explained. On the other hand, as Greenwater case material will show, both aspects may be present in a particular incident.

In sum, Navajo conceptions of uncooperative behavior are embodied in negative prescriptions which state that "mean," "jealous," "stingy," and "mad" behavior are disapproved. These same characteristics are part of the cultural definition of *witch* or *werewolf*. In other words, all the uncooperative, antisocial attributes of behavior are epitomized in this prototype of the "anti-Navajo": the *witch* and *werewolf*.

CONCEPTIONS OF AUTONOMY AND CONSENSUS

As one aspect of the Navajo cultural system, I have discussed the generalized obligation to cooperate along with Navajo conceptions of uncooperative behavior. Another dimension of the cultural system is that concerning concepts which involve: (1) an individual's rights over the allocation of goods and services (which stress autonomy) and (2) mechanisms for recruiting joint action (which stress consensus).

The Navajo phrase which fuses both autonomy and consensus conceptions is *t ?áá bee bóholníih*, which has been translated as *he is the boss* (Wall and Morgan 1958:23), but is more accurately rendered by, *It's up to him to decide, It is his business,* or *It's his area of concern.* The phrase describes the individual's "right to make a decision" (1) over the use and disposal of his possessions, and (2) over his own actions and the allocation of his time.

The use of *t ?áá bee bóholníih* to indicate an individual's exclusive rights over possessions is congruent with the fact that most movable property (including livestock, jewelry, medicine pouches, cars, and wagons) is individually owned. Rights with regard to objects are expressed, not through a concept of ownership as in our phrase, "He owns it," but through such phrases as *da dibésh nee hóló? Do sheep exist by means of you?*, or *da tsinabạạshish síńtł ?ạ? Do you cause a wagon to be at your disposal?* (Haile 1947:4 and 1954:24).

Ownership is also designated by noun-possession as in *his car (bichidi), his sheep (bidibé), his livestock or horse (billíí?)*.[10] Houses, farmland, and grazing areas are thought of in terms of "use-rights" rather than ownership. One can say, *his house (bighan), his field (bida ?ak ?eh),* or *his land (bikéyah),* but the meaning here is that an individual has the right to use the field and grazing area; if vacated, land can be claimed by other Navajos. Houses are at the disposal of the nuclear family, and, in case of divorce, the spouse with whose relatives the couple is living retains the right to stay there (Haile 1954:10–13). Examples of "decision right" over possessions include the following instances taken from interviews with Greenwater informants. If someone comes to borrow a shovel or wagon that belongs to the mother of the household, a daughter might say *shimá bóholníih (my mother, it's her business), ?éí ?aa diní (you ask her).* If the mother is not at home, the individual making the request must return later, since no one except the owner has the right to dispose of the property or to allow others to use it. Likewise, a sheep in the residence group herd cannot be butchered or sold without the owner's consent.

With regard to the allocation of his time and energy, an individual has "decision right" and is *t ?áá bee bóholníih* over his own actions insofar as they do not harm others. For instance, if a Navajo wishes to make a trip to the trading post or to visit a relative, the trip is his business and not that of others. Conversely, if an individual's services are desired, he has the right to decide to contribute time and effort; there is no obligation to do so as a consequence of his particular kinship status or the specific situation. A Navajo prefers to wait for a demonstration of generosity, (i.e. an offer for help in response to a generalized obligation once the needs of the situation are known) rather than make a more direct request (Aberle 1961:162). This preserves the "decision right" of the person being asked, as well as maintaining a general atmosphere of cooperativeness.

Further evidence for the importance of decision right over one's own actions is provided by Robert Young (1961:508–10). Sentences like "I made the horse trot," or "I made my wife sing," can only be rendered in Navajo by "I made the horse trot, even though he did not want to do so," and "Even though she did not want to do so, she sang when I told her to do so." Where the subject is an agent causing an action to be performed by another agent, the latter's will or desire must be considered. One does not make the horse trot, because a horse has a will of his own. He may trot even though he does not want to do so, "but he still has the freedom of choice to refuse or decline to trot" (Young 1961:510).

Similarly, Navajos are reluctant to report the opinions of others or account for their actions. In reply to my questions concerning a kinsman's views on a topic or on his actions in a particular situation, my informants often stated, *I don't know, ask him (doo shił bééhósin da, ʔéí ʔááji bidiní)*, indicating that speculation would infringe on the "business" or "concerns" of another.

The first two uses of the phrase *tʔáá bee bóholnííh* stress autonomy, or the individual as a free agent where his possessions and his own actions are concerned. This autonomy has been cited as a significant aspect of Navajo culture by Ladd (1957:292) and Leighton and Kluckhohn (1947:107), and its importance has consequences for the nature of collective action. In a society where the emphasis is on autonomy, joint action is gained by the consent of other free agents. The third use of *tʔáá bee bóholnííh* indicates this complementary aspect: decisions which imply consensus, the mechanism for mobilizing support from a number of individuals. The ways in which consensus is implied by *tʔáá bee bóholnííh (It's up to him to decide)* or *(tʔáá ʔááji bidaholnííh (It's up to them to decide)* are illustrated by examples of marriage negotiations, ceremonial activities, and chapter meetings in Sheep Springs.

First marriages are traditionally arranged by the parents of the couple[11] (Haile 1954:13–15), but second or third marriages are considered the business of the couple themselves. In such non-arranged marriages, there is no bride-price or traditional ceremony, and the marriage is initiated by the couple coming to live together (Aberle 1961:123–28), but like first marriages, parental support and consent is an important factor. As one young Greenwater woman said, in discussing the pos-

sibility of a second marriage, "If somebody wants to get married with me, I'd say *shimá bóholnííh* or *shizhéʔé bohólnííh (It's up to my mother or my father to decide)*. Making such a statement implies both the girl's own willingness and that her parents must be asked also. If she had no interest in the marriage, she would discourage the suitor immediately.

The same elements of making a decision and then asking for consent by stating "It's up to X to decide," are present in ceremonial cooperation. The following example was given by a Greenwater informant. If a man is asked to be Stick Receiver for an Enemy Way Ceremony (also known as a Squaw Dance),[12] he might explain to the emissary making the request, *shi doo shóholnííh da, ʔááji bidaholnííh (I am not the boss, those over there, it is up to them*, referring to other relatives such as his mother, sister, and sister's husband). Another man might refer to his grown children as being *bidaholnííh*, if they would be the main relatives to give cooperation during the ceremony. When these individuals agree, the man originally asked agrees to be Stick Receiver. The reference to his relatives already indicates that he is willing to accept the obligations of carrying out the ceremony, but he needs the consent and the assurance of aid from his closest kin. If he had not been willing to expend the time and effort on the ceremony, he would have immediately refused by giving an excuse.

The same pattern of using the phrase *tʔáá bee bóholnííh* to indicate an individual whose consent is needed is evident in chapter affairs. If someone comes to the chapter secretary asking to be placed on a list of workers for the next Tribal Works Project, the secretary may say, *Nléí bóholnííh ʔááji bidiní (That one, he is the boss, ask him)*, referring to the chapter president. Upon asking the president, the individual will be given the same answer and sent back to the secretary or to the vice-president. This seems like the proverbial "run-around," but if all three officers indicate agreement, the name will be added to the list. In other words, the individual will be sent back and forth until it is clear that none of the officers object and consensus is reached.

In addition to situations involving a small group of kinsmen or chapter officers, consensus is sometimes required of the whole community. In chapter meetings there is an ethic that "it is up to the people to decide." For instance, in speaking about proposals for a Tribal Works Project, a chapter member might say *Jó nihi nihidaholníih (It is up to us to decide)*. This calls for consensus in the sense of unanimity, that is, supporting decisions on the part of a group of autonomous individuals.

The relation between autonomy and consensus which is expressed in the three uses of *t ?áá bee bóholníih* implies authority relations which differ from those in our own society. Most social scientists conceptualize authority in terms of institutionalized power relationships. Parsons, for instance, first defines power as "the capacity to secure the performance of binding obligations," (1963:237) and then describes authority as the legitimate use of power in a system of social roles. "Authority, then, is the aspect of a status in a system of social organization ... by virtue of which the incumbent is put in a position legitimately to make decisions which are binding, not only on himself but on the collectivity as a whole and hence its other member units ..." (1963:244).

Rather than such hierarchial authority where *A*'s decision is binding on *B* or a group of *B*s, Navajo authority is egalitarian. *A* makes a decision and requests a similar one from *B*. If *B*'s decision is congruent with *A*'s, it obligates both to participate in joint activities. In contrast to the Parsonian definition, in Navajo society there are relatively few statuses and roles where a single incumbent has the right to make decisions binding on others (the parent-child relationship, at times, is the major exception). "Bindingness," however, is achieved through the consensus mechanism. If there is general agreement on an issue or course of action, all those in favor are obligated to "go along" with the joint decision. Those opposed may be persuaded to join also, but there is no notion of "majority rule." An individual who disagrees may always decide not to participate, and this preserves his right of autonomy, even in the face of group pressure. As a result of this attempt to reach consensus, action is never taken if there are two opposing factions on a given issue or if near unanimity is lacking.

In sum, the phrase *t ?áá bee bóholníih* combines Navajo emphasis on both autonomy and consensus and entails egalitarian rather than hierarchial authority relations. Like the generalized obligation to cooperate, the phrase summarizes conceptions not specific to particular situations and to particular kin roles, but applicable to all adult Navajos in any setting.

CONCLUSIONS ABOUT COOPERATION AND AUTONOMY CONCEPTS

At the beginning of this article, I described diffuse positive obligations to *help others* and *take care of others* and contrasted these with a number of negative prescriptions which define "uncooperative behavior." Such an undifferentiated system of obligations fits well with what Marshall Sahlins, in analyzing varieties of exchange relationships, has called "generalized reciprocity." By this he means "putatively altruistic transactions of assistance given and if possible returned." Examples are "the pure gift," "sharing," "hospitality," "free gift," "help," and "generosity" (1965:149 and 1968:82).

In further defining the concept, Sahlins says:

At the extreme, say voluntary food-sharing among near kinsmen—or for its logical value, one might think of the suckling of children in this context—the expectation of direct material return is unseemly. At best it is implicit. The material side of the transaction is repressed by the social and is typically left out of account. This is not to say that handing over things in such form, even to "loved ones," generates no counter-obligations. But the counter is not stipulated by time, quality, or quantity: the expectation of reciprocity is indefinite. (1965:147)

In contrast, "balanced reciprocity" refers to direct exchange where there is a balance between goods given and goods received, and the reciprocating transaction is made without delay.

Balanced reciprocity is less "personal" than generalized reciprocity. From our own vantage point it is "more economic." The parties confront each other as distinct economic and social interests. The material side of the transaction is at least as critical as the social: there is more or less precise reckoning, as the things given must be covered within some short term. (Sahlins 1965:148)

Sahlins (1965, 1968) and Service (1966) have used the concept of generalized reciprocity to describe kinship relations in both hunter-gatherer and tribal societies. Like generalized reciprocity, Navajo notions of cooperation provide diffuse obligations where the exact nature and timing of requests and counter-requests are not calculated and need not be exactly equivalent. In other words, Navajo ideology of kinship cooperation can be viewed as an instance of a very widespread method of interpreting and regulating the exchange of goods and services and the organization of tasks among kinsmen.

There is also evidence that concepts of autonomy and consensus are found in other tribal and band groups, especially in North America. The importance placed on individual autonomy has been recognized in studies of American Indian personality (Dorothy Lee 1959; Hallowell 1955), especially among Plains and Eastern Woodland groups. Political leadership in many of these same societies was weakly developed, and decision-making was based on consensus among equals, often in the context of a council of peace chiefs (as among the Cheyenne, Hoebel 1960) or sachems (as among the Iroquois, Morgan 1851). In other words, the Navajo concepts I have outlined are not an isolated instance of combining autonomy with consensus but exemplify a pattern found in other North American societies.

It would seem that an obligation to help others and not be mean, stingy, jealous, or in any way appear uncooperative would conflict with an emphasis on autonomy where individual "decision rights" are highly prized. Choices which are based on an individual's own interests could be construed as legitimate from the point of view of autonomy, but looked on as "selfish" from the point of view of generosity obligations. There are important ways, however, in which these two sets of concepts, one emphasizing an individual orientation and the other a collective orientation, are mutually compatible. First, the concepts of cooperativeness are highly generalized, and this lack of

specificity itself preserves individual options. Second, cooperativeness is mainly defined by what is uncooperative. By emphasizing undesirable behavior and by defining the limits on behavior negatively rather than positively, the individual is left with a great number of choices and hence more autonomy.

Furthermore, uses of the phrase *t'áá bee bóholníih* fuse both individual rights to decide and the necessity of having others agree on the same course of action where collective activity is concerned. This fusion of individual and group interests into the same native phrase leaves room for cooperation while preserving autonomy. The conceptions implicit in such Navajo phrases as *shiká 'anájah (they are helping me)* and *t'áá bee bóholníih (it's up to X to decide)* appear on the surface to be distinct and opposing, but in actuality they are complementary. Each provides for the possible implementation of the other.

In sum, a system which emphasizes generalized reciprocity can also stress individual autonomy, egalitarian authority relations, and consensus decision-making. Generalized reciprocity *need not* be associated with an emphasis on autonomy and consensus, but the combination of these elements in the same cultural system has important consequences for the recruitment of aid within a system of overlapping sets of kin which link together a network of residence groups.

THE PUBLIC COMMUNICATION OF COOPERATION CONCEPTS

Navajos in Greenwater continually seek to communicate and define the conceptions of cooperative and uncooperative behavior which I presented in the beginning pages of this article. This communication and specification takes place both in public gatherings and in face-to-face interaction situations involving two Navajos or a small group.

Two important examples of public expression of cooperative concepts are: (1) the Navajo girls' puberty ceremony where behavior prescriptions are specifically taught to the young girl, and (2) public speech-making at large curing ceremonies such as the Enemy Way and nine-night versions of the Night Chant and the Mountain Chant, when cooperative behavior is enjoined and disruption condemned.

Kinaaldá is the name of the four-day ceremony given for a girl at the time of her first menstruation. It culminates in the making of a large cornmeal cake (*ʔałkaan*), which is baked overnight in the ground while songs from the Blessing Way are sung over the girl in the ceremonial hogan. The following morning the cake is cut and distributed to those who sang and helped. During the four days, the girl must help with corn-grinding and other preparations for the cake, and she must adhere to many behavioral prescriptions. Some of these relate to physical attributes since it is believed that a girl's "bones are soft," and what she does during those four days will influence her health. Navajos believe that obeying various prohibitions will provide the girl with positive physical attributes (such as good teeth, straight back, tall build, strong legs, and long hair) (Keith 1964:32).[13]

Other prescriptions (both positive and negative) are related to cooperation and interpersonal relations, i.e., fulfilling the role of a cooperative Navajo. Keith provides a list of prescriptions gleaned from interviews with adolescent girls which I have translated into Navajo (1964:32). These are similar to statements by my own informants when describing what a girl is taught at her *kinaaldá*.

The first four prescriptions are negative in form and concern the undesirability of laziness, stingi-ness, meanness, and ridicule. The remaining six are positive statements which encourage the girl to be helpful and take care of others. These statements are explicitly taught to the *kinaaldá* girl by the women around her, particularly her mother, maternal grandmother, and mother's sisters. Other older women who are present may also lecture the girl on these topics. It is believed that if the young Navajo girl follows these prescriptions during the ceremony, she will have the appropriate social attributes for the rest of her life. As Keith states:

> . . . the girls do not actually learn much that is new. Rather, the *kinaaldá* is a summary, or a way of giving meaning to skills and values learned gradually in childhood. The kind of behavior that will be most important to her as an adult is reviewed in a short space of time; and general rules such as "Be kind and helpful," are formulated. (1964:35)

In sum, notions of cooperative and uncooperative behavior are communicated, and the ideal of the "sociable" Navajo is explicitly defined both to the pubescent girl and to those attending the ceremony.

Similar communication is part of the speeches made during the last night of the Mountain Chant (Fire Dance) and the Night Chant (*Yeibichai*). Speeches are also given each night of an Enemy Way (Squaw Dance) after the bonfire has been lighted and before dancing begins (Jacobson 1964: 10). The speaker is usually a male relative of the patient, the patient himself, or a chapter officer or

Keith's Prescription	Navajo Phrase	Translation
1. Work hard	*doo jił hóghéé da*	*One is not lazy*
2. Be generous	*doo ʔaa jichį̂ da*	*One is not stingy with something*
3. Don't be mean	*doo hánahaʔchííh da*	*One is not mean*
4. Don't laugh too loud	*diné (sániida) doo baazhodloh da* (Haile 1943:85)	*One does not laugh about men (and women)*
5. Be helpful	*ʔaká ʔanjilgho*	*One helps someone*
6. Be happy and cheerful	*ʔił hózhǫ́ dooleeł*	*One will be happy*
7. Be gentle with children	*ʔáłchíní baa hojílyą́*	*One takes care of children*
8. Be dependable	*hojoolíí ʔ*	*That someone might depend on someone*
9. Be respectful	*ʔáchʔį̨ʔ hasti ʔ*	*Respectability*
10. Be kind	*baa jijoobaah*	*One is kind to him*

tribal councilman.[14] Examples taken from the literature and speeches I heard at Greenwater ceremonies all follow a common pattern. The speaker usually takes this opportunity to thank everyone for food, help with the cooking, and other contributions; or he may enjoin everyone to "help each other" and "take care of yourselves." There is emphasis on seeing that everything "goes well" and that the ceremony continues smoothly. *Nizhónígo*, which means *pleasant-conditions-being* or *may everything be pleasant*, and *yá?át?ééhgo* meaning *it-is-good-being* or *may everything be good*, are the most frequently used phrases which stress the importance of this atmosphere of cooperativeness. Negatively valued behavior is mentioned as undesirable. For example, the speaker may tell those assembled "not to drink" and "not to fight each other" (e.g., the speech recorded in Harmon 1964:24). These public speeches are the most explicit statement of the importance of cooperation where joint activities are carried out with a minimum of disruption and a maximum of mutual aid.

THE PRIVATE COMMUNICATION OF COOPERATION CONCEPTS THROUGH GOSSIP

More frequent than public statements are the communication and definition of Navajo concepts through face-to-face interaction, where judgments are made about uncooperative behavior. During visits, when giving rides, while engaged in conversations at the trading post or chapter house, or while participating in a ritual or economic activity, Greenwater Navajos communicate the latest "news," including events at their own residence group or details which they have recently heard about the lives of other Navajos. Often this news or gossip (*?aseezį*) deals with troubles (such as an illness, accident, or death) or with disputes. Although gossip may be sympathetic, the speaker often emphasizes negative aspects and communicates his disapproval of any conflict behavior involved.[15] The negative judgment may be made as an explicit statement, where a norm describing uncooperative behavior of the form "One is not X" is transformed into a positive statement of the

form, "He or she is X" and attributed to a participant in the incident. The most common statements of this kind are:

1. *He is stingy* (about it)   *baa nichį?*
2. *He is mean*   *?ayóo bá hachį?*
3. *He is mad*   *báhóóchįįd; hashke*
4. *He is sex-jealous*   *łe? nizin*
5. *He is jealous* (of   *?oołch?įį*
   someone's possessions)
6. *He is lazy*   *bił hóghéé?*

An additional concept which is sometimes used to describe undesirable behavior is that of "craziness," expressed by two different phrases: *doo ?áhályá da* and *t?óó diigis*. One Greenwater informant explained the differences between the two concepts in the following way: *t?óó diigis* means *You don't know what you are doing, like if you are doing something and you are all shaky; you can't even hold things together. Doo ?áhályá da* means *half out of his mind.* From Kaplan and Johnson's analysis of Navajo psychopathology it is evident that these phrases may be used to describe various forms of mental illness (schizophrenia, epilepsy, the "fits" of violence and "spells" of being out of control associated with moth craziness, ghost sickness, and crazy violence) (1964:212–20). In Greenwater the two terms are also applied to drunks, someone joking at an incorrect time, or other instances of inappropriate behavior. If someone participates in a dispute, becomes angry, and refuses to cooperate, a Navajo, in relating the incident, might say "He is crazy," thereby labeling the behavior as undesirable.

Other phrases used to register the speaker's disapproval are:

1. *doo ya?ashǫ́ǫ́da*   *I don't like it* or *It's bad*
2. *t?óó baa?ii*   *It's ugly or in poor taste*
3. *bąąh yishį*   *I'm against it*
4. *doo shił ?aaniida*   *It's not true with me*
5. *doo yá?át?ééh da*   *It's not good* (more often used to disapprove of objects or a plan of action than to object to an individual's behavior)

All of the above phrases are not applied to a particular individual at one time. Rather, when *A* relates to *B* an incident involving *C*, he often ends the description with the judgmental statement appropriate to the behavior concerned: "He's just too mean," if there has been an argument; "He's just jealous, I guess," if there are difficulties between a husband and wife; or "He's too stingy," if someone has failed to contribute money or food for a ceremony. If the individual relating a dispute is directly involved, he may make a general statement of his own position by saying, "I don't like it" or "It's too bad" (i.e. the behavior is in poor taste). In addition to situations where behavior is discussed among Navajos, these phrases were used when I posed questions to my informants. "Maybe he's jealous" or "He's just mad, I guess" were given as explanations of why someone had behaved in a particular way.

It is important to emphasize that statements that a Navajo is "mean," "jealous," "crazy," or "stingy," are rarely face-to-face accusations. They are part of a direct confrontation *only* at the peak of an angry argument between close kin (e.g., parents and children, husband and wife). For instance, an accusation "You're crazy" indicates that the misdemeanor is a very serious one, and that the speaker is directly sanctioning the behavior of the accused. More typically these statements are used in private to relatives when news is being communicated, and they are formulated as declarative sentences and statements of fact rather than of judgment.

During my first months in Greenwater I thought that many of these phrases described individual personality traits. Later I discovered that their use was situational and determined by the relationship between the speaker and the individual to whom he referred rather than to any inherent, stable personality characteristics. In other words, the attribution of "meanness," "stinginess," or "jealousy" either (1) points to *X*'s momentary relation with *Y* and the recent events which have altered a congenial relationship or (2) indicates the kinship distance between *X* and *Y*, where *X* is more likely to ascribe a negative characteristic to a distant kinsman or nonkinsman than

to a parent, child, sibling, or grandchild. The Navajo language has few terms for emotional states or behavior characteristics, and Greenwater Navajos seem more concerned with using what terms they have for defining behavior which is disapproved than for describing individual personalities and inner feelings.

Judgments about uncooperative or antisocial behavior are often conveyed more indirectly than by using these key words and phrases. At times, none of the phrases I have mentioned are used, and the speaker simply relates an incident without comment; however, the fact that he or she has taken it upon himself to describe a set of events surrounded by conflict and disruption indicates disapproval. Whether or not judgmental phrases are used, disapproval can be subtly suggested through intonation, gesture, and other paralinguistic devices.

Gossip may be sympathetic, but more often it highlights disruption and brings pejorative judgments about individuals. Engaging in these negative aspects of gossip is undesirable, according to Navajo belief, and is labeled as "talking against someone." The injunction, "Don't talk against someone" is often included in a list of Navajo prohibitions. The clearly stated norm not to indulge in derogatory gossip does not, however, explain why Navajos continually break this rule and talk about others with the view of judging their behavior in a negative fashion.

Some suggestive answers can be given by viewing gossip as information management. Drawing on aspects of the recent exchange between Gluckman (1963, 1968) and Paine (1967)[16] on the analysis of gossip, I find it useful to see Navajo gossip as forwarding an individual's self-interest through impression management with the unintended consequence that Navajo concepts of cooperative behavior are defined and become part of a widely shared cultural system.

Paine's interpretation of the flow and control of information through gossip is readily applicable to the Navajo. Since they live in a dispersed settlement pattern, individuals in one residence group know very little about what is happening in other residence groups, particularly those of nonkinsmen. Gossip, then, is an important method of transmitting what *is* going on. However, the transmitter of gossip may not, in fact, know many of the details of the incident he is reporting, or if he was immediately involved he may only present those details favorable to his own position. It is this latter type of "impression management," in an effort to further self-interest, that Paine stresses. If *A* is reporting to *B* his dispute with *C*, it is in his interest to demonstrate that *C* was at fault and guilty of "mean," "jealous," or "crazy" behavior.

However, in an egalitarian society like the Navajo with the stress on harmonious social relationships, an individual gains little long-run advantage in boosting his reputation or status at the expense of others.[17] It is important to see that in addition to the component of self-interest which Paine emphasizes, the unintended consequence of gossip is the perpetuation of a cultural system of shared ideas, norms, and conceptions. In other words, through gossip, concepts concerning appropriate and inappropriate behavior are defined. Concrete acts are interpreted as "mean," "mad," "jealous," "crazy," or "stingy," and in the flow of such interpretations from one Navajo to another, the concepts become part of a shared cultural system.

The details of an incident, therefore, are not as important as the interpretation or judgment which is passed on the alleged behavior of an individual. What matters is not whether an individual actually behaved in a particular way, but that the disapproval of this type of action is communicated. This is especially important among the Navajo, where the obligation to cooperate is very general and where individual autonomy is highly valued so that there is a great deal of latitude in acceptable behavior. Like Paine, I see gossip as information management, but this control has two aspects: the pursuit of self-interest through impression management and the communication of what constitutes valued cooperative behavior through the use of judgmental words and phrases.

The dual role of gossip can be more clearly seen in discussing the communication of disputes which surrounded the deaths and funerals of two Greenwater Navajos. I have selected these two

examples because I was able to fully document both cases and because they illustrate aspects of gossip present in other dispute cases not connected with death or funeral arrangements.

CASE 1: SILVERSMITH'S DEATH AND FUNERAL

After a long illness, Silversmith died in August 1966 in a Public Health Service Hospital two hundred miles from his home. A burial service was held at the Mormon Mission (twelve miles from Greenwater) by the Greenwater Mormon elders with the help of the resident missionaries at the mission.

Silversmith's own residence group consists of his wife, two of her married daughters with children, and two married daughters-in-law with children (see genealogy in Figure 1). One sister of Silversmith lives in another residence group with her son (Benally) and his wife. A second sister (Zonnie) lives with clan relatives (Edna and her mother) in a third camp. One of Zonnie's daughters (Betsy) lives in a community fifty miles away with her husband (Edward); another daughter (Mrs. Sage) lives in a fourth residence group with her husband and adult son not far from where Zonnie lives. A son of Mrs. Sage and his wife were visiting from Wyoming at the time of the funeral.

Most of the funeral arrangements were made by Edward (ZD's husband) and Benally (ZS). These arrangements included retrieving jewelry from pawn shops in Gallup and purchasing new clothes.

I first heard of a dispute between Edward, Benally, and his mother on one hand and Silversmith's wife on the other from Pearl, whose father belonged to the same clan as Benally (making them *bizeedi* or *cross-cousins*) and who has frequent dealings with Benally and his wife during the summer when Pearl uses the wife's nieces as sheep-herders. Pearl reported to me that she had visited Benally's camp the day before the funeral. They (presumably Benally, his wife, Edward, and his wife Betsy) had complained that Silversmith's wife would not help buy clothes in which to bury her husband or provide mutton for the mourning period. Pearl, acting as an intermediary, went to the wife's camp

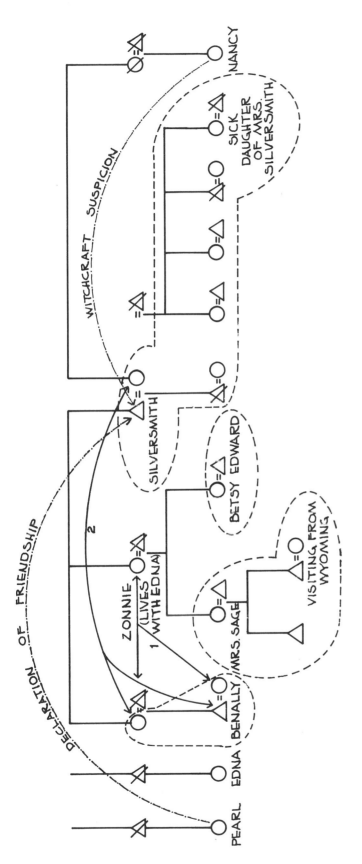

NOTE: Dotted lines indicate members of the same residence group.

DISPUTES:

1. Silversmith's sister and her son Benally vs. Zonnie (between sisters, and between mother's sister/sister's scn)

2. Silversmith's sister and Benally vs. Silversmith's wife (between affines)

INFORMANTS:

1. Pearl: Cross-cousin of Benally, since her father was the same clan as Silversmith. She acted as intermediary in the dispute between Benally, his mother, and Silversmith's wife and made a declaration of friendship for Silversmith.

2. Edna: Cross-cousin of Benally, since her father was the same clan as Silversmith and Zonnie. Zonnie lives with Edna and her mother. Edna reported the dispute between Zonnie and Benally's mother and took Zonnie's side.

3. Nancy: Daughter of Silversmith's wife's sister. She accused Silversmith of sorcery.

Figure 1 Silversmith's Genealogy

and asked her to help. The wife (who is a woman of seventy) explained that she was "too sick" and could not do anything. Pearl mimicked the old lady's voice and mannerisms, thereby indicating that she felt this was a feeble excuse. Benally had mentioned the railroad retirement pension, which Silversmith's wife would soon be receiving; he threatened that if the wife did not help and come to the funeral, they would have the money cut off. As it turned out, Silversmith's wife never appeared at the funeral, and only one of the stepdaughters attended (although Edward stopped by the camp to offer a ride to any who wanted to come). The wife, however, did provide two sheep to Benally and his mother so that the mourning period could be observed at their camp for two days. Pearl's account is an example of reporting a dispute as "statements of fact." Rather than specifically accusing Silversmith's wife of being too "stingy" or "mean," she implied this by hinting that the wife's excuse was not a legitimate one and by emphasizing the direct sanctions which Benally and his mother threatened.

A second dispute was reported to me by Edna, who provides shelter and occasional help to Zonnie, Silversmith's sister. Edna (who is also *bizeedí* to Benally) reported that Zonnie had been to Benally's camp two days before the funeral. They asked her to help with the groceries and provide a sheep to be butchered. Edna said they were "too mean" (*ʔayóo bahoóchįįd*), and Zonnie had refused. Zonnie did not want to go to the funeral because of the dispute with her sister and sister's son; she said she would just "stay home and cry and be sorry for her brother." On the day of the funeral she went to the camp of her daughter (Mrs. Sage), which was nearby, in order to avoid Benally's mother and wife, who arrived in the car with me in order to go to the funeral.

Edna's report of the dispute lacked many of the details of the conversation between Zonnie and her relatives. Edna clearly took Zonnie's side (as she has done in other disputes between the same individuals), with an overall condemnation that they were "too mean." Presumably, she felt they had made unwarranted demands on Zonnie, which were beyond her abilities to meet. This

example shows that the details of the argument are not as important as Edna's judgment about the argument itself. The judgment condemned those who presumably started the quarrel and at the same time explained the rift, which resulted in Zonnie avoiding the funeral and not contributing groceries for the mourning period. In sum, Edna's commentary has two aspects; on one hand it exemplifies impression management, since her statement was made to justify Zonnie's actions. On the other it defines the kinds of actions which are uncooperative and undesirable.

Similar patterns of communication about disruptive behavior are evident from the events which surrounded the suicide and funeral of John Begay.

CASE 2: JOHN BEGAY'S DEATH

John Begay's suicide and the events which followed it were the object of much discussion during July 1966. The family was well known for its disputes and drinking. John, his second wife, and her three daughters lived on the edge of the Greenwater area with John's daughter by a previous marriage, Ruth (see genealogy in Figure 2). Ruth died in January 1966, leaving two small, fatherless children in the care of John and his wife. Another of John's daughters, Lucy, had moved out of the residence group in the spring of 1965. She had refused to pay rent for using her brother and sister-in-law's house while they were living in California, feeling that she did not have the money and that they should let her "borrow the house" rent free. Lucy had argued with Ruth over Ruth's lack of cooperation in fixing the road which led from the residence site to the main road. Lucy also openly criticized her father and stepmother for drinking, and her report to me of a ceremony emphasized all the work she had done, in contrast to the fighting and drinking in which her relatives were engaged.

Besides these disputes, which were reported to me by members of John's residence group, I was told of a dispute with John's neighbors, the Salts. The Salts' married daughter reported that when members of the residence group were building a new house for her, John came to tell them not to build it, since it was located on "his land," not

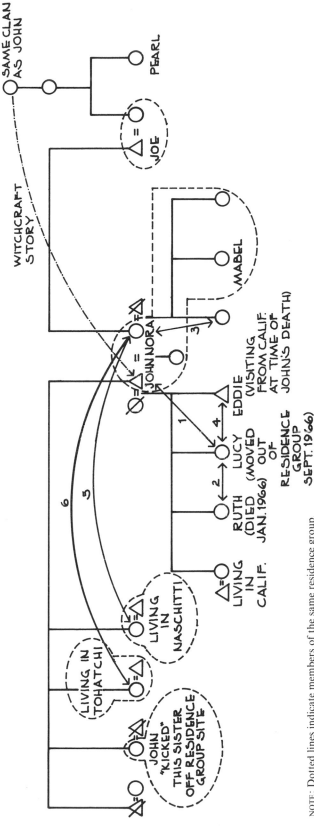

NOTE: Dotted lines indicate members of the same residence group

DISPUTES:

1. Lucy vs. John and his wife
   (between daughter and father/stepmother)

2. Lucy vs. Ruth (between sisters)

3. Nora vs. her daughter (between mother and daughter)

4. Lucy vs. Eddie and his wife
   (between sister and brother/sister-in-law)

5. Nora vs. John's Naschitti sister (between affines)

6. Nora vs. John's Tohatchi sister (between affines)

7. John vs. Salts (between neighbors)

Figure 2   John Begay's Genealogy

INFORMANTS:

1. Mabel: John's stepdaughter. She reported the incidents surrounding John's death, deemphasized disputes within the residence group, and emphasized a dispute with John's sister.

2. Pearl: same clan as John. She reported her grandmother's story of John's wealth, implying witchcraft.

3. Edna: a non-relative. She reported John's death as suicide because of jealousy.

4. Mormon elders. They reported details of the funeral and the dispute between Nora and John's Tohatchi sister.

5. Lucy: John's daughter. She reported disputes with her father, stepmother, and siblings.

theirs. This behavior was defined and communicated as *mean (bá hachį́ʔ)*. I was told by other nonrelatives that John's *mother's brother (bidaʔį)* was the first to settle at John's winter camp site. John later "kicked off" all his brothers and sisters from the land so that he was the only one left. Thus, even before his death, John had gained the reputation of often being drunk, stingy, and quarrelsome.

After John's death, there was some question as to whether it had been a murder or suicide. He had been shot in the head with a rifle, and, to some, the position of the wounds indicated that they could not have been self-inflicted.

I talked with Mabel, John's stepdaughter, (aged fourteen) two days after the funeral, and she gave me the following details. She said John had gone off with a gun; he often went out shooting, so the rest of the camp did not suspect anything. When John did not return, they went looking for him. The next day, when they had almost given up the search, Nora (John's wife), told Eddie and his wife to look once more; if they did not find John she said they should call the Navajo Police. The couple searched again and found John's body near some rocks where he had fallen. Eddie wanted to bring the body back to the camp site, but Nora told him to call the police from the nearby fire lookout.

The Navajo Police arrived to investigate the incident and removed the body to the hospital several miles away. Mabel commented that the police thought one of the adults in the camp had shot John. That's why they asked the family so many questions. She claimed there had been twelve policemen on the scene.

Mabel reported that John's sister had come and "that lady said a lot of mean things." The sister accused the adults of the camp: "You killed my brother." Mabel maintained that the sister wanted all the sheep, but the woman's daughter persuaded her to leave rather than continue the argument. The sister threatened to return for the sheep later, and Mabel indicated that the police had remained all night at the camp, partly to protect them from the sister's threatened return.

Mabel also gave an account of a meeting of relatives and chapter officers which was held two days after the funeral to discuss what should be done with John's property and with the two small children of John's deceased daughter. The meeting was attended by members of the residence group, the wife's brother and mother, and various clan relatives of John, in addition to some of the chapter officers from Naschitti. The sister's claims were not honored, and it was decided that the sheep, field, and other possessions should go to John's wife. Eddie's wife wanted to take the two children to California with her. The little girl, however, said she wanted to stay with her grandmother; when Eddie's wife tried to take the boy, he cried to stay with the grandmother also. According to Mabel, the decision was left to the children rather than to the adults present at the meeting.

Mabel's story deemphasized any disputes within the camp that may have precipitated John's death or that created dissension at the meeting to dispose of John's property. On the other hand, she stressed the argument with John's sister over the livestock and labeled the woman's behavior as "mean." Mabel never questioned the theory that John had shot himself, while others who reported the incident were more likely to suggest murder or to emphasize *sexual jealousy (łeʔ nizin)* as a motive for suicide.

For instance, Pearl, who is the granddaughter of a woman in John's clan, thought that the two stepdaughters always wanted to "run off with boys." John did not like this and would not let them go. They ran off to the Squaw Dance on Saturday night, and John got mad at them. Pearl hinted that the girls had killed him because he would not let them go off, and they wanted to get rid of him.

Edna, who is a nonrelative, had heard from the wife of John's brother's son that they were all drunk. John wanted to marry Mabel. (It had been rumored for several months that he had been giving his wife some jewelry for the sex rights to Mabel's older sister.) Mabel was scared and ran away to the Squaw Dance. John got mad; he shot the dog first, then the cat; then he went off by himself with the gun. They found him shot the next day. Edna herself felt that it was suicide because John was jealous *(łeʔ nizin)* over his stepdaughter.

I heard of one additional dispute which occurred at the funeral, a graveside service conducted by the Mormon elders. There was an argument between John's sister from Tohatchi and Nora, John's wife. The former noticed that John was being buried with only one turquoise bracelet. She seemed to think that there should be two bracelets, and that Nora was keeping one for herself.

As an outsider, I am inclined to believe the suicide rather than the homicide theory of John's death. However, the actual facts of the case are not as important as the impression each gossiper wished to communicate in relating either the cause of death or the disputes which surrounded it. Those closest to the incident tended to play down any dissension except that which would justify their own counterclaims. For instance, Nora's brother, who had been present in the camp following the shooting, was unwilling to give any hint of disputes.

Affines, neighbors, clan relatives, and nonrelatives were much more willing to communicate a negative picture of John, his wife, or stepdaughters, both in discussing past disputes in which they had been involved and in giving their theories about the shooting. Disputes occurred (1) between kinsmen (e.g. Lucy and her father and stepmother; Lucy and her sister; and Lucy and Eddy and his wife, Nora, and her daughter) and (2) between affines (e.g. Nora and her husband's two sisters). The manner in which both kinds of disputes were discussed was similar in that the gossiper put forward the impression that his or her claims were legitimate and those of the other disputants were not. It is equally important to emphasize that gossip about John and his relatives also was used to communicate concepts of meanness and jealousy. Claims on goods or service which were thought to be illegitimate, such as John's desire for more land and his sister's claim to the livestock, were considered evidence of "meanness." Jealousy was used as an explanation for otherwise unaccountable behavior (suicide).

The two cases show how the same kin relationships can be the focus either of cooperation or disruption. Both Silversmith and John Begay were old men who died leaving several siblings, a wife,

children, and stepchildren. Silversmith's funeral was arranged by his matrilateral kin (sister, sister's son, sister's daughter, and her husband). The major disputes were between these kin and another sister, on one hand, and the widow, on the other. In John Begay's case, the funeral arrangements were made by conjugal kin, i.e., wife, children, and stepchildren, with major disputes arising between the widow and John's two sisters. A man's ties to his wife, children, siblings, and siblings' children are all potentially important, but among any of these relatives there may be mutual aid or disruption. The sets of kin of Silversmith and John Begay were structurally similar, but the pattern of cooperation was quite different in each case. However, the same notions of cooperative and uncooperative behavior were used to communicate disputes of those who gossiped about various incidents. On a manifest level, these gossipers often look after their own interests, but the unintended consequence of their gossip is the maintenance of aspects of the Navajo cultural system relevant to cooperation. The two cases illustrate both the diversity and variation which are characteristic of actual social relations and the uniformity characteristic of the cultural system used to interpret these relations.

WITCHCRAFT SUSPICION
AND
UNCOOPERATIVE BEHAVIOR

Witchcraft suspicion, like the reporting of disputes, is communicated in a face-to-face interaction situation, serves to define uncooperative behavior, and, by negative example, serves to reinforce the commitment to an ethic of cooperation. As already pointed out, the Navajo *witch* or *werewolf* is the prototype of antisocial, anti-Navajo, and even antihuman behavior, and there is a clear connection between meanness, jealousy, and *thinking against someone*, and witchcraft practices. Beliefs which describe the practices of *werewolves* and their role in causing illness are very explicit and widely held, but living persons are rarely accused of engaging in these activities. Navajos are very reluctant to discuss witchcraft, (Kluckhohn 1944:13–20), but when they do, it is in terms of vague statements, e.g., that X's illness was caused by witchcraft or sorcery. Less common are statements that *X*'s illness was caused by *Y*, or that *Y* is a *werewolf*. Even these statements are qualified as hearsay (by using the Navajo phrase *jíní (it is said)*, so the speaker does not put himself in the position of making a direct accusation.

The vagueness of Navajo witchcraft is related to its function as an explanation for illness, where it is more important to prescribe the appropriate ceremonial cure than to punish a culprit. Likewise, it is more crucial to communicate the notion of a *witch* or *werewolf* as the ideal type of social deviant than to punish actual uncooperative, antisocial Navajos. In this regard, witchcraft beliefs serve only as indirect sanctions and are more important for the maintenance of a whole system of ideas about cooperation than as a mechanism for directly sanctioning behavior.

Examples of ways in which witchcraft suspicion defines uncooperative, mean behavior can be seen by further examining the cases of Silversmith and John Begay.

Silversmith was accused of sorcery *(bee ʔiińzįįd)* in a story told to me by Nancy, the niece (ZD or *bichʔéʔé*) of Silversmith's wife (see Figure 1). About the time of Silversmith's death, Nancy had performed a divination for a child of Silversmith's stepdaughter, in order to discover the cause of a recent illness. Looking into the *glowing coals (tsiíd)*, Nancy had seen a stone with markings on it. A search of the area around the family hogan uncovered a broken piece of metate which Nancy said came from the grave of Silversmith's wife's mother. Carved on one side was a picture of the stepdaughter and her sick child; on the other side was a picture of the father and other children. This stone had been placed there by Silversmith and was causing the child's illness, Nancy maintained. She had discovered this by seeing Silversmith's face in the coals. Nancy commented that she also had seen Silversmith's face in the coals several times when her husband's father was ill, and she labeled as "sorcery" Silversmith's alleged role in causing sickness.

Silversmith's relatives, in contrast to Nancy, who was aligned with his affines, had a much more positive picture of the old man. According to Pearl (the classificatory cousin mentioned above), he was a good friend. She told me that he used to stop by their house on the way to the trading post and, if he did not have a sack in which to carry his groceries, they would give him a burlap bag. She thought he was "a real nice man." In other words, Silversmith's reputation in the community varied, and the communication of a positive or negative evaluation is primarily determined by the speaker's relation to Silversmith rather than by the old man's actual behavior. In general, the more distant the social relationship, the greater the likelihood of witchcraft suspicion. As with disputes, affines and nonkin are more likely to circulate rumors about witchcraft than are kinsmen, although accusations by close kin such as a brother, sister, father, mother's brother or cross-cousin, have been recorded (Kluckhohn 1944:59–60).

In Silversmith's case, witchcraft was suspected as an explanation for a particular illness. For John Begay, accusations were much more vague and related to his general reputation for "meanness." The stories which circulated after his death concerning past disputes and possible reasons for his suicide contributed to a picture of a quarrelsome, jealous man. My own observations indicate that he and his wife were social isolates, having sporadic and often quarrelsome relations with several close relatives over the years.

Rumors that John was a *yeenaaldloozhii* can be related to a story of his wealth, which was reported by a clan "sister" who attended the meeting concerning the disposal of John Begay's property. John reportedly had two sealskins, two buffalo skins, two deerskins, two mountain lion skins, several strings of turquoise beads, several bracelets, rings, and many ceremonial fetishes. In addition, he owned many sheep and horses. The report fits the description of a rich Navajo who possesses all the traditional kinds of wealth; it is believed that such wealth is often obtained through stinginess rather than generosity, or by those who transform themselves into *werewolves* and rob graves. The story is in contrast to the signs of John's poverty which the trader reported and which I had observed while staying at their winter camp during my first months in Greenwater.[18]

Again, the actual facts of the case are not as crucial as the image communicated. Stories about John Begay combine jealousy, meanness, and stinginess with a great amount of traditional wealth. To the Navajo, such accumulation indicates someone who has not been generous and cooperative but who has acted in terms of his own desires rather than those of his kinsmen. While the judgment of Silversmith varied, the suspicion of John as a witch was more generally believed. He exemplifies the social isolate who is the epitome of the uncooperative Navajo, and gossip about him defines and communicates the nature of undesirable behavior in its most extreme form.

My interpretation of Navajo witchcraft supports some of the conclusions found in Kluckhohn's classic study (1944). Kluckhohn emphasized the psychological functions of witchcraft for dealing with aggression and anxiety, but he also pointed out the social functions that witchcraft beliefs have in (1) defining what is "bad," (2) preserving equilibrium in an egalitarian society, and (3) providing a technique of social control (1944:110–13). In other words, Kluckhohn recognized the importance of witchcraft beliefs for stating conceptions of undesirable behavior and for exerting pressure for appropriate behavior. However, even though he presented evidence for the indirectness of Navajo witchcraft accusations, he did not recognize the important connection between this indirectness and the system of generalized reciprocity which characterizes Navajo cooperative activities. Furthermore, Kluckhohn did not see the relationship between witchcraft beliefs and statements that "*X* is mean, mad, jealous, crazy, or stingy," which are part of Navajo gossip and which also define negatively valued, uncooperative behavior.[19] Witchcraft for Kluckhohn was a set of beliefs to be explained in terms of very broad, general psychological and sociological functions. He failed to see Navajo witchcraft as part of a system of shared ideas relevant to particular situations, especially the organization of concrete cooperative activities through the recruitment of kinsmen.

CONCLUSIONS

In this article, I have described aspects of the Navajo cultural system which are utilized by residents of an eastern reservation community. I have presented conceptions of cooperative and uncooperative behavior and have shown how they constitute an ethic of generalized reciprocity. Another set of equally important and complementary concepts deals with individual autonomy and with consensus as a mechanism for achieving joint action among autonomous individuals. These two sets of concepts are balanced against each other, in part because the notions of cooperativeness are defined in terms of uncooperative behavior. The relative lack of specific obligations to "Do X," in contrast to several injunctions, "Don't do X" or "X is not done," preserves individual autonomy and decision rights by allowing for an indefinite variety of appropriate cooperative actions. On the other hand, cooperation is also assured by the Navajo phrase which describes autonomy and simultaneously implies the need for consensus and joint effort.

The positive obligations of *helping* others and *taking care of* others, as well as injunctions against uncooperative behavior are communicated in public statements at various Navajo ceremonies. The attributes of uncooperative behavior (including meanness, jealousy, stinginess, laziness, and craziness), along with the attributes of witches and werewolves who epitomize antisocial Navajos, are continually defined in face-to-face interaction, where disputes are reported and witchcraft suspicion is discussed.

A cultural system of generalized reciprocity and universally applied concepts of cooperative and uncooperative behavior is congruent with a social system based on ego-centered recruitment of aid that in turn creates an unbounded network of residence groups. In a social system where obligations to provide goods and services are not part of a well-defined set of kinship roles or large corporate groups, it is advantageous to have as many kinsmen as possible available to help and to have obligations which bind all equally, regardless of kinship role or type of task. A generalized notion that "everybody helps" combined with concepts of unhelpful behavior, which are also not role-specific, provide the very diffuse system of norms and sanctions necessary to "back up" an open-ended, flexible social system.

Although much of my analysis is based on comments from Greenwater informants and on case material describing Greenwater situations, it has implications for other present-day communities and for Navajo society as a whole. Factors of population density, ecological adaptation, and degree of acculturation affect patterns of social organization so that there are differences between communities with regard to residence choices, marriage practices, the expansion and fission of domestic groups, and the organization of coopera-

tion in concrete activities. In contrast to the social system, there may, however, be more uniformity in the aspects of the Navajo cultural system discussed in this article. In Greenwater itself, cooperation and disputes followed very different patterns in two structurally similar sets of kin, while the same shared concepts were used to interpret these diverse situations. I have found supporting data for my analysis in publications based on research in other communities and covering a time span of several decades. This suggests that the conceptions which I found important at Greenwater may be shared by most Navajos and that the analysis presented here may be applicable to Navajo culture in general.

NOTES

[1] The major studies of Navajo social organization are Adams 1963, Aberle 1961, Collier 1966, Kluckhohn and Leighton 1946, Levy 1962, Reichard 1928, Ross 1955, and Shepardson and Hammond 1970. A more complete bibliography can be found in Aberle 1961 and Lamphere 1967.

[2] In addition, the Navajo have dispersed matrilineal clans which regulate marriage and hospitality but do not function to organize social activities, either as a whole or in localized segments (e.g. the Local Clan Element, Aberle 1961).

[3] Due to the frequency of uxorilocal residence and the primacy of a mother's ties with her children over those of a father with his children (Witherspoon 1970), an individual's set may have a matrilateral bias, with ties to patrilateral kin becoming of secondary importance.

[4] The distinction between the social system and the cultural system has been made by Parsons and Shils 1951, Geertz 1957, and Schneider 1968. Geertz refers to cultural systems of cognitive and expressive symbols as "programs"; they provide a "template" or "blueprint" for the organization and interpretation of social processes (1964:62).

[5] I use the terms "cooperative" and "uncooperative" not as logical opposites, but as convenient cover terms for Navajo words and phrases which describe *helping* and *caring for*, on one hand, and

behavior which characterizes someone who does not help, on the other.

[6] The name Greenwater is a pseudonym used to protect the identity of the community and my informants.

[7] One informant explained in English the two words for jealousy. "For instance, if some man sees that I have a butane tank out there and keep my house warm with gas or have a nice pickup truck or car, then maybe he is jealous *(ʔooɫchʔíí)*. There is another kind of jealousy; when a man and woman are married, maybe she knows another man and they get together. Then the husband is jealous of his wife *(ɫe nizin)*. Nizin* means *he's thinking; ɫe* means *he can't control his mind.* For example, *Haitao ninizin* means *What do you think about it?*

[8] Although witches often deal with the dead, they are not to be confused with ghosts *(chʔįįdii)*, a malevolent aspect of a deceased human which may cause sickness.

[9] Handtrembling is one of the three forms of Navajo divination. The practitioner's hand and arm is possessed with a violent shaking and is passed over the patient's body, allowing the hand-trembler to "see" or diagnose the cause of the illness and prescribe the appropriate ceremonial cure (Kluckhohn and Leighton 1946:146–49).

[10] The prefix *bi* or *ba* does not always indicate possession, but may refer to kin relationships as in *bamá* or *bizhé'é* (his mother, his father).

[11] Children are not full-fledged members of the society and are considered ethically incompetent in some instances (Ladd 1957:272). In other instances, notably the arrangement of a first marriage or the organization of a ceremony for the child, the parents are *bóholníih* for children. A Navajo child, however, has greater autonomy than in our own culture. A child may go where he wants without asking permission and may often choose which parent to live with if there is a divorce. In arranging a first marriage, if the girl objects strongly, the marriage probably will not take place.

[12] The Enemy Way is a three-day ceremony to cure illness caused by the ghost of an alien or enemy. It requires the participation of two local groups (that of the patient and that of the Stick Receiver, who lives at some distance from the patient and his relatives).

[13] As in the Navajo ideology of sickness and disease as it relates to witchcraft, this is a post hoc theory of causation. A woman with a "mean" personality may be said to have been mad at someone during her *kinaaldá*. Present behavior is explained in terms of a past event, and it is immaterial whether she actually was angry with someone during those four days. The breaking of an injunction did not *cause* the subsequent behavior; rather the behavior is *explained* because of a broken prescription.

[14] No particular person is obligated to speak, so that the number and kinship or political status of speakers varies from occasion to occasion. If no one steps forward, there are no speeches on that particular night.

[15] News or gossip is told to the anthropologist in much the same way as it is to other Navajos. Although I have evidence of some Navajos reporting only what they thought I wanted to hear and thus grossly distorting an episode of drunken fighting and driving, I have reason to believe that many other informants were telling me the same details they communicated to others. Much of my data on disputes and gossip were gathered by having an informant translate actual conversations where one Navajo was relating recent events to another of his own accord.

[16] In my opinion the two points of view are complementary, since Gluckman concentrates on the latent or unintended functions of gossip for the group, while Paine elucidates the manifest and relatively conscious functions of gossip for the individual. In discussing gossip with respect to the Navajo cultural system, I have drawn on perspectives used by both authors.

[17] A comparison of the Navajo with Colson's study of the Makah (1953) is instructive. Crucial differences between Makah backbiting and scandal and Navajo gossip are related to the importance of social ranking among the Makah versus the egalitarian quality of Navajo society. Navajo gossip is indirect, diffuse, and subtle by comparison with the Makah, where attacks on another's reputation are often made in face-to-face situations and gossip is much more vicious and more clearly related to defining one's social position as higher than that of others (Colson 1953:228–230).

[18] Economically, John and his wife were not well off. Their income came from his social security payments ($60 a month) and his wife's weaving (approximately $1,000 per year). They had only a few sheep, no pickup truck, electricity, or other modern conveniences which the wealthier Greenwater households have.

[19] Keith Basso's excellent analysis of Western Apache witchcraft (1969) also shows a relationship between behavior criteria and the concept of a witch. Apaches clearly define a witch in the abstract on the basis of such concepts as "stinginess," "anger," and "meanness" and make concrete accusations in light of disputes (1969:40–59). Since Basso's data are much more detailed than my own, I find he not only corroborates the point of view I propose, but offers many suggestions for further investigation of witchcraft among the Navajo.

REFERENCES

ABERLE, DAVID F.

1961   The Navaho. *In* Matrilineal Kinship, David Schneider and Kathleen Gough, editors. University of California Press, Berkeley.

ADAMS, WILLIAM Y.

1963   Shonto: A Study of the Role of the Trader in a Modern Navaho Community. Bulletin of the Bureau of American Ethnology 188. Smithsonian Institution, Washington, D.C.

BASSO, KEITH H.

1969   Western Apache Witchcraft. Anthropological Papers of the University of Arizona 15. University of Arizona Press, Tucson.

COLLIER, MALCOLM CARR

1966   Local Organization Among the Navaho. Human Relations Area Files Flex Book, NT 13–001. Yale University, New Haven, Connecticut.

COLSON, ELIZABETH

1953   The Makah Indians. Manchester University Press, Manchester, England.

EVANS-PRITCHARD, E. E.

1937   Witchcraft, Oracles and Magic among the Azande. Clarendon Press, Oxford, England.

GEERTZ, CLIFFORD

1957   Ritual and Social Change: A Javanese Example. American Anthropologist 59:32–54.

1964   Ideology as a Cultural System. *In* Ideology of Discontent, D. Apter, editor. The Free Press [Macmillan], New York.

GLUCKMAN, MAX

1963   Gossip and Scandal. Current Anthropology 4:307–15.

1968   Psychological, Sociological and Anthropological Explanations of Witchcraft and Gossip: A Clarification. Man, n.s., 3, No. 1:20–34.

HAILE, FATHER BERARD

1943   Soul Concepts of the Navaho. Annali Lateranensi 7. Tipografia Poliglotta Vadicana. Rome.

1947   Learning Navaho. Vol. 3. St. Michaels Press, St. Michaels, Arizona.

1954   Property Concepts of the Navaho Indians. Catholic University of America Anthropological Series 17. Washington, D.C.

HALLOWELL, A. IRVING

1955   Culture and Experience. University of Pennsylvania Press, Philadelphia.

HARMON, ROBERT

1964   Change in a Navajo Ceremonial. El Palacio 71, No. 1:20–26.

HOEBEL, E. ADAMSON

1960   The Cheyennes, Indians of the Great Plains. Holt, Rhinehart and Winston, New York.

JACOBSON, DORANNE

    1964   Navajo Enemy Way Exchanges. El Palacio 71, No. 1:7–19.

KAPLAN, BERT AND DALE JOHNSON

    1964   The Social Meaning of Navaho Psychopathology and Psychotherapy. *In* Magic, Faith and Healing, Ari Kiev, editor. The Free Press [Macmillan], New York.

KEITH, ANNE B.

    1964   The Navajo Girls' Puberty Ceremony: Function and Meaning for the Adolescent. El Palacio 71, No. 1:27–36.

KIMBALL, SOLON T. AND JOHN H. PROVINSE

    1942   Navajo Social Organization in Land Use Planning. Applied Anthropology 1:18–30.

KLUCKHOHN, CLYDE

    1944   Navajo Witchcraft. Beacon Press, Boston.

    1954   Some Navaho Value Terms in Behavioral Context. Language 32, No. 1:140–45.

KLUCKHOHN, CLYDE AND DOROTHEA LEIGHTON

    1946   The Navaho. Harvard University Press, Cambridge, Massachusetts.

LADD, JOHN

    1957   Structure of a Moral Code. Harvard University Press, Cambridge, Massachusetts.

LAMPHERE, LOUISE

    1967   Social Organization and Cooperation in a Navajo Community. Unpublished Ph.D. thesis. Harvard University, Cambridge, Massachusetts.

    1970   Ceremonial Cooperation and Networks: A Reanalysis of the Navajo Outfit. Man, n.s., 5:1:39 59.

LEE, DOROTHY

    1959   Freedom and Culture. Prentice-Hall, Inc., Englewood Cliffs, New Jersey.

LEIGHTON, DOROTHEA AND CLYDE KLUCKHOHN

    1947   Children of the People. Harvard University Press, Cambridge, Massachusetts.

LEVY, JERROLD

    1962   Community Organization of the Western Navajo. American Anthropologist 64:781–801.

MORGAN, LEWIS HENRY

    1851   League of the Ho-do-no-sau-nee, or Iroquois. Reprinted 1962 by Corinth Books, Inc., New York.

PAINE, ROBERT

    1967   What Is Gossip About: An Alternative Hypothesis. Man, n.s., 2:278–85.

PARSONS, TALCOTT

    1963   On the Concept of Political Power. Proceedings of the American Philosophical Society 107, No. 3:232–62.

PARSONS, TALCOTT AND EDWARD A. SHILS

    1951   Toward a General Theory of Action. Harvard University Press, Cambridge, Massachusetts.

REICHARD, GLADYS

  1928   Navajo Social Organization. Columbia University Contributions to Anthropology 7. New York.

ROSS, WILLIAM T.

  1955   Navajo Kinship and Social Organization: With Special Reference to a Transitional Community. Unpublished M.A. thesis, University of Chicago.

SAHLINS, MARSHALL

  1965   On the Sociology of Primitive Exchange. *In* The Relevance of Models for Social Anthropology, Michael Banton, editor. Association for Social Anthropologists Monograph 1. Tavistock, London.

  1968   Tribesmen. Prentice-Hall, Inc., Englewood Cliffs, New Jersey.

SCHNEIDER, DAVID

  1968   American Kinship: A Cultural Account. Prentice-Hall, Inc., Englewood Cliffs, New Jersey.

SERVICE, ELMAN R.

  1966   The Hunters. Prentice-Hall, Inc., Englewood Cliffs, New Jersey.

SHEPARDSON, MARY AND BLODWEN HAMMOND

  1970   The Navajo Mountain Community: Social Organization and Kinship Terminology. University of California Press, Berkeley.

WALL, LEON AND WILLIAM MORGAN

  1958   Navajo-English Dictionary. U.S. Department of Interior, Bureau of Indian Affairs. Navajo Agency, Window Rock, Arizona.

WITHERSPOON, GARY

  1970   A New Look at Navajo Social Organization. American Anthropologist 72, No. 1:55–65.

YOUNG, ROBERT

  1961   Navajo Yearbook, 1951–61. Navajo Agency, Window Rock, Arizona.

YOUNG, ROBERT AND WILLIAM MORGAN

  1943   A Dictionary of the Navaho Language. *In* The Navajo Language by Young and Morgan. U.S. Indian Service, Washington, D.C.

Chapter 10

WAGE LABOR AND THE SAN CARLOS APACHE

Part I by
William Y. Adams*

Part II by
Gordon V. Krutz

Authors' Note

A little less than a century ago, the "Apache problem" ceased for all practical purposes to be a military problem and became a social and economic one. Some place had to be found within the American system for a defeated and disarmed, but culturally unassimilated, enemy. The "melting pot" ideal, which seemed to be working well in the case of European immigrant groups, was clearly inappropriate to the circumstances of the "primitive" Indians; there was, in the beginning, no thought of turning them loose to sink or swim in the American economic mainstream without guidance or protection.

The solution which was originally conceived for the Apache, as for most other Indian groups, was the reservation system. In theory the Indians were granted for their exclusive use, and in perpetuity, a tract of land sufficiently large to permit them to maintain an independent, agrarian society. To tide over the initial crisis of adjustment to a new way of life, an outright subsidy of basic foodstuffs and clothing ("rations") was issued to each Apache family for a full generation after their subjugation (1870–1903).

For the San Carlos Apaches and many other Indians, the agrarian ideal which underlay the reservation system proved unrealistic. The Indians would not or could not settle down to a life as small farmers at a time when such a means of livelihood was already becoming outmoded in surrounding America. For Apache and Anglo alike, a growing dependence on manufactured goods created a need for cash, which could not be provided through sub-

sistence farming. In these circumstances, many Apaches turned from farming to temporary wage work in the nearby Arizona communities as a principal source of livelihood.

Entry of the Apaches into the Arizona job market was encouraged from the beginning by officials of the Bureau of Indian Affairs. Fostering of wage work became, in time, a major policy of the Indian Bureau, and it remained so throughout the first half of the twentieth century. In effect, the bureau abandoned its original ideal of social and economic separatism in favor of a strategy of assimilating the Indians into the regional labor force. Under the labor-short conditions prevailing in Arizona's pioneer days, the assimilationist policy seemed to offer every hope of success.

In the long run, however, the ideal of economic assimilation of the Apache as an unskilled labor force proved as illusory as had the earlier goal of agrarian self-sufficiency. After expanding throughout the first two decades of the twentieth century, Apache wage work fell off to almost nothing in the 1930s, and it failed to revive even in the booming wartime and postwar labor markets of the following decades. By the 1950s the Indian Bureau had largely given up its efforts to stimulate Indian employment and had in fact reverted to its earlier, agrarian ideal.

For a brief period it appeared that a modern, well-managed cattle industry on the San Carlos Reservation might, after all, permit the Indians to achieve economic self-sufficiency through their own resources. That dream, too, went up in smoke. While today's Apaches derive some income from their cattle operations and some from wage labor, the combination of the two does not provide them with an adequate living. The deficit, amounting to about one-third of San Carlos Apache tribal income,

*Biographical Note on page 77

115

is made up largely by public Welfare in one form or another. In effect, then, the rations system has been reinstituted, and the "Apache problem" is for all practical purposes back where it began one hundred years ago.

In the two studies which follow, the rise and fall of Apache wage labor is viewed from two different points in time and from two different points of view. In a study made fifteen years ago (but not previously published), Adams reviews the historical development of Apache wage labor and assesses the reasons for its low state of development in 1954. In a study made in 1970, Krutz finds the conditions not greatly different from those in 1954. However, what was seen by Adams as the failure of an American policy of assimilation and Apache reaction to that failure is seen by Krutz as a successful and persisting strategy of resistance to assimilation on the part of the Apache.

While there are differences of interpretation between Adams and Krutz, it is also true that American failure and Apache resistance are to some extent opposite sides of the same coin. The economic and social relations between the two peoples have, at all events, reached a stalemate after a century of thrust and counterthrust. From the Anglo's standpoint, at least, there is still no permanently viable solution to the "Apache problem" in sight.

I. The Development of San Carlos Apache Wage Labor to 1954

William Y. Adams

THE APACHE ECONOMIC TRADITION

The Western Apache in prereservation times had an unspecialized subsistence economy; an annual round of farming, hunting, gathering, and raiding in which all families participated equally. Seasonal group migration to harvesting and hunting grounds was a regular and universal feature. Farming activities were consequently limited in scope, and there was relatively little possibility for the production of a surplus. The Western Apache cannot be regarded as fully agricultural peoples; their farming appears more in the light of a specialized phase of the gathering cycle, and was, like its other phases, geared to a subsistence level (Goodwin 1942:155–60).

The extended family, commonly matrilocal, was the basic economic unit. It held common title to cornfields and other productive resources, and in normal conditions functioned throughout the year as a self-sufficient productive unit, engaging collectively in economic activities. Within the group were specializations: hunting and raiding for men, some types of gathering for women. Younger members in general probably took a larger part in subsistence activities than did their elders (Goodwin 1942:155–60; 374–84; 473–76; 535–40).

Minimum economic units, functioning as dependent members of the extended family, were the nuclear families. Undoubtedly each was responsible first and foremost for its own maintenance,

NOTE: This study is based on an investigation carried out in 1954. Its immediate purpose was to trace the historical development of wage labor as a source of Apache livelihood in the reservation era. A wider objective was to determine, if possible, how successfully the Indians had been integrated into a national or regional economy following the destruction of their native subsistence base.

Information on the early development of wage labor was obtained from rather meager documentary sources, which are cited in the text. Data on the modern economic situation were obtained from firsthand interviews as well as from employment records. Major informants were the chairman and another member of the San Carlos Tribal Council; the tribal business manager; the managers of the Tribal and Tiffany trading posts at San Carlos; officials of the Arizona State Employment Service in Globe and Safford; the secretary of the Mine, Mill and Smelter Workers' local in Globe; and the Placement Officer of the U. S. Bureau of Indian Affairs in Phoenix. Much background information was also provided by Professors Harry T. Getty and Edward H. Spicer, both of whom were engaged in field research on the San Carlos Reservation during the same period.

with disparities in productive ability leveled to some extent by communal exchange within the group. It can probably be said of the Western Apache and of all other groups who exhibited a well-marked division of labor by sex and age that there was no conception of the individual as an economic unit.

Social units beyond the extended family level seem to have been of less immediate economic importance. Nearly every extended family belonged to a local group, to which it was vaguely united by kinship. Economic interchange within these groups occurred regularly, but it was not of a compulsory nature and did not amount to interdependence, except perhaps in emergency situations. Self-sufficient extended family groups were united in a wider social scheme by voluntary association, which was formalized by voluntary economic interchange (Goodwin 1942:123–29).

The first goal in Apache culture, as in all culture, was the satisfaction of immediate bodily needs through subsistence activity and marriage. On this elemental level only the extended family was a functional necessity. It was on a higher level, beyond the satisfaction of biological needs, that other social institutions became important. Through the operation of regular economic interchange between extended families, productive activity could be geared to a wider social horizon. Food and other goods were distributed in such a way as to cement social relations and establish interactive patterns throughout the local group and perhaps with even more extended groups.

The economic goal, nevertheless, was limited to subsistence; to the satisfaction of immediate needs at the highest possible level of fulfillment. Throughout Apache productive activity there seems to be little concept of the production of surplus, or provision for the future through the acquisition and maintenance of exchangeable property. Emphasis was on production for immediate consumption at a high level, not on production for acquisition. The limited resources of the Western Apache imposed severe restrictions on the accumulation of property, and it is not surprising that property played little part in the economic scheme. The traditions of the culture, in any event, showed

comparatively little concern for or interest in the distant future; attention and interest were focused on the needs of the present (Goodwin 1942: 541–43).

The concept of capital, in the modern sense, was unknown to the Apache of prereservation times. Lacking conservable media of exchange, security and status were rooted instead in the extension and maintenance of lines of social interaction and economic obligation. The direction of such lines was governed primarily by kinship; consequently the superordinate goals of Apache life have often been expressed as "having a lot of relatives." The statement can presumably be read to mean having regular interaction with a lot of relatives. There can be little question that social and economic I.O.U.'s constitute the intangible capital of San Carlos life, and their maintenance and extension is an overriding goal. They are probably also the main road to prestige (Goodwin 1942:541).

In short, it appears that the maintenance of social relations, rather than the acquisition of property was the primary objective in Apache culture beyond the minimum subsistence level. The rationale for such relations was partly, but not entirely, economic. There is a suggestion of considerable cultural emphasis on socializing for its own sake. Likewise, fairly large groups were probably necessary for ritual activity, which was an important cultural focus. In these respects social interaction between extended families was a noneconomic necessity. Such obligations had an important role in limiting productive activity; in many instances their fulfillment probably took precedence over material ends.

THE ECONOMY OF THE MODERN SOUTHWEST

The coming of American settlement after the Civil War brought the American capital economy to Arizona and transformed the region into a producer of raw materials for distant markets. Mining, agriculture, lumbering, construction, and transportation became, and remain, the chief enterprises of the state. Like all raw material production enterprises, they are dependent on a large supply of hand labor. To that extent, they presented an important new economic opportunity to Arizona's native inhabitants (Wyllys 1950: 239–98).

Dependence on world commodity markets makes for an unstable economy, and Arizona's raw material industries have had their share of ups and downs in the past seventy-five years. Mineral strikes have come and gone, agricultural prices have fluctuated widely, and construction projects have been temporary by nature. In consequence, labor demand in Arizona has been inconsistent both in time and in space. The state's industry has come to rely heavily on two basic sources of labor: a highly mobile and essentially rootless labor force and a series of localized parttime labor forces. These conditions are less true today than formerly, but over the past half century it is safe to say that either high mobility or some amount of independent resources was generally necessary to large-scale participation in the Arizona labor force (Wyllys 1950: 329–62). That such a demand can be made is a reflection of the fully capitalized quality of the American economy, with its concomitants of specialization and interdependence. These characteristics have become commonplaces of American life, but they obviously represent a radical departure from the economic traditions and motivations of the prereservation Apache.

HISTORICAL DEVELOPMENT OF APACHE WAGE LABOR

1872–97. The two and one-half decades following the establishment of the San Carlos Reservation might be called a "shakedown period" for the Apache people. During that time the last outlaw bands surrendered, and the last practical hope of an independent future vanished. The conversion of Apaches into Americans began. Rations were issued throughout the period, and local agriculture was extensively fostered. The two formed the basis of San Carlos subsistence for a generation, augmented by some continuation of gathering activity from time to time.

Wage labor was inaugurated by the employment of scouts, at thirteen dollars a month plus an additional twelve dollars for the use of a horse. In the 1880s this employment was apparently so popular that nearly every youth on the reservation volunteered for it (U.S. Govt. 1886:40–41). Nevertheless, the number actually involved cannot have been very large, and inevitably it diminished as the Apache wars came to an end.

Construction and maintenance of the San Carlos Agency and the gradual development of the reservation offered a considerable number of jobs throughout the period from 1872 to 1897. Various government reports mention the employment of Indians in constructing roads, dams, ditches, and buildings, and as teamsters, herders, and butchers. The maintenance of a military establishment on the reservation created a labor demand which was later withdrawn.

The first mention of off-reservation wage work appears in 1878, when Agent Hall noted that a number of Indians were regularly employed in Globe and McMillans (an old silver-mining camp about ten miles from Globe, which was of considerable importance at the time) and at various mining camps and ranches near the western boundary of the reservation. They were employed to collect wood and hay, make adobes, herd cattle, and to perform other casual labor. According to Hall, "They are almost without exception willing to work, and could constant employment be found for them they would be easily made self-supporting" (U.S. Govt. 1878:7).

Again in 1883 the agent's report indicates that the services of Apaches were often sought by nearby ranchmen for ditching, woodchopping, adobe-making, and so forth. The report implies, however, that such opportunities were limited, and that economic conditions on the reservation were severe at the time. The agent goes on to present a stereotype of the Apache as a laborer: indolent, shiftless, and undependable (U.S. Govt. 1883: 7–10). At later dates there are occasional references to small numbers of individuals working in nearby towns, with the suggestion that their services were sought by the local residents. The report for 1897 mentions an increase in the number of Apaches employed in Globe and notes that their behavior was generally good (U.S. Govt. 1897:112).

Apache labor seems to have played no part in the early development of the upper Gila valley, which occurred primarily between 1880 and 1885.

Mormon colonists in the region were having their share of Apache troubles throughout this time, primarily because their settlements lay directly in the path of marauding expeditions which originated on the reservation. Then, too, Mormon pioneer farming is not notable for its dependence on outside labor.

Apache labor was likewise apparently unimportant in early copper development in the area, which began in the 1870s and continued to expand throughout the remainder of the century (Wyllys 1950:284–87). There were evidently other sources of cheap labor. At Clifton "Chinamen were employed as laborers, and if occasionally a few were killed no questions were asked" (Colquhoun 1924:13). Apparently, at a later period, the Clifton mines were worked by Anglos, whose number included a sizable group of desperados (Colquhoun 1924:32–44). There is evidence to suggest that these men may have been unemployed cowhands left over from the collapse of the Arizona cattle boom in 1892 (Wyllys 1950:250). At any rate, by 1914, Mexicans and Italians provided the bulk of the labor at Clifton and Morenci (Cleland 1952:170).

The period from 1872 to 1897 may be summarized as the time when San Carlos Apaches were first introduced to wage labor through various construction projects on the reservation, with off-reservation work probably limited to the casual and economically unimportant employment of individuals.

1898–1916. The Apache got their first taste of large-scale wage work with the construction of the Gila Valley, Globe and Northern Railroad (later absorbed by the Southern Pacific) across their reservation in 1898; a new economic era was inaugurated. Railroad-building had begun in Arizona in 1879 and continued until well after the turn of the century. The original construction gangs consisted of Mexicans and Orientals, who had been brought in for the purpose (Wyllys 1950:273–78). Completion of the transcontinental lines by 1885 left a large surplus labor force available for work on the numerous subsidiary lines built in later years. Hence, it was not until track was actually laid across the San Carlos Reservation

that the Apache found employment in railroad construction.

According to Agent Corson, Apaches supplied at least fifty percent of the labor employed in building the line from Bylas to Globe (U.S. Govt. 1898:130). Discovery of the sulphuric process for reducing low-grade ores had given a tremendous impetus to the copper industry at the same period (Colquhoun 1924:62), and for a time there was a wide-open labor market in the area. Apparently, almost overnight, wage labor became a basic feature of the San Carlos economy. By 1901 the agent reported that his wards ". . . eagerly seek work on the railroad, among the white farmers, at the mines, and, in fact, anywhere they can hear of a job. They have established a reputation as good workers, and their capacity runs from railroad work to washing dishes. There are several who are capable of running and caring for stationary engines, and quite a number are familiar with the use of drills and dynamite in mining" (U.S. Govt. 1901:190).

In the following year a large party of Apaches worked on the construction of a road near Bowie, and another group worked in the Pinal Mountains, receiving $1.25 a day. Employment of the latter group was formally protested by the Metal Miners' local at Globe, but the protest was overruled. Many individuals also served in section gangs on the Southern Pacific, at $1.00 a day. These jobs were evidently at a considerable distance from the reservation, as the Southern Pacific Railroad did not acquire control of either the Gila Valley, Globe and Northern or the Florence-Ray-Winkelman line until some years later. Agent Corson reports that a large gang at Tucson had stayed on the job, but that other Apaches relegated to the Colorado Desert gangs had returned almost immediately to the reservation. There begin to emerge in the report some of the characteristics of Apache labor that are commonly cited today: "The principal trouble is that they get tired and come back to the reservation, and can not be depended on for continuous work" (U.S. Govt. 1902:161–62).

Nevertheless, Corson thought that wage work was the answer. While conceding that the resources of the San Carlos Reservation were inadequate for the support of its population, he was convinced that the labor demand was ample to supply the difference, and recommended that rations be terminated. His judgment was apparently vindicated when the recommendation was carried out in the following year without significant economic effect for the Apaches (U.S. Govt. 1908:152).

The protest of the Globe mine union in 1902 sheds an interesting light on the efflorescence of Apache wage labor at this time. The period at the turn of the century was one of intensive unionization of all Arizona labor. As early as 1896 there was a strike at Globe, protesting the employment of Mexican labor, and, according to Wyllys (1950:291), it was in the long run successful. There was a similar strike at Morenci in 1903. Corson's report (U.S. Govt. 1908) suggests that in 1902 the union was sufficiently powerful so that the Globe local considered itself to have complete control over the labor market in the area. (The Metal Miners' Union, which made the protest, was later affiliated with the I.W.W., but it is questionable whether the connection existed in 1902. The older established mine union in Arizona was the Western Miners' Federation, which later became the Mine, Mill and Smelter Workers' Union.)

In view of the mounting power of the unions, it seems probable that by the turn of the century the Apaches were left as the principal source of cheap, unorganized labor in southeastern Arizona. This condition, coupled with suspicion of the rapidly growing I.W.W. and a disinclination to hire union members whenever it could be avoided, goes a long way to explain the economic role of Apache labor during most of the next two decades. It suggests that there was probably little opportunity for Apaches to work in the mines and other better-paid occupations until late in World War I, when the power of the union was broken (Cleland 1952:169–92).

In 1903, rations having been terminated, Agent Kelly reported continuing work on the railroads and at the Salt River dam site. In the latter case the work must have been in stripping and road-building, for construction of the dam did not begin until three years later (Barnes 1934:160). No mine work was mentioned in this or subsequent reports. However, the agent observed that there

was work for everyone, and that it was eagerly sought, so that the reservation was largely depleted of able-bodied males. Most of them took their families with them (U.S. Govt. 1903:152).

By 1905 Apaches could not supply the local labor demand, created principally by the Salt River Project, and Mexicans and other Indians had to be imported. As noted by the agent, "In railroad work the Apache becomes easily dissatisfied if the men over him are not to his liking, and changes from one work gang to another. With no one to look after his interest his pay accounts are often in confusion. When hot weather comes in July they [sic] quit work and move to the mountains, remaining there until September" (U.S. Govt. 1905:176).

Publication of agents' reports ceased in 1906, and information on Apache wage work in subsequent years is much less complete. It seems probable, however, that the year 1906 marked the end of extensive railroad work and the beginning of the shift of Apache labor to highway construction. By that year most of Arizona's trackage had been laid, and Apaches were proving unsatisfactory in way maintenance because of their mercurial habits.

In any event, the construction of Roosevelt Dam and the Apache Trail provided ready employment for a large part of the Apache labor force at a short distance from the reservation. For the next few years it was probably the locus of the bulk of Apache employment. The dam was commenced in 1906 and completed in 1911, but Apache labor seems to have been expended largely on road construction connected with the project rather than on the dam itself.

Louis C. Hill, supervising engineer on the dam construction, was among the first to use Apaches in large numbers for day labor. Hill gave the following account of his Apache workers: "They used to work all day on the road like the white men, but when the day was finished and the foreman yelled 'All off,' the Indians started for home up the canyon and ran to the top of the hill and on over to their camp at a good fast dog trot. They ran from about where the foot of the grade is now clear up to the old town of Roosevelt near Cottonwood Creek. My opinion is that if they had been properly treated by giving them time and thought and interest, so that they would feel they were getting somewhere, there would never have been any trouble" (Lockwood 1938:335). What sort of trouble there was and when it occurred is not recorded. Hill's statement seems to suggest the old story of high turnover and desertion.

After the Apache Trail came other highway construction projects. The first federal highway aid bill was passed in 1907, and thereafter railroad-building was succeeded by a vast expansion of highway construction throughout the next two decades. In the years immediately preceding World War I it undoubtedly presented the Apaches with their primary employment opportunity. As there was no state highway system and no state highway commission until after 1920, roads were built mostly on limited county programs. In the early years of hand labor, counties seem to have followed the railroad practice of doing their own construction; contracting came in later, with the development of earth-moving equipment.

An article in the *Literary Digest* in the mid-1920s probably reveals most accurately the role of Apache labor in Arizona road construction in the early decades of the present century. The author states that Apache labor was indispensable to highway construction in Arizona, making possible many roads that otherwise would not have been built. "Weather conditions are such that the labor problem is acute during some months of the year. The white man cannot be induced to remain on the job, so the builders are obliged to turn to the races of darker skin" (*Literary Digest* 1924:25). With regard to the Apache Trail: ". . . if the government had been forced to resort to modern methods of road building the cost of construction would have been prohibitive" (*Literary Digest* 1924:25). The author concluded that the Apache was Arizona's finest labor asset, apparently because of his willingness to work under conditions unacceptable to others.

It is certain that agricultural labor furnished no appreciable economic opportunity for the San Carlos Apache prior to World War I. Most of the state's cultivated acreage was in alfalfa, cereals, and irrigated pastureland, industries which do not create a large labor demand (Wyllys 1950:265).

The upper Gila valley was having various difficulties at this time, and settlements there were even threatened with extinction for a while because of water contamination produced by the spreading tailings of the Clifton smelter (McClintock 1924: 250–59).

The years from 1898 to 1916 may be summed up as the period when wage labor, mostly on more or less temporary construction projects, became and remained a basic economic activity of the San Carlos Apache, possibly because they became the best source of cheap labor in their area. The people seem to have worked here and there on a variety of short-term projects, often taking their families with them and establishing their own communities. The average duration of any particular stretch of work was probably not more than a few months, with seasonal retreats to the reservation. During this time there grew up an experienced and annually available construction labor force.

1917–29. Specific information for this period is extremely scarce, except for the previously noted allusion to continued road construction through the early 1920s.

World War I certainly brought a critical labor demand in Arizona, and it seems probable that the position of the Apache in the Southwestern economy was materially altered. Dislodgement of the I.W.W. from the mines, the vastly increased demand for copper, and the beginnings of large-scale cotton cultivation and concomitant irrigation projects all offered the Apache opportunity to extend their participation in the unskilled labor market (cf. Wyllys 1950:331). From a marginal position they moved, at least for a time, to an equal footing with other labor forces. As a result of the war boom, there was an outpouring of San Carlos families to productive areas throughout east-central Arizona between 1915 and 1930.

Lockwood (1938:334) mentions a demand for Apaches as miners in Globe and other towns at this time. Considering the extent of copper mining in the area, it is virtually certain that mining became an important Apache activity during and after World War I. The establishment of Apache community clusters in various off-reservation areas made possible not only mine work but all sorts of other hand-labor employment. What came about was a geographical extension of Apache society, with a consequent widening of economic opportunity. The elimination of dependence on a social framework confined to the reservation enabled large numbers of Apaches for the first time to participate in the Arizona labor market on a fulltime basis.

World War I was followed by a temporary recession, and many copper mines were shut down for a time in 1920 (Colquhoun 1924:124). The setback probably forced most Apaches to return to the reservation; it is difficult to see how they could have done otherwise. The temporary slack was soon taken up by the great postwar expansion, and the Apache returned to their wartime economic position. Throughout the remainder of the twenties, they maintained a high level of participation in the Arizona labor market. After 1923 the San Carlos Agency included a fulltime employment officer, who apparently succeeded in finding work for all applicants.

The final phase of San Carlos Apache wage labor during the 1920s came about with the building of Coolidge Dam in 1924–30. Precise information on the number employed is lacking, but the project, carried on within sight of the San Carlos Agency, probably furnished jobs for a large part of the resident labor force throughout the five years of construction. There can be little doubt that Coolidge Dam made by far the most significant single contribution to Apache wage earnings between 1915 and 1930.

A highly conjectural summary of the years from World War I to the Great Depression suggests that in this era the San Carlos Apache moved from a marginal to a fairly significant position in the Arizona labor force. A generation had grown up to accept wage work as a necessity of subsistence and had voluntarily expanded its horizon of participation. This period marked the peak of Apache integration into the Anglo's economic scheme.

More or less concurrent with the end of construction on Coolidge Dam came the Great Depression, and overnight the Apache lost their position in the Arizona labor market.

1930–40. Off-reservation wage work in the 1930s was virtually nonexistent. During this decade nearly every member of the Apache Tribe returned to the reservation, where economic support was provided by a large-scale program of construction and development and by the founding of the modern cattle industry.

While the Apache were absent from the labor scene, a number of important changes took place in the Arizona economy which affected their future stake in it. In the early years of the decade, depression was so severe that more than fifty thousand people left the state. Nearly all copper mines were closed from 1931 until 1934 (Clifton-Morenci until 1937), and cotton fell to four cents a pound (Wyllys 1950:352).

While the native labor force emigrated in droves, a new group came on the scene, uprooted by the Dust Bowl in the lower Midwest and the bottomless depression in the South. "Okie" and Negro migrants have been an important feature of the Arizona labor force ever since, and the so-called Big Swing has come into full operation. Agricultural employers, assisted by farm labor bureaus and a complex system of reciprocal labor contracting, have systematized and scheduled their seasonal labor demands in such a way that they are now assured, under normal conditions, of a regular annual supply of migrant labor. Consequently, opportunities for localized parttime labor forces have been limited.

Depression, moreover, put an end to Arizona's total dependence on raw material production. While the "Five C's" of cattle, cotton, copper, citrus, and construction, plus lumbering have remained the economic base, diversification has been a prominent feature of Arizona's economic rehabilitation and expansion since the late 1930s. Insofar as new opportunity has been created, it has been essentially for diversified, specialized, and skilled or semiskilled labor. The unskilled labor market in the state is probably smaller today than it was in 1929.

Developments at San Carlos during the 1930s were equally important to the future of Apache wage labor. During this decade a process of what may be termed cultural withdrawal and resistance was under way. It probably derived its original impetus from the construction of Coolidge Dam and the resulting condemnation of a large part of the Apaches' farm acreage during the late 1920s. It was certainly augmented by generally depressed economic conditions and vanishing labor opportunities in the thirties. Possibly significant as well was the termination of national alcoholic prohibition—but not Indian prohibition—which reemphasized the apparent legal inferiority of Indians. For whatever cause or causes, there developed at San Carlos an increasingly strong and articulate body of anti-Anglo sentiment; a withdrawal from the Anglo world and rejection of its values. There arose instead a desire among the Apache to maintain a separate economic and social existence, geared to their own aspirations.

An opportunity to maintain such a separate existence seemed to be presented in the 1940s by the establishment of the modern cattle industry, which made the San Carlos Reservation potentially self-supporting for the first time in its history. Economic dependence of the Apache on the surrounding Anglo community, for the first time since the termination of rations forty years earlier, was reduced to minor proportions. From 1940 onward the San Carlos people were able to participate in the outside labor market very largely on their own terms.

1940–54. World War II and the continuing postwar boom reopened the Arizona labor market to all comers. By and large since 1940 there has been, at least in theory, continual employment opportunity for the entire San Carlos labor force. Nevertheless, the level of realization has been consistently low, and wage work has never regained the position of importance in Apache life which it held before 1930.

Wartime and postwar labor experience is perhaps best indicated in a survey of the San Carlos labor force conducted by Edward H. Spicer for the Stanford Research Institute in 1954. Spicer's figures show that 33.8 percent of the group has been employed in agriculture and livestock enterprise; 20.2 percent in mining; and 14.5 percent in construction. In view of the general youth of the

labor force it seems safe to assume that the great majority of this experience has been gained since 1940. As the figures do not differentiate between on-reservation and off-reservation employment, however, it is difficult to evaluate them in terms of the latter alone. The high figure for agriculture and livestock undoubtedly reflects primarily the recent importance of the Apache cattle industry, rather than widespread participation in off-reservation harvests. Mining opportunities, on the other hand, have been almost entirely in off-reservation communities. There has been construction activity both on and off the reservation.

Two other categories of employment loom fairly important in Spicer's survey: wholesale and retail trade, and public administration, with roughly 10 percent of the labor force each. The latter represents almost entirely employment at the San Carlos Agency. Wholesale and retail trade can probably be read as clerking, working in stockrooms, and generally assisting, largely in stores on the reservation (Stanford Research Institute 1954).

World War II also brought, for the first time, an opportunity for large-scale employment in agriculture. Although cotton had been grown extensively in the upper Gila valley since 1917, the area had relied on migrant labor throughout the twenties and thirties. Only when the war boom dried up the flow of migrants did the Safford farmers turn to the wholesale recruitment of Apaches. Thereafter several hundred families picked cotton for an average of two months out of every year throughout the war and subsequently. Agricultural employment, in fact, reached its peak in 1951 and 1952, when over one thousand Apache individuals are said to have worked in the Safford area. This was apparently the biggest single source of postwar employment. Workers and their families were regularly recruited and transported to the Safford area, where they set up their own camps. The cotton-picking force was composed largely of younger people, aged eighteen to forty, who moved in nuclear family groups and usually brought their children with them. During their six weeks' to two months' stay at Safford they made frequent return trips to San Carlos on weekends, resulting inevitably in a considerable turnover, as many neglected to return. Some families commuted daily from Bylas.

After 1951 cotton-picking fell off drastically at Safford; at the peak of the 1954 season fewer than three hundred Apache individuals were employed. However, this work continued in limited volume and was the only regular seasonal wage work of any significance for the Apache in 1954.

Off-reservation agricultural work for the San Carlos Apache from 1940 to 1954 seems to have been confined pretty exclusively to the Safford cotton harvest. Other opportunities were numerous, but they were not embraced. From time to time during the war and as late as 1952 cotton and vegetable growers from the Salt River Valley sent recruiting expeditions to the San Carlos Reservation, but without success.

In 1953 the Arizona State Employment Service reported:

During the January–June period, 17 employers placed 27 different clearance orders for approximately 3,000 seasonal agricultural workers. During the July–December period, 29 employers placed 33 orders for approximately 3,600 seasonal agricultural workers. Arizona, alone, could use all of the Indians available to assist in the cotton harvest, but past experience has shown that very few are willing to work in the cotton fields. At least 1,000 Indians could have been used for the carrot harvest at Phoenix. In December, another 300 workers were needed in Pinal County for the carrot harvest. Arizona orders for Indian workers in cotton and carrots exclusively far exceed the number of Indians willing to work in these jobs. (Arizona State Employment Service 1953:4)

The years from 1940 to 1954 were a period of almost continuous economic opportunity, when the sheer pressure of labor demand, if nothing else, drew the Apaches to some extent back into the labor force. Developments in the decade from 1930 to 1940, however, wrought a fundamental change in the nature of participation. Cattle-raising supplanted wage labor as the basic subsistence activity. This condition, coupled with the well-developed resistance to Anglo institutions, acted to limit drastically the Apaches' realization

of their labor opportunities, and to minimize the economic importance of wage work to the reservation.

WAGE LABOR IN 1954

In 1954 the general desire of the San Carlos Apache to withdraw from the Anglo world and to maintain a separate economic and social existence was very much in evidence. A comparison with their condition of thirty years before, moreover, showed that they had been largely successful in achieving this goal. Cattle, farming, and other home industry and employment comprised a substantial, if not totally adequate, economic base, and there were plans for the extension of reservation enterprise and productivity in the future. Participation in the outside economy had been reduced to the level of a secondary and largely nonessential activity, operating inconsistently and at a generally low level.

Mining. The largest continuous employer of Apache labor was the Inspiration Mine and Smelter at Miami, which in 1954 carried some sixty individuals on its payrolls. Semiskilled capacities predominated; the number of skilled workmen was small.

The great bulk of the Inspiration labor force of Apaches lived in the Apache community of Hollywood, consisting of some thirty-five frame shacks scattered over a hillside near Claypool. The full population of the community was said to comprise some two hundred individuals, residing in nuclear family units. Distribution of the houses suggests that there might have been a smaller number of more extended social groupings present. Children were sent to school in Miami.

Hollywood apparently functioned as an Apache community in its own right, and might be described as the normal residence of that part of the San Carlos population which was employed or potentially employed at the Inspiration Mine. It was said that the actual volume of employment rarely approached the proportions of the potential labor force which was at times resident in the community. It has varied roughly from twenty to eighty percent since 1954.

Families were likely to spend periods of temporary unemployment on the reservation, but there was apparently little actual turnover in the population of Hollywood. All of its resident families, however, had homes at San Carlos as well, and most had cattle. In addition to Hollywood there were three families, apparently comprising a single extended unit, living on the creek immediately west of Miami. It was said that all of these transplanted families were seen regularly at San Carlos and often spent weekends there. A half dozen Apaches commuted daily from San Carlos to the Miami mines.

Other colonies of Apache copper miners and smelter workers in 1954 were located at Morenci (thirty individuals), Superior (thirty), and Hayden-Winkelman (ten). These families were seen less frequently on the reservation and were apparently fairly permanent residents of the communities in which they worked. Although most were cattle-owners, the cattle were apparently cared for by, and went to support, relatives at home.

Of the two asbestos mines on the reservation, one was not operating through most of 1954. The Metate Mine, near Cutter, regularly employed around ten Apaches, who commuted daily from San Carlos. Labor turnover was said to be high, but the mine was committed to the employment of Apaches.

Agriculture. From 250 to 300 Apaches picked cotton in the Safford area between October and early December 1954. Of these, 75–100 were from the Fort Apache Reservation. San Carlos Apaches came in nuclear family groups about equally from San Carlos and Bylas. The former brought their children with them. Part of the group was housed in two rather small (ten to fifteen families) camps maintained by farmers. The remainder, largely from San Carlos, occupied a large encampment on unoccupied land, which was set up by the Apaches themselves some years ago and which served as a central labor pool.

Apache participation in the Safford cotton harvest declined sharply after 1950 and was eventually reduced to a nucleus of the steadiest workers, who returned annually to the same employers. The latter almost always furnished transportation, sometimes working through an Apache contact man who acted as labor contractor and transporter. It was through these circumstances that the central Apache camp was able to function as an effective institution.

Apaches no longer constitute a majority of the labor force at Safford, being outnumbered in 1954 not only by migrants but also by Navajos. All but two of the largest cotton-growers have shifted entirely to the use of migrant and Navajo labor; it is mainly the small-time operators who employ Apaches.

There was no other significant off-reservation agricultural employment in 1954.

Other Work. There were no major construction projects off the reservation during 1954. Mechanization of highway construction has evidently eliminated the demand for Apache labor in that field; construction on the Cutter-to-Bylas grade on U.S. 70 seemed to have furnished no jobs whatever. It is said that ten or fifteen individuals from Bylas were employed temporarily on various small constructions around Safford, and probably there was some such casual work in the Globe-Miami area also. In November, ten men were hired to work on the El Paso Natural Gas Company right-of-way not far from San Carlos. Four or five Apache families constituted the Southern Pacific section gang at Cutter. There were said to be a few other Apache individuals in other gangs on the same line.

Individual Relocation. The persistent efforts of the Indian Bureau's placement service led to the successful relocation of half a dozen San Carlos Apaches in jobs in the Los Angeles area, out of some twenty-eight who were sent there at various times. All but two of the individuals were accompanied by their families. One such successful placement was made in 1954.

About twenty individuals, some accompanied by their families, were said to be employed in various fulltime capacities in the Phoenix area. They were without exception young, mostly veterans with an unusually high level of education.

Like the relocatees in Los Angeles, most of them did not have cattle on the reservation.

Other San Carlos individuals and families have been and possibly are still relocated at Albuquerque, Payson, Tucson, Prescott, Yuma, Sacramento, and in Washington state. A majority of this group are Yavapais or mixed bloods.

Labor Supply and Demand. Participation of the San Carlos Apache in the off-reservation economy in 1954 seemed to be becoming stabilized at a low level. Although Arizona's productive industry offered potential employment opportunity for the entire San Carlos labor force, at least seasonally, there was persistent disinclination on the part of the Apache to seek such employment in 1954. As a result, they were apparently largely discounted as a labor source; there was little recruiting and virtually no specified demand for Apache labor.

The stereotype of the Apache laborer as undependable, unpredictable, lacking in incentive, and hard-drinking was found to be all but universal. Above and beyond the lack of specific demand for Apache workers, there was a common disinclination to employ them in any circumstances where it could be avoided. Positive as well as negative sanctions acted to limit the role of Apache labor in 1954.

In sum, by 1954 the Apaches had ceased to constitute a significant labor force; there was neither effective supply nor specific demand for them. Their economic contribution was confined to their immediate local area; the area's potential was sharply limited, and its position was marginal in both the Apache and Anglo economies.

Economic Significance. It is very difficult to evaluate the true contribution of wage work to the total San Carlos economy in 1954. Kelly's figures indicate that in 1953, 325 out of 933 nuclear families on the reservation were totally or partially supported by it and that the median income from such work (plus the total of all other nonagricultural income) was $750 annually, compared to a median income from farming and cattle of $1,350 (Kelly 1953:20). The former figure can be taken as an upper limit only, since it includes a sizable block of unearned income from Welfare payments as well. Moreover, it includes labor both on and off the reservation, of which the former was at least equally significant with the latter. The total cash value of off-reservation wage work was evidently small, comprising probably less than ten percent of the total annual income of the tribe.

It was widely recognized that Apache off-reservation wage work resulted in no capital return to the reservation. Since Apache savings accounts were few and, such as they were, had been built up from cattle sales, the conclusion is inescapable that wage work resulted in no capital return of any sort. It was also stated by several observers that distribution of wage income was generally confined to the immediate nuclear family. Traders on the reservation saw no evidence of individuals there being supported even to a limited extent by the activities of relatives in outside communities.

The contribution of wage work seemed to be no more than the support of the individuals actually engaged in it and their immediate families at the time of employment. It was an occasional subsistence activity, and its contribution to the reservation economy could be measured only in terms of a lessening of the number of individuals who must be supported by reservation resources.

ANALYSIS AND PROSPECTS

It is more or less implicit in the cross-cultural nature of San Carlos Apache off-reservation labor that its development has been governed and limited by three fairly distinct sets of factors:

1. Persisting traditions and motivations of native Apache culture, or what may be considered internal factors. Basically, these affect the supply and potential of Apache labor.

2. Characteristics of American culture as reflected in the economic development of the modern Southwest (external factors), affecting the demand for Apache labor.

3. Historical developments (chance factors) affecting economic conditions both off and especially on the reservation, which have governed both the supply and demand for Apache labor.

The interaction of these three sets of forces has inevitably added up to a highly unstable and inconsistent history of San Carlos wage labor over the past half century.

Through all the vicissitudes of Apache participation in the American capital economy, however, one basic trend seems to emerge: it has come to be governed less and less by external factors, and more and more by internal ones. In the last analysis this is perhaps a reflection of the change from a buyer's to a seller's labor market. In the early decades of the twentieth century the San Carlos Reservation could not support itself; there was incentive and, to a large extent, a necessity to participate in the off-reservation economy. Subject to certain overriding traditions of Apache life, the limiting conditions to wage labor were largely external. If Apache activity during those years was fluctuating and uncertain, the labor demand was at least equally so.

The decade from 1930 to 1940 wrought a fundamental change in the economic role of the San Carlos Apache. Establishment of a quasi-self-supporting reservation industry coupled with the articulate rejection of the Anglo world created both incentive and opportunity for the maintenance of an independent Apache social and economic life. There was a tremendous reduction in dependence on, and willingness to depend on, the off-reservation economy at a time when opportunity in that field was high. The result was that the limiting factors to wage labor in 1954 were to be found largely, if not entirely, within the structure of modern Apache life. Succeeding discussion will attempt to isolate and examine the more important of these factors.

The Subsistence Tradition. After a half century of exposure to the American capital economy, Apache productive activity remained geared to a subsistence level, as it was in prereservation times. The Apache had apparently never accepted the concept of capital. The underlying motivation for all economic activity was the maintenance of as high a level of immediate consumption as is practicable. Even though capitalization provided the potential means, the production of surplus seemed to be as little contemplated in 1954 as it was a century earlier.

The importance of the subsistence tradition cannot be overstated. It has operated as the overriding limitation on the economic potential of Apache wage labor throughout its history. Taken in conjunction with the superordinate values of Apache life considered below, it accounts for most of the universally described characteristics of Apache labor—"undependability," "unambitiousness," and "laziness," which can all be read more accurately as "low level of aspiration." No matter in whose economy he participates, the Apache is bound to be governed by Apache motivations, and these, as we have seen, are oriented to the maintenance of a maximum subsistence level. In prereservation times, this was attained through a seasonal round of temporary productive activities, interspersed with periods when other enterprises necessary to a satisfactory life were carried on. The activities involved have changed in modern times, but the pattern remains essentially the same. Short tenure and high turnover are all but universal features of Apache wage labor.

Social and Ritual Obligations. Surviving with the subsistence tradition have been the superordinate values of Apache life—the maintenance of a high degree of social interaction beyond the family level, and, probably, a degree of regular ritual participation. Lacking the capital concept, the Apache still apparently measures security and status largely in these terms.

Social and ritual necessities have acted to limit off-reservation wage work in several ways. Since a certain degree of continuous socializing seems to be an absolute necessity of Apache life, a minimum limit is set on the size of work groups. Successful employment of Apache labor has always involved groups of considerable size, most commonly families. Hence, individual relocation, involving long periods of separation from spouse and kin, has been and continues to be a negligible phenomenon.

Social obligations have likewise limited the geographic range of Apache labor. The standards of satisfactory life at San Carlos seem to demand at least occasional participation in a wider social context than can be found in most work communities. The individual must return to the reservation for such participation. The net result is that the effective range for the employment of Apache labor has been and continues to be limited to about seventy-five miles from the reservation, except for extremely brief periods. This radius may increase with the construction of better and faster highways.

Social obligations act to limit wage work in degree as well as in kind. Above the minimum subsistence level they are likely to take precedence over materially productive activity; and above the maximum subsistence level they regularly do so.

Finally, the importance of liquor must be mentioned. The place of alcoholic beverages in Apache life is a subject for a study in itself; all that can be said here is that it has apparently always been important, and has become increasingly so in modern times. The extensive use of intoxicants was a regular feature of most San Carlos Apache social activity in 1954, and the net effect was a considerable, if unintentional, enhancement of the already undependable quality of Apache labor.

Subsidiary Role of Wage Work. By 1954 cattle-raising had become the base of the San Carlos economy, with wage labor relegated to a secondary and often nonessential role. The former posed far fewer conflicts with the major traditions of Apache life. Wage work was no longer required to supply the basis of subsistence, but served merely to defray the differential between cattle income and the desired subsistence level. For many families cattle income alone was sufficient, and the volume of labor was limited in consequence.

Lack of Organization. The San Carlos labor force has always been unstructured. Its mobilization in the past has commonly required an original external impetus, usually in the form of active recruiting and judicious application of pressure by traders and Indian Bureau officials.

In their altered role, Anglos are no longer capable either of recruiting successfully or of applying such pressure. Insofar as there remains an unrealized labor potential at San Carlos in spite of the conditions described above, it can only be mobilized successfully by an impetus from within the Apache Tribe. In 1954 the machinery for mobilization was lacking. The Tribal Council, aware of the general unpopularity of wage work, was understandably reluctant to assume such a role despite repeated urgings by Indian Bureau officials.

Cultural Withdrawal. While no particular stigma attaches to wage work for subsistence purposes, there is a definite feeling that the conditions are objectionable in many cases. The average Apache would undoubtably prefer to make his living with as little dependence on, and contact with, Anglos as possible. Hence, there exists a powerful positive sanction against wage labor, particularly off the reservation.

II. San Carlos Apache Wage Labor in 1970

Gordon V. Krutz

GORDON V. KRUTZ, as coordinator of Indian programs at the University of Arizona, worked with Arizona tribes in providing University services. He spent three years as health educator for the Indian Health Service in Nevada and Arizona, his experience including the training of San Carlos Apache health aides in a trachoma control program, a report of which was prepared to appear in *Revue Internationale Du Trahome*.

The preceding historical description of San Carlos Apache economy by Adams illustrates how this group withdrew from an external wage market system in order to maintain an internal system of ritual and kinship obligations, a process greatly facilitated by the development of an on-reservation economy. It is also clear from Adams' account how basic Apache values have discouraged the accumulation of wealth for future use, the severance of kin ties, and the concept that the solitary individual is a primary unit of economic production. The purpose of this study is to review 1970 economic conditions at San Carlos in order to determine if Apaches have continued to reject off-reservation employment for the same reasons they did in 1954. In other words, are Apache workmen refusing to work off the reservation because of social and ritual factors and, if so, how is the process facilitated?

THE SETTING

Over the past sixteen years there have been many economic and physical changes at San Carlos. The latter include an increase in the number of Apache-built homes. Forty-five homes were completed through the Mutual Self-Help Program with an additional 27 near completion, and plans call for a total of 350 houses, 68 to be completed by 1970 (Bureau of Indian Affairs 1969; personal communication 1970c). Approximately half of the homes at San Carlos have access to running water, but many are without electricity and indoor plumbing.

The Indian Health Service completed a thirty-five-bed hospital at San Carlos in 1961, and a

contract with the tribal council was signed to provide five jobs for native health aides to work in the field health program (personal communication 1970d).

Public school districts receiving Johnson-O'Malley funds have displaced the on-reservation Bureau of Indian Affairs schools. Lutheran and Catholic mission societies also operate on-reservation schools, which are attended by nearly 250 Apache students. Three hundred Apache children go to off-reservation boarding schools run by the BIA, and another 50 have been placed in various cities in the care of Mormon foster parents. In 1969, San Carlos had 52 college-bound students, 65 high school graduates, 96 eighth grade graduates, 1,374 students enrolled in elementary school, and 1 college graduate (Bureau of Indian Affairs 1969).

The labor force at San Carlos over sixteen years of age is 2,200, of which 640 are employed (Bureau of Indian Affairs 1969). The estimated annual family income is $2,620, with a per capita income of $524 (Bureau of Indian Affairs 1969). Employment services are provided by the State of Arizona and the BIA.

The two principal industries at San Carlos are cattle, with a herd of 12,000, and timber, with a production of eight million board feet annually. An Economic Development Act grant for $220,000 was released for the development of an industrial park on the reservation near Globe, Arizona. EDA also provided $572,000 for the development of San Carlos Lake and $542,000 for the development of Seneca Lake to provide recreational areas on the reservation (Bureau of Indian Affairs 1969). The tribe has a revolving credit fund of $185,000 for economic development on deposit with the BIA (Bureau of Indian Affairs 1969).

OFF-RESERVATION EMPLOYMENT

The total number of Apaches who work off the reservation is unknown. Some San Carlos Apaches work in Arizona mines at Miami, San Manuel, Morenci, Superior, and Hayden, while others work in the lumber mill at Payson, on cattle ranches near the reservation, and as laborers at Safford and Phoenix.

There are Apaches living at Hollywood and Payson, Arizona, in small Apache communities, where families live in extended groups, speak Apache, and avoid social contact with Anglos. It is rare to find Apache families living in isolation from other Apaches in Arizona cities; those who live in metropolitan areas maintain close social ties with reservation relatives.

There are Apache workmen in Phoenix, Tucson, Los Angeles, Oakland, and Chicago. The Employment Assistance Officer at San Carlos placed 207 Apaches in urban areas last year. He said recently, "Apaches are happier living as a group while away from the reservation. Rarely, do they spend more than a year away from the reservation" (personal communication 1970a).

In most cases, Apaches refuse to accept off-reservation employment which requires lengthy separations from family members, a fact expressed in the words of the State Employment Officer at San Carlos: "I have on the average 150 available jobs in my files which go unfilled because everybody wants to stay home." An Apache himself, he further states, "I could place every able-bodied man on the reservation in employment if there were enough jobs to go around, but most of the requests I get are for off-reservation employment, and the bad thing about it is that they pay less than most people get from welfare."

During an interview with the State Employment Officer, two Apache men refused to accept employment at Seneca Lake, forty miles to the north, because it was too far from home. When asked to comment on their refusal, the officer said:

> There's a lot of fear of the outside world by our people. It might be easy for you to get a job with the White man because you've got education and experience. Most of the people that come in have no employable skills, no education above eighth grade. They are afraid of failure, what the White man's going to think of them. It's a lot easier to stay at home where you know what to expect.

Some Apaches are successful in long-term off-reservation employment, but these individuals still maintain close social ties with kinsmen and friends through frequent visits to the reservation. One Apache who lived in Tucson for more than a year made personal contact with relatives on the reservation at least twice a month; his wife and children spent greater periods of time on the reservation. Although there is a desire for off-reservation employment by younger Apaches, this is seldom allowed to interfere with on-reservation social obligations.

ON-RESERVATION EMPLOYMENT

Lack of employable skills limits many Apaches from holding on-reservation jobs. In 1969, only one graduated from college and a limited number completed vocational training. Most tribal leaders have come up through the ranks with little formal education. The Apache's unwillingness to spend extended periods of time in schools away from the reservation further limits job preparation.

San Carlos Apaches play subordinate roles in on-reservation federal employment. There are no Apache physicians, pharmacists, nurse supervisors, or hospital administrators. Apaches work as janitors, drivers, clerks, and practical nurses at the hospital. The BIA superintendent is an Indian from the outside, and the highest position held by an Apache in the bureau is that of an administrative assistant. However, Apaches do hold responsible positions in tribal employment, where they serve as councilmen, committee members, OEO directors, store managers, and herd managers. A group of Apaches contracted to build a sixty-five-mile roadway, which was satisfactorily completed in 1969.

Earned salaries at San Carlos in federal and state employment in 1969 totaled $1\frac{1}{2}$ million, of which nearly half went to Apache workers (personal communication 1970b). A part of this income ($227,000) came from the work projects of Tribal Work Experience Program (BIA), the Manpower Development Program (Arizona), and the Title 5 Work Experience Program (OEO) (personal communication 1970b). The tribe paid $98,500 in salaries to Apache employees. Other forms of salaried income came from projects sponsored by Community Action Project ($115,000), Neighborhood Youth Corps ($40,100), and Job Corps ($56,400) (personal communication 1970b).

Tribal income from mining, cattle, timber, and recreation for 1969 was $2,017,900 (personal communication 1970b). Cattle sales totaled $961,500, of which $667,700 was paid to cattle-owners and $293,800 to the tribe for grazing fees and sales tax (personal communication 1970b). A 1961 tribal report states that of 503 families involved in cattle sales less than three percent received over $5,000 (San Carlos Tribal Council 1962).

During the fiscal year 1969 yearly $1 ⅓ million was paid to San Carlos Apaches in payments for the blind, old age, dependent children, general assistance, child welfare, social security, veterans' benefits, and unemployment compensation (personal communication 1970e). This represents an increase in unearned income of one-half million over 1961.

A simple economic profile for Apache earned and unearned income at San Carlos for 1969 is as follows:

Tribal income—wages, enterprises,
  mining, cattle, etc. $2,017,900
Estimated salaries—state, federal
  work projects 450,000
Unearned income—tribal, state, and
  federal payments; social security;
  veterans; unemployment; surplus
  food 1,300,000
  _____
  Total $3,767,900*

It is difficult to accurately assess the economic profile at San Carlos, since there are no figures for craft sales, temporary parttime employment, or charges for transportation. There are also other benefits usually not listed, such as the indirect costs of the boarding school, which are absorbed by the BIA and foster families, and the operation

*This is an approximate figure for San Carlos Apache income which averages out to $800 per capita, thus disagreeing with the Bureau of Indian Affairs estimate of $524.

of the public schools at San Carlos, funded through the Johnson-O'Malley Fund in lieu of property taxes not paid by Apache residents.

Individual family income can range from the conservative $2,620 suggested by the BIA to the high estimate of $4,000 indicated in the review of income above. Although these income figures are below the national average, it should be mentioned that most Apaches own their own homes and pay no property tax.

CULTURAL REINFORCEMENT

The term "reinforcement" will be substituted here for Adams' term "withdrawal," since the behavior that most concerns us may be viewed as an attempt by Western Apaches to prevent the disintegration of their existing culture.

As Adams' historical review makes evident, the Apache laborer has compartmentalized a work role within Anglo society which requires a minimum of commitment outside the Apache social system. Clearly, the fact that Apaches choose on-reservation employment in order to remain near their families indicates a strong and basic desire to remain Apache. It is not that Apaches refuse to utilize the material advantages of the modern world. This they do like other Americans. What they refuse to do is to prostrate their own values in the process.

A brief visit to San Carlos gives some indication of how Apache culture is being reinforced. Here Apache families continue to live in "clan" camp groupings, separated from other "clan" camps, in small houses constructed of wood in clapboard style. Many of the families in these camps hesitate to utilize modern facilities, since they require a regular financial commitment.

Within each Apache camp there usually lives an older woman, who exerts authority over the families of her daughters and who plays a primary role in instructing her grandchildren in appropriate forms of behavior. Apache is the primary language of the camp, and English is used only to communicate with Anglos. Child-rearing practices tend to be permissive, but deviant behavior is curbed with negative sanctions in the forms of criticism and gossip. Family ties are close in the

Apache camp, and individuals strongly identify as members of particular clan groupings. Rules for behavior within the camp are clearly articulated, a fact which, in turn, leads to the reinforcement of tribal identity. Many Apaches participate in a complex system of aid to needy kinsmen which, despite the emphasis on matrilineal descent, may be extended to include agnatic and affinal relatives.

The tightness of this system of reciprocities was made clear during a visit to Globe with an Apache friend. A movie company was filming a scene in which Apaches were employed. Before we had walked one block my friend was asked by four other Apaches for a small loan to buy beer. The friend said, "Let's go to the car. I can't afford another block of this." In the car, when asked if he could refuse the requests, he responded, "They are my relatives, and you don't turn them down. The Apaches got a way of making you uncomfortable if you don't help. They talk about you and get to other members of your family. Pretty soon they'll make you not want to come back, and that would be just too bad."

During the past year there have been several girls' puberty ceremonies held at San Carlos, which were well attended and costly affairs, attesting to the willingness of Apaches to support ritual obligations. At one such event, nearly five hundred Apaches attended a four-day ceremony held at Beaver Springs, south of San Carlos, which also served as a training experience for several budding medicine men in their apprenticeship to an older shaman.

The support for ritual at San Carlos is also found in the operation of several "holy grounds." At one such ground an Apache family spends most of its time guarding and maintaining the sacred territory.

There are many overt expressions of hostility against outsiders at San Carlos which reinforce Apache identity. Many Apaches blame Anglos for their deprived economic status and fear to leave the reservation to compete in the labor market. There is limited social interaction between Apaches and agency personnel who reside in the federal compound. Apache hostility as felt by federal employees was expressed by a nurse who worked at the San Carlos Indian Hospital as follows:

There is a hostility towards Whites at San Carlos which isn't difficult to detect. I used to work at the hospital as supervisor of nurses. I knew this one Apache LPN for over five years, did special favors for her and thought we were good friends. Even after all of these close contacts, this woman never talked to me on the street; she walked by me like I never existed.

Quite often Apache hostility is not limited to federal employees. While training Apache health aides, I learned of the fear on the part of the trainees to enter strange camps to discuss health programs. One trainee said, "I just don't want to go into that camp. I know that they don't like me, and I'm not sure I want to talk about this White man disease to Apaches."

CONCLUSION

The combination of an on-reservation earned and unearned income has enabled the Apache laborer at San Carlos to remain at home and thus contribute to the maintenance of a critical internal system of social and ritual obligations. Apache identity is reinforced in the fulfillment of these obligations, a fulfillment requiring a minimal commitment to an off-reservation economic system. This process was threatened by the termination of the ration system in 1903, but was activated once again in the New Deal era through the Work Projects Administration and development of the cattle industry. Concomitantly, acculturation resulting from off-reservation employment was diminished by the expansion of an on-reservation economic system which provided earned and unearned income from tribal, state, and federal sources.

It is difficult to predict the future of the San Carlos Apache wage-earner. Clearly, his desire to remain an Apache takes precedence over—but does not obliterate—his wish to enjoy the material benefits of modern society. The historical and cultural factors that have produced this situation continue and, in fact, may be more strongly felt today than at any time since the establishment of the San Carlos Reservation.

REFERENCES TO PARTS I & II

ARIZONA STATE EMPLOYMENT SERVICE
  1958   Expanded Employment Service to Reservation Indians in Arizona. Mimeographed. Phoenix.

BARNES, W. C.
  1935   Arizona Place Names. University of Arizona General Bulletin 2. Tucson.

BUREAU OF INDIAN AFFAIRS
  1969   Fact Sheet for Fiscal Year 1969: San Carlos Agency. Washington, D.C.

CLELAND, R. G.
  1952   A History of Phelps Dodge. Alfred A. Knopf, New York.

COLQUHOUN, J.
  1924   The History of the Clifton-Morenci Mining District. John Murray, London.

GOODWIN, G.
  1942   The Social Organization of the Western Apache. University of Chicago Press, Chicago. Reprinted 1969, University of Arizona Press, Tucson.

KELLY, W. H.
  1953   Indians of the Southwest. First Annual Report of the Bureau of Ethnic Research. Department of Anthropology. University of Arizona, Tucson.

LITERARY DIGEST
  1924   The Apache Indian as Roadbuilder. 83, No. 4:25 26.

LOCKWOOD, F. C.
  1938   The Apache Indians. Macmillan, New York.

McCLINTOCK, J. H.
  1921   Mormon Settlement in Arizona. Manufacturing Stationers, Inc., Phoenix.

PERSONAL COMMUNICATIONS TO GORDON V. KRUTZ
  1970a Bureau of Indian Affairs, employment assistance officer, San Carlos, Arizona.
  1970b Bureau of Indian Affairs, planning officer, San Carlos, Arizona.
  1970c Bureau of Indian Affairs, welfare director, San Carlos, Arizona.
  1970d service unit director, Indian Health Service, San Carlos Agency, Arizona.

SAN CARLOS TRIBAL COUNCIL
  1962   Provisional Overall Economic Development Program for the San Carlos Apache Reservation Redevelopment Area. Tribal Council, San Carlos, Arizona.

STANFORD RESEARCH INSTITUTE
  1954   Characteristics of the Labor Force. Stanford Research Institute, Mountain States Branch, Progress Report 5. Mimeographed. Portland, Oregon.

Chapter 11

WHITE MOUNTAIN APACHE MEDICAL DECISION-MAKING

Michael W. Everett

MICHAEL W. EVERETT, assistant professor in the Department of Anthropology at the University of Kentucky, includes work with Navajos and Western Apaches in his past ethnographic research. Dr. Everett has published a paper on the comparative analysis of social pathology among the San Carlos and White Mountain Apache and has coauthored (with Jerrold Levy and Stephen Kunitz) several articles dealing with Navajo homicide and alcoholic cirrhosis. Lately, his research has dealt with White Mountain Apache suicide.

The description and analysis of native medical systems is of increasing concern to modern investigators. Studies within this area have fallen largely into two somewhat discrete categories. Most have been objective examinations, describing the components of particular medical systems and their various interrelationships (Spencer 1941; Ritzenthaler 1953; Clark 1959; Van Amelsvoort 1964; Kelly 1965; Blum and Blum 1965). More recently, however, with the development of ethnographic semantics as a methodological and theoretical tool, a few researchers have begun to explore medical systems with explicit reference to native cognition. The primary focus in these studies has been to discover what, in fact, defines and constitutes the domain "illness" and how this domain is partitioned internally (Frake 1961; Glick 1967; Shaw 1968). Implicit in this strategy is the assumption that the human mind acts as an

information-processing device which encodes data relevant to particular decision-making events and generates a series of rules upon which behavior is then predicated (Geoghegan 1968, 1969). Despite the promise of such an approach, it is noteworthy that, so far, the application of decision-making methodology to the study of native medical systems has been limited (Metzger and Williams 1963; Nash 1967).

This study presents a strategy for deriving a decision-making model from a corpus of native medical data. Epidemiological information and native cognitive distinctions are combined with behavioral data to produce a formal description of medical decision-making which is sensitive to acculturation differences.

Data gathered in the course of eight months' fieldwork in 1969–70 on the Fort Apache Indian Reservation in east-central Arizona are presented. At the outset, three communities were selected on the basis of apparent differences in acculturative level. These were systematically sampled for medical data by interview schedule and by examination of medical records in a nearby U.S. Public Health Service hospital. In addition, a non-random survey of native ceremonial therapy occurring over the period of fieldwork was made, focusing primarily on the least acculturated of the three communities.

Whiteriver, which has the largest population (approximately 1,800 persons), contains the federal government agency compound and is the location of tribal administrative headquarters. It is essentially an artificial settlement in the sense that it was not traditionally inhabited and had its genesis as an agency town. Many residents here are transient, maintaining one dwelling in the

NOTE: The fieldwork on which this study is based was made possible by grants from the Comins Foundation and the U.S. Steel Foundation. Their support is gratefully acknowledged, as is the kind cooperation rendered by the staff of the Whiteriver U.S. Public Health Service Hospital in allowing the use of medical records. I would like to express my thanks for the valuable criticism and suggestions offered in regard to an earlier version of this paper by Keith Basso, Clifford Barnett, and Jane Underwood. The final form of the study, however, is the sole responsibility of the author.

vicinity of wage-work employment centers and another in their home districts. Three miles to the south, with camps strewn for several miles along a small river, is East Fork, a traditional agricultural settlement. One-third the size of its northern neighbor, this district exists as an economic isolate, with farm labor, seasonal wage work, and Welfare providing the subsistence base. Seven Mile, with a population of about four hundred, is located adjacent to the bottomland tilled by the residents of East Fork. Somewhat less farming is practiced here. The presence of a modern elementary school and a Christian faith-healing church mark this district as distinctive from the others.

Disease Ecology

Ascertaining the occurrence and frequency of disease among White Mountain Apaches presents two problems. The major one is cognitive and

focuses on the discrepancies that exist between Apache and Anglo medical categories. Let us set this topic aside for the moment and confront the second problem. By what means are we to reliably establish and quantify the prevalence of disease types as defined by Anglo categories? The technique that offered the highest degree of reliability was the examination of medical records and the clinical diagnoses of complaints as reported by Anglo physicians. Table I summarizes these data for a standardized corpus of medical categories used by the U.S. Public Health Service at the Whiteriver Hospital.

On the basis of these figures, it appears that three major Anglo categories account for over seventy percent of Apache illnesses. The characteristic features of these categories are readily definable. In one—"injuries"—there is an obvious impairment of locomotor functions (e.g., a

TABLE 1   Selected Disease Frequencies from U.S. PHS Inpatient Medical Statistics, Fiscal Year 1967

Type of Disease	Frequency No.	%*
1. Infective and parasitic (tuberculosis, hepatitis, dysentery, measles, etc.)	62	6
2. Allergic, Endocrine, Nutritional (allergy, diabetes, avitaminosis, etc.)	18	2
3. Mental Disorders (mainly effects of alcohol)	37	3
4. Nervous System and Sense Organs (vascular lesions, meningitis, eye diseases, otitis media, etc.)	44	4
5. Circulatory System (rheumatic diseases, etc.)	36	3
6. Respiratory System (upper respiratory infections, influenza, pneumonia, bronchitis, etc.)	330	30
7. Digestive System (gastroenteritis, liver diseases, gallbladder diseases, etc.)	208	19
8. Gastro-Urinary System (nephritis, etc.)	46	4
9. Skin and Cellular Tissue	60	5
10. Bones (arthritis, rheumatism, etc.)	17	1
11. Injuries (fractures, dislocations, sprains, lacerations, contusions, burns, etc.)	226	21
Total cases	1084	98

*Column does not total one hundred percent due to rounding.

sprained ankle) or a disturbance in the normal condition of body surfaces (e.g., a laceration). In the "digestive system disturbances" category, gastrointestinal ailments, marked by diarrhea, vomiting, and abdominal pain, also exhibit obvious bodily malfunctions. Another attribute of this category is the sometimes chronic, but not necessarily acute, nature of its salient symptoms. This is also true of the third category—"respiratory complaints"—in which symptoms defining influenza, pneumonia, and upper respiratory infections are either perpetual or critical, but not necessarily both. It should be stressed that, in comparison to these physiological categories, there is a marked absence of psychoneurotic and psychopathological diagnoses in the hospital treatment sample. These data indicate a peculiar type of skewing which appears to result from the interplay of at least two factors: (1) only certain types of medical complaints are brought to the attention of Anglo physicians, and (2) some instances of those ailments which appear from the records to be normally treated at the hospital are in fact not treated there.

Assuming that there are two basic types of diseases which affect Apaches—physiological and psychological—what are the media by which these are transmitted? By conventional Anglo standards, the physical setting of the human ecosystem at Fort Apache is deficient in many ways. Much of the population is housed in haphazardly built frame structures that are poorly ventilated and insulated. The families inhabiting them must contend with a frequently contaminated water supply, an unsanitary system of waste disposal, and inadequate provision for food storage. Even where facilities exist, they are apt to be poorly understood and, as a consequence, frequently fall into disrepair. Irrigation-ditch water (used for domestic purposes), outdoor privies, inadequate clothing, poor dietary regime, irregular medical care, and notoriously inclement weather—all of these factors contribute to a favorable atmosphere for the growth and perpetuation of disease.

Sociopathological factors serve to further intensify the effects of such conditions. The major problem is the type of adjustment Apaches have achieved in the face of formidable acculturative pressures. With some allowance for traditionally defined goals, modern Apaches are relentlessly persuaded to adhere to Anglo socioeconomic norms. However, a double conflict occurs here: (1) the means which would normally facilitate this adherence are as yet only minimally developed, and (2) even in those rare cases where they are, they frequently collide with a set of deeply rooted Apachean values. Faced with this conflict, the Apache takes the path of least resistance—procrastination and indecision—which, in turn, fosters apathy, self-directed aggression, social factionalism, problem drinking, and the continued inability to extricate himself from a disintegrating state of affairs.

The case of X illuminates some of the complex media through which disease travels at Fort Apache.

X, a sixteen-year-old high-school dropout, gave birth to an illegitimate baby girl. Her parents, Christian converts, were very upset and the girl moved out with the child to the home of an older sister. She made several attempts to give the child up for adoption, because she did not desire the added responsibility it brought. For two weeks, the baby had been "sick." X took the infant to the hospital for medicine several times. Then a close kinsman of X died, and she was required to participate in the wake and funeral proceedings, an affair which lasted several days. The baby, taken from place to place during this hectic period, was poorly cared for, and its condition worsened. X brought the child again to the hospital, asking that it be admitted. She was given more medication and sent home. The next morning the baby died.

Perhaps even more graphically exposed in the following instance are the cultural and social elements which can affect the physical and mental health of modern White Mountain Apaches.

Y is a forty-six-year-old Apache cowboy. This is the only work he is trained to do and in which he can exhibit some expertise. Aggressive, single, and living under economically deprived conditions, Y has developed a drinking problem over the years. Once a community leader of sorts, with an admirable wartime service record, he is no longer respected and spends his days in an alcoholic fog seeking out the company of others with similar inclinations. Recently, his drinking problem became uncontrollable. The first day of roundup at the cow camp, *Y* exhibited alcoholic withdrawal symptoms, behaved "crazily," and had to be hospitalized. Unable to work after that, he remained constantly intoxicated. Although he frequently requested medical assistance for his "mental condition" on a veterans' program, he could not sober up enough to be accepted for treatment. This is the current pattern of *Y*'s life, in which his two younger brothers and a sister are also inextricably involved.

Medical Cognition

The role of cognitive factors in medical decision-making is a critical one for, as mentioned earlier, it is on the basis of culturally relevant definitions of "illness" that decision-making paradigms are most successfully formulated. Anglo medicine has attempted to circumvent this problem through the use of absolute symptomological criteria which are thought to be culture free. The initial question that confronts the ethnographer, however, is not whether "vomiting" or "sores" are categories with general cross-cultural validity, but what constitutes "sickness" per se to the members of the society under investigation (see Frake 1961; Glick 1967). The following cases give some indication of how Apache notions of "illness" vary from conventional Anglo conceptions.

The seven-year-old daughter of *X* began acting strange recently. She was scared at night, tried to run away, and behaved "crazily." The child's grandfather, seeking an explanation for this behavior, approached a medicine man, who, upon dreaming about the girl's condition, diagnosed the problem as "bear sickness," saying she had been frightened by the animal. On the basis of this information, another medicine man later performed curing chants over the girl. The grandfather, however, perhaps doubtful of the original diagnosis, sought the assistance of another eminent native practitioner and was told that his granddaughter was merely suffering from the "flu."

Y is a sixty-nine-year-old man who night and day walks the road in front of his house. People say he is "crazy." Recently, a curing ceremony was held for *Y* by a medicine man

who believed the man's problem stemmed from disrespect to a set of anthropomorphic mountain spirits known by the Apache as *gan*. Another medicine man, however, noting that *Y* had just returned from a tuberculosis sanitorium, said it was too late to help the man, that the disease had damaged his brain. This diagnosis was identical to the one made by Anglo physicians.

Traditionally, the physical and psychological well-being of adult Apaches was a direct function of their relationships to supernatural *powers (diyi?)*.[1] An individual who possessed *power* was believed to be able to avoid many of the natural pitfalls of life, ward off malevolent supernaturals, and maintain for himself and his close kinsmen a reasonably secure existence. Those individuals who chose to use their *power* on behalf of others—most conspicuously in curing ceremonies—were called *diyín* or *medicine men*. The manipulation of *power* for destructive purposes, such as causing sickness, distinguished the medicine man's negative counterpart, labeled *iłkəšn* or *witch*. Without appropriate care and attention, the individual's relationship to his *power* could be upset, thereby bringing misfortune upon him, most commonly in the form of illness.

Let us proceed now to a brief characterization of the Apache domain labeled *nezkai*. Although the English term "illness" can serve here as an adequate gloss, it is essential to understand that in response to queries regarding the causes of illness and what a medicine man can accomplish with his power, a whole range of essentially nonmedical data emerges. Apaches view illness as but a single component in a multilevel taxonomy which may be glossed as *trouble* or *evil (náonk?lək?)*. Thus, *sickness* contrasts with such categories as *fighting, cut, bruise, gunshot wound, witchcraft, going to jail, owl it looks at me, bad luck, sores*, and so on. Only at a lower level of contrast does Apache mapping coincide with established Anglo medical categories; members of the contrast set *nezkai (illness)* include *pain, fainting, crazy, broken bone, syphilis, colds, sores*, etc. The first of these—*pain*—is the only taxon which appears to be more specifically differentiated; thus, it is possible to distinguish by body locale several varieties of *pain*. This taxonomy is presented in Figure 1.

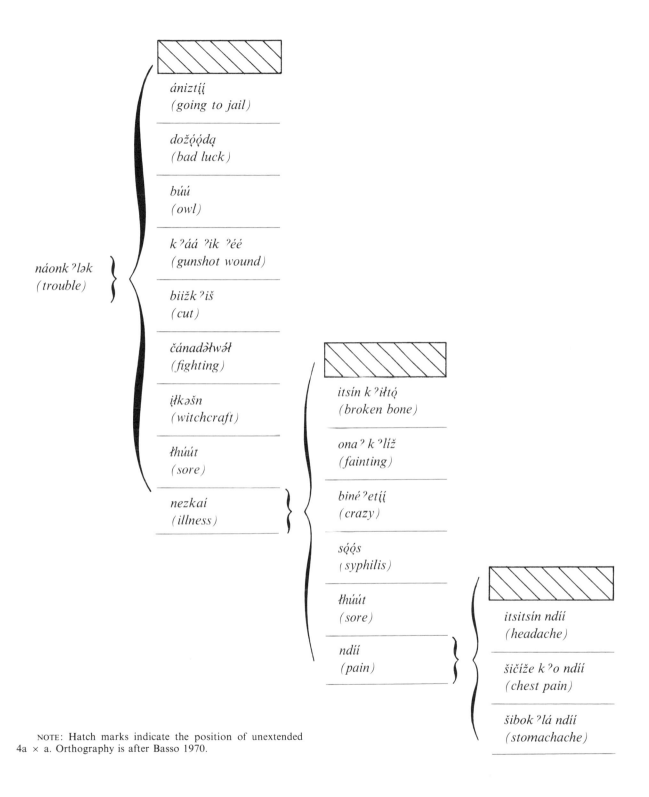

NOTE: Hatch marks indicate the position of unextended 4a × a. Orthography is after Basso 1970.

Figure 1 Taxonomic Structure of White Mountain Apache Medical Domain

In view of the fact that Anglo medical categories intersect and overlap Apache categories, it is reasonable to expect that the selection of appropriate treatment procedures is based only in part upon symptomological criteria. Consider, for example, the Apache category *sores (łhúút)*, which operates at two levels of contrast. At level one, the reference is to *sores* whose effects are described as minor and/or temporary. At level two, however, where *sores* is a member of the subset *illness (nezkai)*, their effects are described as chronic and acute. This suggests that the intensity or seriousness of an illness is of central concern to Apaches, and, indeed, the most common response to a new case of sickness is to inquire about its intensity. It is also noteworthy that the prescription of appropriate ceremonial therapy frequently hinges upon the perceived seriousness of the affliction.

In addition to symptomological criteria such as intensity, there is considerable evidence to show that disease cause plays a significant role in Apache decision-making. Some sets of disease symptoms are labeled in terms of their causal agents (e.g., *bear sickness*), and several types of ritual therapy are predicated not only on the seriousness of the ailment but also upon its cause. Thus, it is not surprising that the feature of disease causation occupies a prominent place within the taxonomic framework of Apache disease categories. A good example occurs on level one, where varieties of *trouble* are labeled by their supernatural causal agents—e.g., *witchcraft* and *owl, it looks at me*—or by some other causal feature, such as *bad luck*.

In order to explore the role of causation in Apache medical cognition more fully, a corpus of field data in which disease symptoms and their causes could be reliably correlated was collected. Of thirty-two cases, fourteen consisted of psychological symptoms caused by supernatural agents; only one psychological symptom was naturally caused; eight physiological symptoms had supernatural causes; and seven physiological symptoms were naturally caused. Since this sample is not a representative one, we must be cautious about accepting these figures at face value. It does seem clear, however, that causal considerations, together with those of a symptomological nature,

are central to an understanding of Apache decision-making. In other words, we should expect diagnostic and etiological discriminations to be made primarily on the basis of the two criterial attributes, symptom and cause.

Therapeutic Behavior

Modern White Mountain Apaches have access to four major institutions which provide medical care once the decision has been made to seek therapeutic assistance for some ailment. Two of these—traditional medicine men and Anglo physicians at the U.S. PHS hospital—have already been noted. Of much less significance are (1) several Christian church groups whose ritual activities include so-called faith-healing and (2) off-reservation Anglo doctors in nearby towns. The pattern of Apache therapeutic behavior vis-à-vis medical decision-making reflects directly their involvement with these institutions.

By far the most intricate and complex form of Apache medical behavior is that in which a decision is made to seek the aid of a native medicine man. Formerly, upon the recognition of some form of *illness*, symptoms were subjected to the diagnostic scrutiny of a medicine man. On the basis of the causal agent involved, another medicine man might be consulted and preparations made to hold a curing ceremony. Once relief was obtained, the patient normally received ritual protection against a recurrence of the malady. At every juncture, decisions had to be made regarding the selection of medicine men, the appropriate form of ritual, and the generation of enough support through kin obligations to accumulate the necessary financial and economic resources for the event.

It should also be noted that medicine men are called upon to provide not only treatment therapy, but also preventive and purificatory services. Thus, one may consult a medicine man (1) in the face of imminent danger and (2) in order to maintain the status quo and avert future misfortune.

For modern White Mountain Apaches, these once-crucial decision-making problems do not occur too frequently. Based on a twenty-one percent questionnaire sample of the three communities described earlier, five percent (Whiteriver), twelve percent (East Fork), and thirty-six percent (Seven Mile) of those adults interviewed had seen a medicine man at least once for treatment or preventive therapy during the past year. These figures change somewhat when we consider total family involvement with traditional healers: thirteen percent (Whiteriver), twenty-eight percent (East Fork), and twenty-five percent (Seven Mile), respectively. Tables 2 and 3 present the type of medical complaint and therapy rendered for the family sample. It is notable that in all three communities, the most common forms of treatment were for ailments subsumed under the categories *pain* and *crazy*, which exhibit almost equal frequencies. Preventive therapy occurred as frequently in Whiteriver as in East Fork, but not at all in Seven Mile.

Data on how modern Apaches perceive disease causation and the effectiveness of native medicine men are summarized in Tables 4 and 5. Once again, community differences are significant. In Whiteriver, the use of Anglo causal categories predominates, although Apache categories are regularly used in conjunction with them. The situation in Seven Mile is the same, except that the frequency of Anglo-Apache conjunctions is significantly greater. In East Fork, the use of Apache categories, separately and by themselves, is considerably greater than in either of the other two communities. Attitudes toward the effectiveness of medicine men are consistent with this pattern (see Table 5). The residents of Whiteriver and Seven Mile place approximately the same degree of credence in medicine men, although the caveat "sometimes" is commonly given. In East Fork, on

TABLE 2   Type of Complaint Occasioning Visit to Medicine Man

Type of Complaint	Whiteriver		East Fork		Seven Mile		Total	
	No.	%*	No.	%	No.	%	No.	%*
Physiological								
Pain	2	22	1	20	2	40	5	26
Other	3	33	2	40			5	26
Psychological								
Crazy, worried, scared	4	44	2	40	3	60	9	47
Total cases	9		5		5		19	

NOTE: These statistics have been drawn from a twenty-one percent questionnaire sample of Whiteriver, East Fork, and Seven Mile.

TABLE 3   Type of Therapy Rendered During Visit to Medicine Man

Type of Therapy	Whiteriver		East Fork		Seven Mile		Total	
	No.	%	No.	%*	No.	%	No.	%
Treatment	9	50	5	45	5	83	19	54
Preventive	5	28	3	27			8	23
Other			2	18			2	6
Unknown	4	22	1	9	1	17	6	17
Total cases	18		11		6		35	

NOTE: These statistics have been drawn from a twenty-one percent questionnaire sample of Whiteriver, East Fork, and Seven Mile.
*Column does not total one hundred percent due to rounding.

TABLE 4 Causes of Disease Among Apaches

Type of Cause	Whiteriver No.	% of Subtotal	% of Total	East Fork No.	% of Subtotal*	% of Total*	Seven Mile No.	% of Subtotal	% of Total
Anglo Concepts									
Weather, temperature	18	19		3	16		1	8	
Alcohol	11	12		5	26				
Eating, drinking	13	14		4	21		4	33	
"Disease"**	12	13		5	26		2	17	
Failure to take care of self	8	8							
Germs, flies, dirt	16	17		2	10		3	25	
Other	16	17					2	17	
Subtotal	94		80	19		46	12		50
Apache Concepts									
Witches	1	100		5	71				
Other				2	28		1	100	
Subtotal	1		1	7		17	1		4
Both Anglo and Apache	23		19	15		36	11		46
Total cases	118			41			24		

NOTE: These statistics have been drawn from a twenty-one percent questionnaire sample of Whiteriver, East Fork, and Seven Mile.
*Column does not total one hundred percent due to rounding.
**A number of informants stated that "disease" causes sickness. The semantic implications are interesting, for this usage suggests that illness symptoms themselves, either in part or whole, are not only indicators of sickness but products of sickness as well.

TABLE 5 Attitudes Toward Efficacy of Medicine Men

Attitude	Whiteriver No.	%	East Fork No.	%*	Seven Mile No.	%
Positive	71	63	32	91	16	64
Qualified		26		9		9
Unqualified		45		23		7
Negative	41	37	3	8	9	36
Total cases	112		35		25	

NOTE: These statistics have been drawn from a twenty-one percent questionnaire sample of Whiteriver, East Fork, and Seven Mile.
*Column does not total one hundred percent due to rounding.

the other hand, a much smaller percentage of individuals deny the success of medicine men and provide more unqualified affirmative responses than in the two companion communities.

Additional information on the topics discussed above, but not derivable from the questionnaire sample, is presented below with reference to a nonrepresentative corpus of data dealing with ceremonial activities.[2] Of ninety-four cases in which a medicine man was sought, thirty-four percent of the patients resided in Whiteriver, fifty-three percent in East Fork, and the remainder in Seven Mile and other areas. As shown in Tables 6 and 7, treatment therapy exceeds other forms of service provided by medicine men in both communities, with preventive ritual playing a noticeably more significant role in Whiteriver. Table 6 displays the strikingly differential distribution of symptom types across communities. Physiological complaints are treated less frequently in Whiteriver by medicine men than psychological problems, while just the opposite is true of East Fork.

The pattern of treatment therapy is rendered more complex by the fact that, under certain circumstances, some ailments are taken to medicine men more than once. Historically, medicine men normally worked over a patient four consecutive times. Although with regard to physiological

TABLE 6 Type of Ritual Therapy

Type of Therapy	Whiteriver		East Fork		Other		Total	
	No.	%*	No.	%	No.	%	No.	%*
Treatment	19	59	43	86	9	75	71	75
Preventive	12	37	4	8	2	17	18	19
Divination			2	4			2	2
Unknown	1	3			1	8	2	2
Other			1	2			1	1
Total cases	32		50		12		94	

NOTE: These statistics have been drawn from a nonrepresentative corpus of data dealing with ceremonial activities in Whiteriver and East Fork. Seven Mile has been grouped with other communities due to the relatively small number of cases there.

*Column does not total one hundred percent due to rounding.

TABLE 7 Type of Medical Complaint by Therapy

Medical Complaint	Whiteriver		East Fork		Other		Total	
	No.	%*	No.	%*	No.	%*	No.	%
Treatment therapy								
Physiological	5	16	27	57	6	54	38	43
Psychological	14	45	16	34	3	27	33	37
Preventive therapy								
Protection	10	32	3	6	2	18	15	17
Purification	2	6	1	2			3	3
Total cases	31		47		11		89	

NOTE: These statistics have been drawn from a nonrepresentative corpus of data dealing with ceremonial activities in Whiteriver and East Fork. Seven Mile has been grouped with other communities due to the relatively small number of cases there.

*Column does not total one hundred percent due to rounding.

TABLE 8 Complaints Occasioning Return Visits to Medicine Man

Type of Complaint	Initial Visit			Return Visit			Total		
	No.	% of Subtotal*	% of Type Total	No.	% of Subtotal	% of Type Total	No.	% of Subtotal*	% of Type Total*
Treatment therapy									
Physiological									
Pain	8	28		3	30		11	29	
Stab	2	7		2	20		4	10	
Broken bone	1	3					1	3	
Fainting	3	11					3	8	
Vomiting	2	7					2	5	
Sores	1	3		1	10		2	5	
Inability to breathe	2	7		4	40		6	16	
Nosebleed	1	3					1	3	
Paralyzed	4	14					4	10	
High blood pressure	1	3					1	3	
Heart attack	2	7					2	5	
General	1	3					1	3	
Subtotal	28		61	10		40	38		53
Treatment therapy									
Psychological									
Lost mind	4	22					4	12	
Crazy	6	33		6	40		12	36	
Acts funny	3	17		3	20		6	18	
Scared at night	4	22		3	20		7	21	
Bad things happen	1	5		3	20		4	12	
Subtotal	18		39	15		60	33		46
Preventive therapy, protective									
Prenatal	2	13					2	13	
Against lightning	2	13					2	13	
Against witch	1	7					1	7	
Against ghost	1	7					1	7	
General	9	60					9	60	
Subtotal	15		83				15		83
Preventive therapy, purificatory									
Post partum	1	33					1	33	
Stay in hospital	2	67					2	67	
Subtotal	3		17				3		17
Total cases	64			25			89		

NOTE: These statistics have been drawn from a nonrepresentative corpus of data dealing with ceremonial activities in Whiteriver and East Fork. A small number of cases came from Seven Mile and other nearby communities.

*Column does not total one hundred percent due to rounding.

complaints this pattern is rarely followed today, it should be noted that a sizable percentage of psychological problems are treated by medicine men on more than one occasion (see Table 8).

Let us move now to a more precise consideration of the role of causal factors in Apache medical behavior. Making use of the distinction between supernatural and natural—the presence of *power* in whatever form as opposed to its absence, Table 9 presents a set of correlations between types of disease symptoms and causal agents, where both are known in the ceremonial sample. Supernatural causes occur three times as frequently as natural causes. More specifically, natural causal agents produce three times as many physiological ailments as psychological ones, while supernatural

agents are responsible for approximately equal numbers of both types of complaints.

The cases of *X* and *Y* exemplify the interplay of symptomological and causal factors in uniquely Apache forms of illness.

X is a twenty-six-year-old man, who, until recently, led a reasonably secure existence. A fulltime job, personal health and well-being, a conscientious wife, two children—all of these were suddenly jeopardized. While attending a feast, *X* was attacked by another male. Later, at a rodeo, he was unable to match his usual high performance as a bull-rider. During a subsequent drinking bout, he and his wife argued violently. As a result of these events, which *X* was unable to account for, he sought the assistance of a medicine man, who told

TABLE 9 Frequency Correlations of Disease Symptoms and Causes

Type of Cause	Type of Symptom		Total
	Physiological	Psychological	
Natural			
Fire	1		1
Hauling water	2		2
Pneumonia	1		1
Flu		2	2
Tuberculosis		1	1
Stab	4		4
Born like that	1		1
Unknown	1		1
Subtotal	10	3	13
Supernatural			
Witch	1	12	13
Ghost		1	1
Lightning	5		5
Bear	2	2	4
Owl	1		1
Snake	3		3
Gan	2	7	9
Water dog	2		2
Subtotal	16	22	38
Total cases	26	25	51

NOTE: These statistics have been drawn from a nonrepresentative corpus of data dealing with ceremonial activities in Whiteriver and East Fork. A small number of cases came from Seven Mile and other nearby communities.

him that a witch was causing the misfortunes. The medicine man prayed for *X*, blessed his rodeo paraphernalia, and requested that he return three more times to complete the ritual treatment. Soon after, *X*'s life returned to normal.

Y is a well-respected forty-seven-year-old man. He and his family live in a wickiup, practice some farming, and travel seasonally by horseback to gather wild plant products. Recently, a bull snake crawled into *Y*'s camp. *Y* removed it unharmed, taking the creature across a nearby stream on a narrow footbridge. The snake returned four times, and each time *Y* removed it. The fourth time, according to *Y*, the snake threw him into the river while he was crossing the bridge. Appearing a fifth time, the snake got so mad that its breath entered *Y*'s lungs and made it difficult for him to breathe. In some physical distress, *Y* sought the aid of two brothers, both of whom are medicine men. Three curing sessions followed, with the result that *Y*'s condition was much improved.

It should be evident that assertions made earlier concerning the differential recognition and treatment of disease among White Mountain Apaches have ample empirical support. Despite some minor variation between the questionnaire and ceremonial samples, both sets of data indicate that certain types of medical complaints are regularly brought to the attention of native medicine men. The question now remains, does the

same pattern appear with respect to the use made by Apaches of Anglo medical institutions? The questionnaire sample shows that thirty-eight percent, thirty-three percent, and thirty-two percent of the adults of Whiteriver, East Fork, and Seven Mile, respectively, went to the U.S. PHS hospital at least once in the past year for treatment therapy. Conversely, eight percent, twenty percent and thirty-six percent made no visits at all. The type of complaint occasioning the most recent visit to the hospital within a one-year period for a fifty percent subsample of the three community populations revealed only one psychological complaint, a most significant discovery. Within the physiological category, most symptoms involved *pain* (see Table 10). Intercommunity variation becomes conspicuous in reference to essentially minor ailments such as colds and coughs, which occur more frequently in Whiteriver and Seven Mile than in East Fork.

Summary and Discussion

Although only a portion of the White Mountain Apache medical decision-making paradigm has been explored and discussed here, it is abundantly clear nevertheless that certain types of medical and nonmedical information are responsible for producing a distinctively Apache pattern of therapeutic action. More specifically, the data reveal the following.

TABLE 10   Most Recent Hospital Visit by Fifty Percent Subsample Within a One-Year Period

Type of Complaint	Whiteriver		East Fork		Seven Mile		Total	
	No.	%*	No.	%	No.	%*	No.	%
Pain	23	40	7	44	3	33	33	40
Cut	5	9	1	6	1	11	7	8
Sores	4	7	3	19	1	11	8	10
Cold, cough	12	21	1	6	2	22	15	18
Swollen extremities	4	7	1	6			5	6
Other	10	17	3	19	2	22	15	18
Total cases	58		16		9		83	

NOTE: These statistics have been drawn from medical records of the Whiteriver U.S. Public Health Service Hospital for a fifty percent subsample of the populations of Whiteriver, East Fork, and Seven Mile.

*Column does not total one hundred percent due to rounding.

Type of Symptom

	Physiological	Psychological
Supernatural	Infrequent	Taken to Apache medicine men
Natural	Taken to medicine men or Anglo physicians	Taken to medicine men or Anglo physicians

Type
of
Cause

Figure 2   Paradigmatic Representation of Apache Illness Classes

1. On the basis of epidemiological investigations, the occurrence and frequency of disease, as classified and measured in accordance with Anglo medical terminology, indicate a predominance of ailments in the injury, gastrointestinal, and respiratory categories, and a paucity of sociopathological and psychopathological problems.

2. However, if we consider symptomology and notions of causation as defined by Apache categories, it becomes apparent that a variety of psychological complaints normally subsumed under the general rubric *crazy* are usually attributed to supernatural causal agents, while physiological ailments may or may not be a result of supernatural action.

3. Combining the dimensions that have been used to order these two sets of data—i.e., type of symptom and type of cause—it is now possible to construct a simple paradigm which represents the four logically possible illness classes on the basis of which treatment-seeking decisions must be made (see Figure 2). We shall assume that the result of each decision is one or the other of two major behavioral outcomes: treatment by an Anglo physician or treatment by a native curer.[3] What follows is an empirical summary of the relative outcome frequencies of each illness class.

a. Psychological problems which are supernaturally caused are consistently brought to Apache medicine men and almost never to Anglo physicians.

b. Psychological complaints which are not attributed to supernatural actions occur so infrequently that this illness class may be considered insignificant.

c. Physiological problems which result from supernatural agents are taken in approximately equal frequencies to medicine men and Anglo doctors.

d. Physiological ailments which are not supernaturally caused are acted upon in a similar fashion, although it is noteworthy that certain kinds of symptoms—especially those which Apaches label *pain*—are regularly attended by medicine men.

4. Although the findings presented above serve to characterize Apache medical behavior at a general level, it is important to take note of cross-community differences.

 a. In Whiteriver, whose acculturated population visits the hospital primarily for symptoms in the *pain* and *cold* categories, complaints taken to medicine men are more frequently psychological in nature, and there is also a high percentage of preventive therapeutic activity. This pattern reflects commonly held attitudes that most diseases are of natural origin and that medicine men are generally ineffective.

 b. The residents of East Fork, more conservative than those of Whiteriver, visit the hospital less regularly, but for somewhat similar complaints. However, the use of medicine men in East Fork produces a markedly different pattern. Here the rate of medicine man consultation is twice that of either Whiteriver or Seven Mile, complaints are as likely to be physiological as psychological, and preventive therapeutic services occur almost as frequently as in Whiteriver. Once again, this pattern may be interpreted as mirroring shared attitudes toward disease causation and the efficacy of medicine men.

 c. Seven Mile appears to be an acculturative anomaly because features of its medical decision-making pattern are both similar to and different from those of the companion communities. Hospital visitation rates are lower, and symptoms treated by Anglo physicians are in most cases physiological. The use of medicine men is much less frequent than in Whiteriver and deals equally with physiological and psychological complaints, but not at all with protective and purificatory ritual. Attitudes with respect to disease causation and the success of medicine men reflect a like equanimity.

We are now in a position to make some general comments about the internal structure of White Mountain Apache medical decision-making. Two dimensions—symptomology and causation—by which classes of ailments are discriminated have

been isolated. The particular features of an illness class, as defined by the intersection of these dimensions are, we assume, responsible for decisions to elect one or the other of two major therapeutic treatment procedures. A stochastic, or ordering, principle is the most appropriate analytic model to utilize here. And the results are striking. As Apache disease symptoms become more psychological in nature, their etiologies or causes assume greater significance, while a concern for type of symptom and its relative intensity is increasingly minimized. Conversely, as physiological symptoms manifest greater intensity, considerations of cause become relatively insignificant. Thus, with respect to weighing the relative importance of the two dimensions, we are forced to conclude that both are dependent variables whose roles in the medical decision-making process are influenced by other factors.

One possible factor, and one to which Apaches attach considerable importance, deals with expectations based on past treatment success and/or failure.[4] It is reasonable to assume that Apaches do not continue to patronize a curing institution which cannot provide relief from their ailments. Thus, it is altogether understandable that native medicine men, trained in the prevention and treatment of supernaturally produced sickness, are regularly selected to deal with all psychological problems and those of a physiological nature whose intensity is not severe. Similarly, it is to be expected that physiological symptoms, especially those of serious intensity, will be brought to the attention of Anglo physicians.

If this hypothesis could be verified with reference to multiple or consecutive decision-making events, i.e., those in which an individual makes use serially of both Anglo and Apache treatment procedures, its implications for the study of Western Apache acculturation would be significant. It has been established that despite long-term contact with Anglo modes of conceptualization, White Mountain Apache medical decision-making continues to reflect a traditional orientation. Like their Navajo relatives,[5] Apaches have not simply replaced native decision-making criteria with Anglo criteria, but have instead combined the two, apparently so that modern decisions take full advantage of new treatment procedures. To what degree the Apache, like the Navajo, have made other structural shifts in decision-making is a problem which now requires immediate confrontation and clarification.

NOTES

[1] For further discussion of traditional White Mountain Apache "religion," see Reagan 1930; Goodwin 1938, 1945; Kaut 1957; Basso 1966, 1969, 1970. The recent work of Basso suggests some major acculturative differences between the more traditional western Fort Apache region and the eastern communities in which the present work took place.

[2] Because of regrettable deficiencies in this sample, e.g., its nonrandomness, the figures mentioned indicate at best relative proportions.

[3] These are by no means all the possibilities, as was indicated earlier. With regard to single decision events, Apaches may elect to see off-reservation Anglo physicians or attend one of the faith-healing churches. Furthermore, there is the important matter of multiple-decision events, where the choice of an alternate route is predicated on the initial decision. For heuristic purposes and because of space limitations, these other situations are not of concern in this investigation.

[4] Other factors which should be considered include (1) the availability of medicine men, (2) the cost of ceremonial therapy, and (3) the accessibility to transportation. There are probably other factors, but these as yet have not been discovered.

[5] It has long been recognized that a major theme in Navajo acculturation has been the addition of new elements to traditional sets of concepts and behavior patterns. With respect to the domain of health and illness, this has been particularly true (Adair 1963).

REFERENCES

ADAIR, JOHN
 1963 Physicians, Medicine Men and their Navajo Patients. *In* Man's Image in Medicine and Anthropology, Iago Galdston, editor. International Universities Press, New York.

BASSO, KEITH H.
 1966 The Gift of Changing Woman. Bulletin of the Bureau of American Ethnology 76. Smithsonian Institution, Washington, D.C.
 1969 Western Apache Witchcraft. Anthropological Papers of the University of Arizona 15. Tucson.
 1970 The Cibecue Apache. Case Studies in Cultural Anthropology. Holt, Rinehart and Winston, New York.

BLUM, RICHARD AND EVA BLUM
 1965 Health and Healing in Rural Greece: A Study of Three Communities. Stanford University Press, Stanford, California.

BURLING, ROBBINS
 1969 Linguistics and Ethnographic Description. American Anthropologist 71, No. 5:817–27.

CLARK, MARGARET
 1959 Health in the Mexican-American Culture: A Community Study. University of California Press, Berkeley.

FRAKE, CHARLES O.

1961   The Diagnosis of Disease Among the Subanun of Mindanao. American Anthropologist 63, No. 1:113–32.

GEOGHEGAN, WILLIAM

1968   Information Processing Systems in Culture. University of California Language Behavior Research Laboratory Working Paper 6. Berkeley.

1969   Decision Making and Residence on Tagtabon Island. University of California Language Behavior Research Laboratory Working Paper 17. Berkeley.

RITZENTHALLER, ROBERT E.

1953   Chippewa Preoccupation with Health: Change in a Traditional Attitude Resulting from Modern Health Problems. Milwaukee Public Museum Bulletin 19, No. 4. Milwaukee, Wisconsin.

SHAW, R. DANIEL

1968   Health Concepts and Attitudes of the Papago Indians. U.S. Public Health Service Health Program Systems Center, Tucson, Arizona.

SPENCER, DOROTHY M.

1941   Disease, Religion and Society in the Fiji Islands. American Ethnological Society Monograph 2. Seattle, Washington.

STURTEVANT, WILLIAM

1964   Studies in Ethnoscience. American Anthropologist 66, No. 3, Part 2:99–131.

TYLER, STEPHEN A., EDITOR

1969   Cognitive Anthropology. Holt, Rinehart and Winston, New York.

VAN AMELSVOORT, V. F. P. M.

1964   Culture, Stone Age and Modern Medicine: A New Guinea Case Study in Medical Anthropology. Van Gorcum, Assen, Netherlands.

Chapter 12

"TO GIVE UP ON WORDS":
SILENCE IN WESTERN APACHE CULTURE

Keith H. Basso[*]

*It is not the case that a man
who is silent says nothing.*

—Anonymous

Anyone who has read about American Indians has probably run across statements which impute to them a strong predilection for keeping silent or, as one writer has put it, ". . . a fierce reluctance to speak except when absolutely necessary." In the popular literature, where this characterization is particularly widespread, the tendency is commonly portrayed as the outgrowth of such dubious causes as "instinctive dignity," "an impoverished language," or, perhaps worst of all, the Indians' "lack of personal warmth." Although statements of this sort are plainly erroneous and dangerously misleading, it is noteworthy that professional anthropologists have made few attempts to correct them. Traditionally, ethnographers and linguists have paid little attention to cultural interpretations given to silence or, equally important, to the types of social contexts in which silence regularly occurs.

This study investigates certain aspects of silence in the culture of the Western Apache of east-central Arizona. After considering some of the theoretical issues involved, I will briefly describe a number of situations—recurrent in Western Apache society—in which one or more of the participants typically refrain from speech for lengthy periods of time.[1] This is accompanied by a discussion of how such acts of silence are interpreted and the reasons they are encouraged and deemed appropriate. I conclude by advancing a hypothesis that accounts for why the Western Apache refrain from speaking when they do and suggest that, with proper testing, this hypothesis may be shown to have relevance to silence behavior in other cultures.

A basic finding of sociolinguistics is that, although both language and language usage are structured, it is the latter which responds most sensitively to extralinguistic influences (Hymes 1962, 1964; Ervin-Tripp 1964, 1967; Gumperz 1964; Slobin 1967). Accordingly, a number of studies since 1960 have addressed themselves to the problem of how factors in the social environment of speech events delimit the range and condition the selection of message forms (see Brown and Gilman 1960; Conklin 1959; Ervin-Tripp 1964, 1967; Frake 1964; Friedrich 1966; Gumperz 1961, 1964; Martin 1964). These studies may be viewed as taking the now-familiar position that verbal communication is fundamentally a decision-making process in which, initially, a speaker, having elected to speak, selects from among a repertoire of available codes that which is most appropriately suited to the situation at hand. Once a code has been selected, the speaker chooses a

NOTE: At different times during the period extending from 1964–69 the research on which this study is based was supported by U.S. PHS Grant MH-12691–01, a grant from the American Philosophical Society, and funds from the Doris Duke Oral History Project at the Arizona State Museum. I am pleased to acknowledge this support. I would also like to express my gratitude to the following scholars for commenting upon an earlier draft: Y. R. Chao, Harold C. Conklin, Roy G. D'Andrade, Charles O. Frake, Paul Friedrich, John Gumperz, Kenneth Hale, Harry Hoijer, Dell Hymes, Stanley Newman, David M. Schneider, Joel Sherzer, and Paul Turner. Although the final version gained much from their criticisms and suggestions, responsibility for its present form and content rests solely with the author.

*Biographical note on page 69

suitable channel of transmission and then, finally, chooses from a set of referentially equivalent expressions within the code. The intelligibility of the expression he chooses will, of course, be subject to grammatical constraints. But its acceptability will not be. Rules for the selection of linguistic alternates operate on features of the social environment and are commensurate with rules governing the conduct of face-to-face interaction. As such, they are properly conceptualized as lying outside the structure of language itself.

It follows from this that for a stranger to communicate appropriately with the members of an unfamiliar society it is not enough that he learn to formulate messages intelligibly. Something else is needed: a knowledge of what kinds of codes, channels, and expressions to use in what kinds of situations, to what kinds of people—as Hymes (1964) has termed it, an "ethnography of communication."

There is considerable evidence to suggest that extralinguistic factors influence not only the use of speech but its actual occurrence as well. In our own culture, for example, remarks such as "Don't you know when to keep quiet?," "Don't talk until you're introduced," and "Remember, now, no talking in church" all point to the fact that one's decision to speak may be directly contingent upon the character of his surroundings. Few of us would maintain that "silence is golden" or "a virtue" for all people at all times. But we feel that it is for some people some times, and we encourage children on the road to cultural competence to act accordingly.

Although the form of silence is always the same, the function of a specific act of silence— that is, its interpretation by and effect upon other people—will vary according to the social context in which it occurs. For example, if I choose to keep silent in the chambers of a justice of the Supreme Court, my action is likely to be interpreted as a sign of politeness or respect. On the other hand, if I refrain from speaking to an established friend or colleague, I am apt to be accused of rudeness or harboring a grudge. In one instance, my behavior is judged by others to be "correct" or "fitting"; in the other it is criticized as being "out of line."

The point, I think, is fairly obvious. For a stranger entering an alien society, a knowledge of when *not* to speak may be as basic to the production of culturally acceptable behavior as a knowledge of what to say. It stands to reason, then, that an adequate ethnography of communication should not confine itself exclusively to the analysis of choice within verbal repertoires. It should also, as Hymes (1962, 1964) has suggested, specify those conditions under which the members of the society regularly decide to refrain from verbal behavior altogether.

The research on which this study is based was conducted over a period of sixteen months (at intervals 1964–69) in the Western Apache settlement of Cibecue, which is located near the center of the Fort Apache Indian Reservation in east-central Arizona. Cibecue's eight hundred residents participate in an unstable economy that combines subsistence agriculture, cattle-raising, sporadic wage-earning, and government subsidies in the form of Welfare checks and social security benefits. Unemployment is a serious problem, and substandard living conditions are widespread.

Although reservation life has precipitated far-reaching changes in the composition and geographical distribution of Western Apache social groups, consanguineal kinship—real and imputed—remains the single most powerful force in the establishment and regulation of interpersonal relationships (Kaut 1957; Basso 1970). The focus of domestic activity is the individual *camp*, or *gowáá*. This term labels both the occupants and the location of a single dwelling or, as is more apt to be the case, several dwellings built within a few feet of each other. The majority of *gowáá* in Cibecue are occupied by nuclear families. The next largest residential unit is the *gotáá (camp cluster)*, a group of spatially localized *gowáá*, each of which has at least one adult member who is related by ties of matrilineal kinship to persons living in all the others. An intricate system of exogamous clans serves to extend kinship relationships beyond the *gowáá* and *gotáá* and facilitates concerted action in projects—most notably in the presentation of ceremonials—requiring large amounts of manpower. Despite the presence in Cibecue of a variety of Anglo missionaries and a dwindling number of medicine men, diagnostic and curing rituals, as well as the girls' puberty ceremonial, continue to be performed with regularity (Basso 1966, 1970). Witchcraft persists in undiluted form (Basso 1969).

Of the many broad categories of events, or scenes, that comprise the daily round of Western Apache life, I shall deal here only with those that are co-terminous with what Goffman (1961, 1964) has called *focused gatherings* or *encounters*. The concept *situation*, in keeping with established usage, will refer inclusively to the location of such a gathering, its physical setting, its point in time, the standing behavior patterns that accompany it, and the social attributes of the persons involved (Hymes 1962, 1964; Ervin-Tripp 1964, 1967).

In what follows, however, I will be mainly concerned with the roles and statuses of participants. This is because the critical factor in the Apache's decision to speak or keep silent seems always to be the nature of his relationships to other people. To be sure, other features of the situation are significant, but apparently only to the extent that they influence the perception of status and role.[2] What this implies, of course, is that roles and statuses are not fixed attributes. Although they may be depicted as such in a static model (and often with good reason), they are appraised and acted upon in particular social contexts and, as a result, are subject to redefinition and variation.[3] With this in mind, let us now turn our attention to the Western Apache and the types of situations in which, as one of my informants put it, ". . . it is right to give up on words."

1. *Meeting strangers (nda dohwáá ʔiłtséédạ).* The term *nda* labels categories at two levels of contrast. At the most general level, it designates any person—Apache or non-Apache—who, prior to an initial meeting, has never been seen and therefore cannot be identified. In addition, the term is used to refer to Apaches who, though previously seen and known by some external

criteria, such as clan affiliation or personal name, have never been engaged in face-to-face interaction. The latter category, which is more restricted than the first, typically includes individuals who live on the adjacent San Carlos Reservation, those who live in Fort Apache settlements geographically removed from Cibecue, and those who fall into the category *kii dòhandáágo (nonkinsmen)*. In all cases, *strangers* are separated by social distance. And in all cases it is considered appropriate, when encountering them for the first time, to refrain from speaking.

The type of situation described as *meeting strangers (nda dohwáá ʔiłtséédạ)* can take place in any number of different physical settings. However, it occurs most frequently in the context of events such as fairs and rodeos which, owing to the large number of people in attendance, offer unusual opportunities for chance encounters. In large gatherings, the lack of verbal communication between *strangers* is apt to go unnoticed, but in smaller groups it becomes quite conspicuous. The following incident, involving two *strangers* who found themselves part of a four-man roundup crew, serves as a good example. My informant, who was also a member of the crew, recalled:

> One time, I was with *A*, *B*, and *X* down at Gleason Flat working cattle. That man, *X*, was from East Fork [a community nearly forty miles from Cibecue] where *B*'s wife was from. But he didn't know *A*, never knew him before, I guess. First day, I worked with *X*. At night, when we camped, we talked with *B*, but *X* and *A* didn't say anything to each other. Same way, second day. Same way, third. Then, at night on fourth day, we were sitting by the fire. Still, *X* and *A* didn't talk. Then *A* said, "Well, I know there is a stranger to me here, but I've been watching him, and I know he is all right." After that, *X* and *A* talked a lot. . . .Those two men didn't know each other, so they took it easy at first.

As this incident suggests, the Western Apache do not feel compelled to "introduce" persons who are unknown to each other. Eventually, it is assumed, *strangers* will begin to speak. However, this is a decision that is properly left up to the individuals involved, and no attempt is made to hasten it. Outside help in the form of "introductions" or other verbal routines is viewed as presumptuous and unnecessary.

Strangers who are quick to launch into conversation are frequently eyed with undisguised suspicion. A typical reaction to such individuals is to assume that they "want something," that is, their willingness to violate convention is attributed to some urgent need which is likely to result in requests for money, labor, or transportation. Another common reaction to talkative *strangers* is to assume that they are drunk.

If the *stranger* is an Anglo, it is usually assumed that he "wants to teach us something" (i.e., give orders or instructions) or that he "wants to make friends in a hurry." The latter response is especially revealing, since Western Apaches are extremely reluctant to be hurried into friendships—with Anglos or each other. Their verbal reticence with *strangers* is directly related to the conviction that the establishment of social relationships is a serious matter that calls for caution, careful judgment, and plenty of time.

2. *Courting (líígoláá)*. During the initial stages of courtship, young men and women go without speaking for conspicuous lengths of time. *Courting* may occur in a wide variety of settings—practically anywhere, in fact—and at virtually any time of the day or night, but it is most readily observable at large public gatherings, such as ceremonials, wakes, and rodeos. At these events, *sweethearts (zééde)* may stand or sit (sometimes holding hands) for as long as an hour without exchanging a word. I am told by adult informants that the young people's reluctance to speak may become even more pronounced in situations where they find themselves alone.

Apaches who have just begun to court attribute their silence to *intense shyness (ʔisté ʔ)* and a feeling of acute *self-consciousness (dàyéézi ʔ)*, which, they claim, stems from their lack of familiarity with one another. More specifically, they complain of "not knowing what to do" in each other's presence and of the fear that whatever they say—no matter how well thought out in advance—will sound "dumb" or "stupid."[4]

One informant, a youth seventeen years old, commented as follows:

> It's hard to talk with your sweetheart at first. She doesn't know you and won't know what to say. It's the same way toward her. You don't know how to talk yet . . . so you get very bashful. That makes it sometimes so you don't say anything. So you just go around together and don't talk. At first, it's better that way. Then, after awhile, when you know each other, you aren't shy anymore and can talk good.

The Western Apache draw an equation between the ease and frequency with which a young couple talks and how well they know each other. Thus, it is expected that after several months of steady companionship *sweethearts* will start to have lengthy conversations. Earlier in their relationship, however, protracted discussions may be openly discouraged. This is especially true for girls, who are informed by their mothers and older sisters that silence in courtship is a sign of modesty and that an eagerness to speak betrays previous experience with men. In extreme cases, they add, it may be interpreted as a willingness to engage in sexual relations. Said one woman, aged thirty-two:

> This way I have talked to my daughter. "Take it easy when boys come around this camp and want you to go somewhere with them. When they talk to you, just listen at first. Maybe you won't know what to say. So don't talk about just anything. If you talk with those boys right away, then they will know you know all about them. They will think you've been with many boys before and they will start talking about that."

3. *Children, coming home (čəgóše nakáii)*. The Western Apache lexeme *iltá ʔinatsáá (reunion)* is used to describe encounters between an individual who has returned home after a long absence and his relatives and friends. The most common type of *reunion*, called *čəgóše nakáii (children, coming home)*, involves boarding-school students and their parents. This type of *reunion* occurs in late May or early in June, and its setting is usually a trading post or school, where parents congregate to await the arrival of buses bringing the children

home. As the latter disembark and locate their parents in the crowd, one anticipates a flurry of verbal greetings. Typically, however, there are very few or none at all. Indeed, it is not unusual for parents and child to go without speaking for as long as fifteen minutes.

When the silence is broken, it is almost always the child who breaks it. His parents listen attentively to everything he says, but speak hardly at all themselves. This pattern persists even after the family has reached the privacy of its camp, and two or three days may pass before the child's parents seek to engage him in sustained conversation.

According to my informants, the silence of Western Apache parents at (and after) *reunions* with their children is ultimately predicated on the possibility that the latter have been adversely affected by their experiences away from home. Uppermost is the fear that, as a result of protracted exposure to Anglo attitudes and values, the children have come to view their parents as ignorant, old-fashioned, and no longer deserving of respect. One of my most thoughtful and articulate informants commented on the problem as follows:

You just can't tell about those children after they've been with white men for a long time. They get their minds turned around sometimes . . .they forget where they come from and get ashamed when they come home because their parents and relatives are poor. They forget how to act with these Apaches and get mad easy. They walk around all night and get into fights. They don't stay at home. At school, some of them learn to want to be white men, so they come back and try to act that way. But we are still Apaches! So we don't know them anymore, and it is like we never knew them. It is hard to talk to them when they are like that.

Apache parents openly admit that, initially, children who have been away to school seem distant and unfamiliar. They have grown older, of course, and their physical appearances may have changed. But more fundamental is the concern that they have acquired new ideas and expectations which will alter their behavior in

unpredictable ways. No matter how pressing this concern may be, however, it is considered inappropriate to directly interrogate a child after his arrival home. Instead, parents anticipate that within a short time he will begin to divulge information about himself that will enable them to determine in what ways, if any, his views and attitudes have changed. This, the Apache say, is why children do practically all the talking in the hours following a *reunion*, and their parents remain unusually silent.

Said one man, the father of two children who had recently returned from boarding school in Utah:

Yes, it's right that we didn't talk much to them when they came back, my wife and me. They were away for a long time, and we didn't know how they would like it, being home. So we waited. Right away, they started to tell stories about what they did. Pretty soon we could tell they liked it, being back. That made us feel good. So it was easy to talk to them again. It was like they were before they went away.

4. *Getting cussed out (šiłditéé)*. This lexeme is used to describe any situation in which one individual, angered and enraged, shouts insults and criticisms at another. Although the object of such invective is in most cases the person or persons who provoked it, this is not always the case, because an Apache who is truly beside himself with rage is likely to vent his feelings on anyone he sees or who happens to be within range of his voice. Consequently, *getting cussed out* may involve large numbers of people who are totally innocent of the charges being hurled against them. But whether they are innocent or not, their response to the situation is the same. They refrain from speech.

Like the types of situations we have discussed thus far, *getting cussed out* can occur in a wide variety of physical settings: at ceremonial dance grounds and trading posts, inside and outside wickiups and houses, on food-gathering expeditions and shopping trips—in short, wherever and whenever individuals lose control of their tempers and lash out verbally at persons nearby.

Although *getting cussed out* is basically free of setting-imposed restrictions, the Western Apache fear it most at gatherings where alcohol is being consumed. My informants observed that especially at *drinking parties (dáʔidlą́ą́)*, where there is much rough joking and ostensibly mock criticism, it is easy for well-intentioned remarks to be misconstrued as insults. Provoked in this way, persons who are intoxicated may become hostile and launch into explosive tirades, often with no warning at all.

The silence of Apaches who are *getting cussed out* is consistently explained in reference to the belief that individuals who are *enraged (haškéé)* are also irrational or *crazy (bìnéʔidíí)*. In this condition, it is said, they "forget who they are" and become oblivious to what they say or do. Concomitantly, they lose all concern for the consequences of their actions on other people. In a word, they are dangerous. Said one informant:

> When people get mad they get crazy. Then they start yelling and saying bad things. Some say they are going to kill somebody for what he has done. Some keep it up that way for a long time, maybe walk from camp to camp, real angry, yelling, crazy like that. They keep it up for a long time, some do.
>
> People like that don't know what they are saying, so you can't tell about them. When you see someone like that, just walk away. If he yells at you, let him say whatever he wants to. Let him say anything. Maybe he doesn't mean it. But he doesn't know that. He will be crazy and he could try to kill you.

Another Apache said:

> When someone gets mad at you and starts yelling, then just don't do anything to make him get worse. Don't try to quiet him down because he won't know why you're doing it. If you try to do that, he may just get worse and try to hurt you.

As the last of these statements implies, the Western Apache operate on the assumption that enraged persons—because they are temporarily *crazy*—are difficult to reason with. Indeed, there is a widely held belief that attempts at mollification will serve to intensify anger, thus increasing the chances of physical violence. The appropriate strategy when *getting cussed out* is to do nothing, to avoid any action that will attract attention to oneself. Since speaking accomplishes just the opposite, the use of silence is strongly advised.

5. *Being with people who are sad (nde dòbiłgožóóda bigą́ą́)*. Although the Western Apache phrase that labels this situation has no precise equivalent in English, it refers quite specifically to gatherings in which an individual finds himself in the company of someone whose spouse or kinsman has recently died. Distinct from wakes and burials, which follow immediately after a death, *being with people who are sad* is most likely to occur several weeks later. At this time, close relatives of the deceased emerge from a period of intense mourning (during which they rarely venture beyond the limits of their camps) and start to resume their normal activities within the community. To persons anxious to convey their sympathies, this is interpreted as a sign that visitors will be welcomed and, if possible, provided with food and drink. To those less solicitous, it means that unplanned encounters with the bereaved must be anticipated and prepared for.

Being with people who are sad can occur on a footpath, in a camp, at church or in a trading post, but whatever the setting—and regardless of whether it is the result of a planned visit or an accidental meeting—the situation is marked by a minimum of speech. Queried about this, my informants volunteered three types of explanations. The first is that persons *who are sad* are so burdened with *intense grief (dòbiłgožooda)* that speaking requires of them an unusual amount of physical effort. It is courteous and considerate, therefore, not to attempt to engage them in conversation.

A second native explanation is that in situations of this sort verbal communication is basically unnecessary. Everyone is familiar with what has happened, and talking about it—even in the interests of conveying solace and sympathy—would only reinforce and augment the sadness felt by those who were close to the deceased. Again, for reasons of courtesy, this is something to be avoided.

The third explanation is rooted in the belief that *intense grief*, like intense rage, produces changes in the personality of the individual who experiences it. As evidence for this, the Western Apache cite numerous instances in which the emotional strain of dealing with death, coupled with an overwhelming sense of irrevocable personal loss, has caused persons who were formerly mild and even-tempered to become abusive, hostile, and physically violent.

That old woman, *X*, who lives across [Cibecue Creek], one time her first husband died. After that she cried all the time, for a long time. Then, I guess she got mean because everyone said she drank a lot and got into fights. Even with her close relatives, she did like that for a long time. She was too sad for her husband. That's what made her like that; it made her lose her mind.

*   *   *

My father was like that when his wife died. He just stayed home all the time and wouldn't go anywhere. He didn't talk to any of his relatives or children. He just said: "I'm hungry. Cook for me." That's all. He stayed that way for a long time. His mind was not with us. He was still with his wife.

*   *   *

My uncle died in 1941. His wife sure went crazy right away after that. Two days after they buried the body, we went over there and stayed with those people who had been left alone. My aunt got mad at us. She said, "Why do you come over here? You can't bring my husband back. I can take care of myself and those others in my camp, so why don't you go home?" She sure was mad that time, too sad for someone who died. She didn't know what she was saying because in about one week she came to our camp and said: "My relatives, I'm all right now. When you came to help me I had too much sadness, and my mind was no good. I said bad words to you. But now I am all right, and I know what I am doing."

As these statements indicate, the Western Apache assume that a person suffering from *intense grief* is likely to be disturbed and unstable. Even though he may appear outwardly composed, they say, there is always the possibility that he is emotionally upset and therefore unusually prone to volatile outbursts. Apaches acknowledge that such an individual might welcome conversation in the context of *being with people who are sad*, but, on the other hand, they fear it might prove incendiary. Under these conditions, which resemble those in Situation 4, it is considered both expedient and appropriate to keep silent.

6. *Being with someone for whom they sing (nde bìdádistááha bigą́ą́)*. The last type of situation to be described is restricted to a small number of physical locations and is more directly influenced by temporal factors than any of the situations we have discussed so far. *Being with someone for whom they sing* takes place only in the context of *curing ceremonials (gòjitáł; èdotáł)*. These events begin early at night and come to a close shortly before dawn the following day. In the late fall and throughout the winter, curing ceremonials are held inside the patient's wickiup or house. In the spring and summer, they are located outside, at some open place near the patient's camp or at specially designated dance grounds, where group rituals of all kinds are regularly performed.

Prior to the start of a curing ceremonial, all persons in attendance may feel free to talk with the patient; indeed, because he is so much a focus of concern it is expected that friends and relatives will seek him out to offer encouragement and support. Conversation breaks off, however, when the patient is informed that the ceremonial is about to begin, and it ceases entirely when the presiding medicine man commences to chant. From this point on—until the completion of the final chant next morning—it is inappropriate for anyone except the medicine man (and, if he has them, his aides) to speak to the patient.[5]

In order to appreciate the explanation Apaches give for this prescription, we must briefly discuss the concept of *supernatural power (diyí?)* and describe some of the effects it is believed to have on persons at whom it is directed. Elsewhere (Basso 1969:30) I have defined *power* as follows:

The term *diyí?* refers to one or all of a set of abstract and invisible forces which are said to derive from certain classes of animals, plants, minerals, meteorological phenomena, and mythological figures within the Western Apache universe. Any of the various powers may be acquired by man and, if properly handled, used for a variety of purposes.

A *power* that has been antagonized by disrespectful behavior toward its source may retaliate by causing the offender to become sick. *Power-caused illnesses (kásiṭí diyíʔbił)* are properly treated with curing ceremonials in which one or more medicine men, using chants and various items of ritual paraphernalia, attempt to neutralize the sickness-causing *power* with *powers* of their own.

Roughly two-thirds of my informants assert that a medicine man's *power* actually enters the body of the patient; others maintain that it simply closes in upon and envelops him. In any case, all agree that the patient is brought into intimate contact with a potent supernatural force which elevates him to a condition labeled *gòdiyóʔ (sacred; holy)*.

The term *gòdiyóʔ* may also be translated as *potentially harmful* and, in this sense, is regularly used to describe classes of objects (including all sources of *power*) that are surrounded with taboos. In keeping with the semantics of *gódiyóʔ*, the Western Apache explain that, besides making patients *holy*, *power* makes them *potentially harmful*. And it is this transformation, they explain, that is basically responsible for the cessation of verbal communication during curing ceremonials. Said one informant:

When they start singing for someone like that, he sort of goes away with what the medicine man is working with [i.e., a *power*]. Sometimes people they sing for don't know you, even after it [the curing ceremonial] is over. They get *holy*, and you shouldn't try to talk to them when they are like that . . . it's best to leave them alone.

Another informant commented along similar lines:

When they sing for someone, what happens is like this: that man for whom they sing doesn't know why he is sick or which way to go. So the medicine man has to show him and work on him. That is when he gets *holy*, and

that makes him go off somewhere in his mind, so you should stay away from him.

Because Apaches undergoing ceremonial treatment are perceived as having been changed by *power* into something different from their normal selves, they are regarded with caution and apprehension. Their newly acquired status places them in close proximity to the supernatural and, as such, carries with it a very real element of danger and uncertainty. These conditions combine to make *being with someone for whom they sing* a situation in which speech is considered disrespectful and, if not exactly harmful, at least potentially hazardous.

Although the six types of situations just described differ from one another in obvious ways, I will argue in what follows that the underlying determinants of silence are in each case basically the same. Specifically, I will attempt to defend the hypothesis that keeping silent in Western Apache culture is associated with social situations in which participants perceive their relationships vis-à-vis one another to be ambiguous and/or unpredictable.

Let us begin with the observation that, in all the situations we have described, *silence is defined as appropriate with respect to a specific individual or individuals*. In other words, the use of speech is not directly curtailed by the setting of a situation, nor by the physical activities that accompany it, but rather by the perceived social and psychological attributes of at least one focal participant.

It may also be observed that, in each type of situation, *the status of the focal participant is marked by ambiguity*—either because he is unfamiliar to other participants in the situation or because, owing to some recent event, a status he formerly held has been changed or is in a process of transition.

Thus, in Situation 1, persons who earlier considered themselves *strangers* move toward something else, perhaps *friend (šìdikéé)*, perhaps *enemy (šìkédndíí)*. In Situation 2, young people who have had relatively limited exposure to one another attempt to adjust to the new and intimate status of *sweetheart*. These two situations are similar in that the focal participants have little or no prior knowledge of each other. Their social identities are not as yet clearly defined, and their expectations, lacking the foundation of previous experience, are poorly developed.

Situation 3 is somewhat different. Although the participants—parents and their children—are well known to each other, their relationship has been seriously interrupted by the latter's prolonged absence from home. This, combined with the possibility that recent experiences at school have altered the children's attitudes, introduces a definite element of unfamiliarity and doubt. Situation 3 is not characterized by the absence of role expectations but by the participants' perception that those already in existence may be outmoded and in need of revision.

Status ambiguity is present in Situation 4 because a focal participant is enraged and, as a result, considered *crazy*. Until he returns to a more rational condition, others in the situation simply have no way of telling how he will behave. Situation 5 is similar in that the personality of a focal participant is seen to have undergone a marked shift, which makes his actions more difficult to anticipate. In both situations, the status of focal participants is uncertain because of real or imagined changes in their psychological makeup.

In Situation 6, a focal participant is ritually transformed from an essentially neutral state to one which is contextually defined as *potentially harmful*. Ambiguity and apprehension accompany this transition and, as in Situations 4 and 5, established patterns of interaction must be waived until the focal participant reverts to a less threatening condition.

This discussion points up a third feature characteristic of all situations: *the ambiguous status of focal participants is accompanied either by the absence or suspension of established role expectations*. In every instance, as we have seen, nonfocal participants (i.e., those who refrain from speech) are either uncertain of how the focal participant will behave toward them or, conversely, how they should behave toward him. Stated in the simplest way possible, their roles become blurred with the result that established expectations—if they exist—lose their relevance as guidelines for social action and must be temporarily discarded or abruptly modified.

We are now in a position to expand upon our initial hypothesis and make it more explicit.

1. In Western Apache culture, the absence of verbal communication is associated with social situations in which the status of focal participants is ambiguous.

2. Under these conditions, fixed role expectations lose their applicability, and the illusion of predictability in social interaction is lost.

3. To sum up and reiterate: keeping silent among the Western Apache is a response to uncertainty and unpredictability in social relations.

The question remains as to what extent the hypothesis stated above is supported by data from other cultures. Unfortunately, standard ethnographies on North American Indians contain very little solid information about the circumstances under which the use of speech is discouraged. Consequently, I have written to a dozen or so ethnographers asking about the types of situations in which members of the groups they are studying keep silent. Additional data are still needed, however, and I am hoping that others will be interested enough to supply me with relevant data.

NOTES

[1] The set of situations described in this study is not the only one in which the Western Apache refrain from speech. There is a second set—not considered here because my data are incomplete—in which silence appears to occur as a gesture of respect, usually to persons in positions of authority. A third set, very poorly understood, involves ritual specialists, who claim they must keep silent at certain points during the preparation of ceremonial paraphernalia.

[2] Work conducted in the 1960s in the sociology of interaction, most notably by Goffman (1963) and Garfinkel (1967), has led to the suggestion that social relationships are everywhere the major determinants of verbal behavior. In this case, as Gumperz (1967) makes clear, it becomes methodologically unsound to treat the various components of communicative events as independent variables. Gumperz (1967) has presented a hierarchical model, sensitive to dependency, in which components are seen as stages in the communication process. Each stage serves as the input for the next. The basic stage, i.e., the initial input, is "social identities or statuses." For further details see Slobin 1967:131–34.

[3] I would like to stress that the emphasis placed on social relations is fully in keeping with how the Western Apache interpret their own behavior. When my informants were asked to explain why they or someone else was silent on a particular occasion, they invariably did so in terms of *who* was present at the time.

[4] Among the Western Apache, rules of exogamy discourage courtship between members of the same clan (*kii ą́łhánigo*) and so-called "related" clans *(kii)*, with the result that *sweethearts* are almost always *nonmatrilineal kinsmen (dòhwàkíida)*. Compared to *matrilineal kinsmen (kii)*, such individuals have fewer opportunities during childhood to establish close personal relationships and thus, when courtship begins, have relatively little knowledge of each other. It is not surprising, therefore, that their behavior is similar to that accorded *strangers*.

[5] I have witnessed over seventy-five curing ceremonials since 1961 and have seen this rule violated only six times. On four occasions, drunks were at fault. In the other two cases, the patient fell asleep and had to be awakened.

REFERENCES

BASSO, KEITH H.

1966   The Gift of Changing Woman. Bulletin of the Bureau of American Ethnology 196. Smithsonian Institution, Washington, D.C.

1969   Western Apache Witchcraft. Anthropological Papers of the University of Arizona 15. University of Arizona Press, Tucson.

1970   The Cibecue Apache. Case Studies in Cultural Anthropology. Holt, Rinehart and Winston, Inc., New York.

BROWN, R. W. AND ALBERT GILMAN

1960   The Pronouns of Power and Solidarity. *In* Style in Language, Thomas Sebeck, editor. MIT Press, Cambridge, Massachusetts.

CONKLIN, HAROLD C.

1959   Linguistic Play in Its Cultural Context. Language 35:631–36.

ERVIN-TRIPP, SUSAN

1964   An Analysis of the Interaction of Language, Topic, and Listener. *In* The Ethnography of Communication, Dell Hymes and John Gumperz, editors. American Anthropologist 66, No. 6, Part 2: 86–102.

1967   Sociolinguistics. Language-Behavior Research Laboratory Working Paper 3. University of California, Berkeley.

FRAKE, CHARLES O.

1964   How to Ask for a Drink in Subanun. *In* The Ethnography of Communication, Dell Hymes and John Gumperz, editors. American Anthropologist 66, No. 6, Part 2:127–32.

FRIEDRICH, P.

1966   Structural Implications of Russian Pronomial Usage. *In* Sociolinguistics, William Bright, editor. Mouton, The Hague.

GARFINKEL, H.

1967   Studies in Ethnomethodology. Prentice-Hall, Inc., Englewood Cliffs, New Jersey.

GOFFMAN, E.

1961   Encounters: Two Studies in the Sociology of Interaction. The Bobbs-Merril Company, Inc., Indianapolis, Indiana.

1963   Behavior in Public Places. The Free Press [Macmillan], Glencoe, Illinois.

1964   The Neglected Situation. *In* The Ethnography of Communication, John J. Gumperz and Dell Hymes, editors. American Anthropologist 66, No. 6, Part 2:133–36.

GUMPERZ, JOHN J.

1961   Speech Variation and the Study of Indian Civilization. American Anthropologist 63:976–88.

1964   Linguistic and Social Interaction in Two Communities. *In* The Ethnography of Communication, Dell Hymes and John Gumperz, editors. American Anthropologist 66, No. 6, Part 2:137–53.

1967   The Social Setting of Linguistic Behavior. *In* A Field Manual for Cross-Cultural Study of the Acquisition of Communicative Competence. Second Draft. University of California, Berkeley.

HYMES, DELL

1962   The Ethnography of Speaking. *In* Anthropology and Human Behavior, Thomas Gladwin and William C. Sturtevant, editors. The Anthropological Society of Washington, Washington, D.C.

1964   Introduction: Toward Ethnographies of Communication. *In* The Ethnography of Communication, Dell Hymes and John Gumperz, editors. American Anthropologist 66, No. 6, Part 2:1–34.

KAUT, CHARLES R.

1957   The Western Apache Clan System: Its Origins and Development. University of New Mexico Publications in Anthropology 9. Albuquerque.

MARTIN, SAMUEL

1964   Speech Levels in Japan and Korea. *In* Language in Culture and Society, Dell Hymes, editor. Harper and Row, New York.

MOWRER, PRISCILLA

1970   Notes on Navajo Silence Behavior. Unpublished manuscript. University of Arizona, Tucson.

NEWMAN, STANLEY

1955   Vocabulary Levels: Zuni Sacred and Slang. Southwestern Journal of Anthropology 11:345–54.

SLOBIN, DAN I., EDITOR

1967   A Field Manual for Cross-Cultural Study of the Acquisition of Communicative Competence. Second Draft. University of California, Berkeley.

INDEX